Stefano Cammelli

The Minaret of Jesus
Twelve Stories from the Near East

to Elsa Dani, with gratitude

Contents

According to an old legend that is very popular in Damascus, when the End of Time comes, that will also be the day of reconciliation between Christians, Jews and Muslims.

That day will be announced by miraculous events: Jesus will come down to Earth and appear on the white minaret of the Great Mosque of the Umayyads.

That is why in Damascus the minaret is called the Minaret of Jesus.

Foreword

Over the course of 2003 I went to Syria with the aim of collecting some life stories. I wanted to use these interviews to contribute to a better understanding of the Near East, overcoming the barriers raised by ideologies and politics. The people I interviewed agreed to work with me knowing in advance that they would receive no monetary reward for this, and that their testimonies would be protected by anonymity.

I asked the individuals I interviewed not to talk about issues directly connected with politics and the international situation. While possibly questionable from a methodological point of view, I believe the request was justified not only on account of the huge differences separating us in that respect, but also in order to avoid revisiting issues that are all too well known (Israel and Palestine) and highly topical but about which it seemed to me that everything had already been said. Besides, politics was not my objective.

The meetings took place in people's homes, in coffee houses, in the street and in the workplace. They often lasted several hours and continued over time. Although French and English are widely spoken in Syria, an interpreter sometimes had to be used to translate from Arabic.

The pages that follow contain the transcription of the interviews which I felt were the most interesting. They are twelve testimonies selected from a much wider collection. Naturally, the names of the speakers have been changed.

In some cases, a narrative intervention has been necessary in order to transpose the testimonies from the spoken language in which they were collected into written form, or to bring together accounts of events and episodes recorded on separate occasions into a single cohesive narrative.

To create the texts, I drew upon a technique that is very well known in the field of folk music studies, an area I worked in for a decade in collaboration with Roberto Leydi. While working on these texts I made every effort to preserve both the contents and the form. Wherever possible, the original document (the oral narrative) was left untouched. In order to produce a lean text, any digressions, repetitions, questions or interruptions were cut, as far as possible, whenever they occurred. Under no circumstances, however, have the stories been edited to correct any errors, inconsistencies or contradictions. These stories must remain the mirror that reflects a given reality as faithfully as possible without being a substitute for it.

For more details about the approach, interested readers will find a preliminary analysis of the collected materials in the afterword at the end of the book.

1 - The Storyteller

I hadn't seen snow falling like this for years, with such big, heavy flakes that stick immediately, just as they did in the old days. Of course, it would have been better to go out with a different pair of shoes, but I don't think it's going to last. It never does, even when it snows this heavily. The snow comes and goes before you know it; it only stays on the Anti-Lebanon Mountains and on Mount Qassioun. It would have been different in the past, when I was a child, Damascus would be covered in a blanket of snow for a few days, and old people complained that it was dangerous to walk. People would stop under the arcades of the indoor *souk*,[1] and in the evening they would go home early. When it snowed there were few customers at the Fountain Café after eight in the evening. The two H. brothers would shift nervously around the room, moving all the waterpipes one by one, putting all the chairs back in place one after the other. They would tell me to wait just a little longer, until a quarter past eight, and then until eight thirty. Then they would tell me to come back another evening. 'You can see for yourself, there's nobody here.' I was a little disappointed; the winter evenings were the best for reading the stories of Antar and Ablah. People were more focused and keener to listen to you. But when the place is empty, I myself don't feel like reading. And it would be pointless anyway. The next day the customers would ask me to start reading again from where I had left off before it snowed. Even so, the café has a strong *hakawati* tradition,[2] and although I may not come up to the standards of old Wahab, I can't lower myself to reading as if I didn't notice that the place was empty. Once I even told the two brothers to get a television and turn it on when there aren't any customers. It's not as if I'm like that man at the Bakery's Coffee House who would wait for people to beg him for hours before he began to read. The fact is that reading when there are people around isn't the same as reading when there aren't. When I reach underneath the chair to take out the big black sword I use to bring the fighting to life, I feel ridiculous. Sitting there, up on the highest chair, handling the sword in a room with just two or three people in it... it's ridiculous. So when it snowed really heavily, I wouldn't even leave the house. But everything is more difficult now. You can never tell if it's really snowing or if it's a false alarm. Sometimes I stay at home and the brothers come and call me over because the café is packed. Other times, like today, I decide to go anyway, only to find that big room almost completely empty.

Of course, Damascus was totally different in the old days. But even if there are millions of us today and not hundreds of thousands as in the past, things are not all that different for me. The millions are almost all outside the city walls; they hardly ever come to the old town and only do so on public holidays. We see them when we get into their car to go somewhere, but no one really notices them in everyday life. Here, we're more or less the same families that have always lived in the neighbourhood; some have left, and a few new ones have arrived. Not that everything is the way it used to be, but it hasn't changed as much as it has in the modern city.

There, everything is different. It has changed enormously. In the old days, when you went outside the old city, around the old citadel and the Umayyad Mosque, there was only greenery. Water was abundant, and there were the farmers' fields and vegetable patches everywhere. We seemed to be surrounded by gardens. Now there are buildings and houses, there's nothing left and even the water isn't clean anymore and not as plentiful as it used to be.

I walk to work whenever I can. I've always liked walking through the old quarters of Damascus where I was born and where I have lived since I was a child. I like hearing the call to prayer from the minarets of the mosques, walking past A.'s bakery and smelling the freshly baked bread. My parents lived in this neighbourhood and obviously I know everyone here.

My father had a barber's shop a few steps away from here, not very far from the Fountain Café. In the evenings when he shut the shop, we would sometimes come here together to listen to the hakawati. As I grew older I was able to stay and listen to the stories by myself. But until I was sixteen years old I had to be there with my father, as the café was not a place for women and children. I kept grumbling about it to my father, telling him that if he had to get back home I could stay behind with someone else. I would beg him to wait at least until the end of the story. Sometimes he would, but more often than not he wouldn't. Dad always had a lot to do; he was a very busy man.

In those days the barber wasn't what he is today, he was an authority. It wasn't enough to be skilled with the scissors and razor. You needed something extra, a vocation, almost a natural prestige. Being a barber was a difficult job and very few people knew how to be good barbers. But I know how to tell stories, and my father knew how to listen. Perhaps he wasn't as outstanding as he seemed to me at the time, I'm sure there were better barbers than him, but there were also many barbers who were not nearly as good as him. Whenever we left the house together to go to his shop, I would realize the extent of my father's prestige, authority and importance by seeing the reactions of the people we met. It wasn't just the fact that everybody greeted him, but it was the way they greeted him.

I've never had any of this, perhaps because I don't take after my father at all, I have a completely different character. People listen to me, they have fun, and sometimes they lead me to believe that I'm quite good. But prestige is something else, that was something my father had, and I don't have.

The other thing I remember about my father, and that everybody remembers about him, is his enthusiasm. Anything he did always became the most important thing of all to him. He would get all worked up, he would worry and become involved as if it concerned him directly and was the most important thing in his life. And when the problem was solved – and he certainly had a lot of problems to solve –, when you expected him to enjoy some much-deserved rest, there was immediately something else to deal with.

His wasn't a wealthy family – ours never has been – but he was quite well off. My grandfather had a grain business not very far from here that had belonged to the family even before his time. When the war broke out,[3] and the Turks introduced the draft, my grandfather received his call-up papers. The matter was discussed at length at home. Doing military service was supposed to be a duty, but leaving the shop would mean condemning the whole family to poverty. So, taking advantage of the fact that my father and my grandfather shared the same name, my father was sent off to enlist in his place. That's one of the reasons why it makes me smile when people say that Damascus had such a large population at the time, and that it was like this and like that, and so on. The way they took the census was fairly approximate; the Turks only had a vague idea about this city even though they had occupied it for centuries.

It's quite funny to think that instead of a thirty-five year old man, the Turks accepted a boy who was only twelve and might have looked sixteen at the most. But I saw some photos of my father at the time and he looked quite grown up. If you didn't look too closely you might have thought he was eighteen. And I am told that's how everything was back then. When the Turks drafted people into the army, the men who enlisted were those that were able to go, not those that were called up. And once the army had one person from each family, the Turks didn't enquire too closely into the identity of the conscript. So, at the age of twelve, my dad left for a war that he has never wanted to talk about and which I don't know anything about. Even though it seems odd, and although there have always been wars – something that unfortunately we know a lot about –, I think my father had a fairly good time of it... Or maybe not, but in any case he never wanted to talk about it. When he came back he was just as he had always been, cheerful and enthusiastic, willing to leave off anything he was doing just to listen to other people. He was happy as long as he was with people and among people.

I never knew whether that's how things really went. When I think back to what happened after the war, it seems more likely to me that it was my dad himself who asked to leave. The grain shop was too limiting for him. Spending all day at the counter and weighing grain was not for him. He wanted to be among people, talking and listening to them; trade was too dry and uninspiring for him. So he asked my grandfather to let him go, and to open a barber's shop for him. I never found out how he learnt to be a barber, perhaps it was during the war. Sometimes I think the Turks had figured it all out, and when they realised they had a young boy who was hardly more than a teenager among them, they put him in the only possible place for someone like him, the infirmary. Maybe that's where my father learnt to treat teeth and sick people, and where he developed a taste for listening to people.

So, as soon as he began to make plans to leave the family and start out on his own path, my grandmother must have thought he was too young, too enthusiastic and maybe also not practical enough to be left completely to his own devices. That's how she set about looking for a woman for him who would help temper his character. So they did the usual things, they gathered some information, made a few proposals, and finally my dad married a young woman whom the family had known since they were children. She was a shy and very devout girl who came from a simple but very respectable family. She was a good woman; I don't think she could be criticized for anything at all. She respected my father and made sure he had everything he needed. They eventually had three children. It seemed to be a moderately happy marriage like many others. Yet Dad wasn't happy. His enthusiasm for life, and for all the things that went on in life, wasn't just a facade for him. Everything was perfect at home, but things like enthusiasm, passion and love never came into the picture at all. His wife ate in silence, as if eating was an inconvenient necessity to be performed as an act of sacrifice. When he got home, everything would be in perfect order, but gloomy and quiet. The food was properly cooked, but without flair or passion. My brothers were well looked after and very well brought up; they were clean, tidy and quiet just like their mother.

My father could never bring himself to love her. He respected her, and he even felt affection for her. He knew she was a good woman, but she didn't know how to laugh, joke or provide companionship. The house seemed as bleak as a mosque, or like certain places near the mosque where women get together to look after the poor and people in need.

He had no intention of giving up love. Living with joy and enthusiasm to him was not a possibility but a necessity. Like air and water. Dad was a passionate man; he loved good and plentiful food, new flavours, and the company of friends. He took every opportunity to invite people around for lunch or to get invited to their house for a meal. In the evening, on the way back from work, he would stop and see friends and people he knew to help solve some problem or difficult situation. There was always an opinion to hear, some advice to give or a suggestion to offer. This was the barber's job, he was a kind of neighbourhood counsellor that all the men who went to his shop turned to, and still turn to, for a chat and to ask questions.

There were no blades back then and even scissors were quite hard to find. You had to go to the barber's to shave almost every day and at least once every ten days to have a haircut. So, with people going so regularly to his shop, a large group eventually formed at the centre of which was the barber. He saw everyone almost daily; he knew them and listened to them. He eventually became the go-to person in the neighbourhood and people very often turned to him whenever they had serious troubles. In those days there were hardly any doctors, and people only consulted them for major issues. But if you had a toothache, or a backache that wouldn't go away, or a headache that lasted the whole day, you went to the barber to have it treated.

My father had his own ideas about medicine. Whatever happened or whatever he had to treat, his cure-all were traditional herbs, the ones you could buy from the souk. And when the problem was difficult to deal with, the ultimate remedy was aspirin.

You had backache? Aspirin! Toothache? Aspirin! A fever? Aspirin! I remember at home once my mum teased him on this point, and my father said something like: 'It doesn't do you any harm, it often does you good, and it's cheap.' Those were dad's therapies.

But then there was everything else, and the scope of everything else was so vast that even we, his children, didn't know where it ended. There was the man who couldn't sleep, the man who kept coughing, and the man who didn't get on in bed with his wife and, very gradually and very coyly, would ask my dad what to do. And then, once you've started talking about your physical issues, the dividing line between different kinds of problems is always quite blurred and shifty. Because there are those who have headache issues, but one thing is a happy person with a headache and another thing is a person whose business is falling apart. And when things don't work out in bed for a man, unless it's on the first wedding night when emotions can play funny tricks, then maybe the wife shares some of the blame, too. I mean, it's worth thinking about. Once I met a man who everyone thought was homosexual; I didn't ask him anything, but when he started talking to me about his wife it didn't take very long for me to realize that he was married to a harpy. And so he obviously didn't feel like doing it. And his wife would go around telling everyone that he was impotent, a half man, the usual things women say in these cases.

The barber knew everybody; he listened to everyone and talked to everyone. He knew about family quarrels, family troubles, about marriages that weren't working out or marriages that people wanted to take place. They didn't ask for very much, but what little they did ask from him was not something you learned, it was something you have from birth. It was the ability to listen, to understand everyone's point of view, and to speak very little and always with common sense. So, when two brothers quarrelled, they would go to the barber to try and find a solution. When a shop wasn't doing well and it was time to close it down or find new partners, the shopkeepers would go to the barber to make initial contact with them. He was the one who would suggest a marriage, a business deal, or some form of mediation to the various families. I don't know if things still work the way they did in my father's days, but it was definitely like that back then.

After closing the shop, my father would go and see one family and then another. People respected him; they knew he personally had nothing to gain from what he did and that he only got involved to protect everyone's interests. And in all of this, he had a natural balance, a kind of moderation and an ability to bring about reconciliation that came naturally to him. People didn't pay him for what he did for them, but they often came to our house with gifts, simple things but which together contributed to improving our family's living standard.

So in the evenings, my father would never come straight home from work. Sometimes he would stop and have dinner with a family or had to go and see somebody; he would listen and offer suggestions and ideas. And when he got home, his wife was the natural partner to share his reflections with.

But what kind of partnership could my father get from his first wife, this devout, unhappy and silent woman, who was irreproachable yet didn't like laughter, noise, rich and plentiful food, and looked almost cross every time he brought someone home with him? So they left each other and, as was the custom at the time, the sons stayed with my father, while their mother moved back to her parents' house. I don't think it was a particularly painful event, they were both tired, and a life together needs something more than silence and mutual respect. My father couldn't live with such lack of love. Not long afterwards she married again, this time to a good craftsman, one of those men who do metalwork. He was no better and no worse than my dad, but he was much quieter, less passionate and less enthusiastic about everything. She had the quiet life she wanted, with a neat and tidy house, always dimly lit, and in her pantry she only had what was strictly needed for an essential meal. She also carried on her usual pious activities, taking care of the poor and looking after the congregation of women who met at the nearby mosque.

My father, now on his own with three boys, also married for a second time. It was a short-lived marriage that only lasted a few months. His new wife wasn't a bad woman; in fact I think she was very good but didn't get on with my grandmother. She was strong-willed and liked to have things her own way. Once there was an argument at home and she asked my dad whether she would have to do everything my grandmother wanted for much longer. My father said that his mother would always be his mother, so she left. They didn't have any children and had done nothing but argue and fight. She may have seemed like the right sort of wife because compared to my dad's first wife she had a stronger personality, was more engaged, and wanted to play a more active role. But this woman, who came into our home as mistress of the house and constantly argued with his mother, couldn't have been so great for my father.

So my father married a third time and everything he had suffered while living with his first two wives was transformed into pure joy with his third wife. His life with my mother was a great and beautiful love story, the kind of relationship that makes men happy and changes people's lives. I'm not saying this just because she was my mother but because even my older brothers, my dad's sons from his first marriage, felt it. My mother and father, who were not so young and had both been married before, had the kind of enthusiasm that people feel the first time around, just like young couples. And their enthusiasm didn't just affect just the two of them. My mother took care of my brothers as if they had been her own sons, and she did it with the kind of sensitivity that only certain women are capable of. When she had to make a decision concerning them she would phone their mother first and ask her what she thought about it. I know for certain that they met each other many times, both at home and outside, to talk about them.

Then, when my brothers' mother fell ill, my mother was the first to go and see her and took care of her as if she had been a friend. She would even stay at her house overnight if she was needed, as she once did after an operation.

She was like my dad; she loved his first wife and his children because she was incapable of doing anything except loving. She was a generous, strong and dynamic woman.

I remember one afternoon when my mother and my father's first wife were at home and they thought I was asleep. Or maybe they thought I wouldn't understand what they were talking about. All I know is that I heard the following sentence very clearly: 'But how did you manage to make him so happy? He seems like a different person. And my sons, too, they seem so happy with you.' Yes, I know, it's the kind of thing people say. But I seem to remember that those words sounded very sincere, she wasn't just saying it. I didn't hear what my mum answered, but I didn't have to, I knew very well how she had done it.

I still remember very vividly when, in the evenings after dinner, they would go into the bathroom. We would hear a crescendo of giggling and laughter. She would pretend to be shocked by something, then everything would suddenly go quiet, and then they would burst out laughing again. And my dad would start screaming 'Help!' followed by more laughter. She would beg him to stop in a way that seemed to urge him to carry on. Then they would come out of the bathroom trying to look composed, both as red as tomatoes.

For almost forty years, things went on just like this. My dad would get home and be overwhelmed by the most alluring smells. He would walk into the kitchen to try and find out what she was cooking, and every time she would push him out firmly but gently. He would come back and join us and say: 'My love, don't make me suffer like this. Tell me what's cooking in the pot, what are you making?' She would peep out of the kitchen door pretending to be angry and say: 'Sit at the table and learn to wait. Don't be such a child!' But as she spoke, my dad would stretch his hand out and pinch her affectionately, and then the door would shut again until the next assault.

My mum was a special woman, or maybe it was just that they loved each other so much and were made for one another. Things then developed naturally, as was bound to happen given their personalities. Just as my father had become the counsellor for all the men in the neighbourhood, his wife naturally became the go-to person for the neighbourhood women. When my father went out of the house, and by that time we boys were grown up, the women would come to see my mum at home. They spoke to her, told her about their situations, their desires, their troubles, and their most serious problems. She would listen, console them and make them feel protected. Then, when my father came home, they compared notes on what they had learned and worked out a solution that would allow family quarrels to be resolved, marriages not to break up, boys to follow the path that one of the parents objected to, and girls to marry the boy that they wanted but didn't dare tell their fathers unless it was through my dad or my mum, the barber and his wife.

Business naturally flourished. Even though my father's profession was apparently more modest than my grandfather's, he eventually managed to buy a house just outside the old town with two apartments, one above the other. So the ground floor became the barber's shop for the men and the top floor was for the women. My father owned both of them, but upstairs it was my mum who pulled the strings.

Things went on like that for many years. When already old and into his eighties, my father still carried on working and being at the centre of life in the neighbourhood and that of dozens of families. He did this with his innate cheerfulness, his ability to remain calm and balanced in all his judgments, which grew with time and coexisted with his formidable appetite, his love of laughter at home with his wife and his children, the squeals in the bathroom, the affectionate pinching and the giggling that we, now grown up, didn't have to pretend not to hear anymore and which went on right up to the last day of this unique and, in its own way, extraordinary couple.

At times I ask myself where my passion for stories began. My mum told us stories every now and then, but although I don't exactly know why, my impression is that she doesn't have anything to do with it. I think there is something else that led me to become a hakawati. Perhaps it's the fact that my dad would drag me away from the Fountain Café as soon as the storytellers had started their readings with the excuse that he had important matters to attend to. Then, after taking me away just when things had started to liven up, it turned out that the "matter" was not so vital as to prevent him from having a long session in the bathroom with my mum, with the usual pinching, giggling and her voice saying 'Hush, the children will hear you!' But I know that, ever since I was a child, that man sitting on the raised chair, with the white cotton hat on his head and his big dark sword, reading his tales became my life's ambition. Obviously, I knew very well it would be a pastime and that real work was something else, and, even if I did become a hakawati myself someday, I would still have to get a job. But whatever that job might be, I only asked for one thing, that I could be free in the evenings, at eight o'clock, to go and sit on that high chair and start reading the tales of Antar.

When I learned to read, I remember I used to force my brothers to sit at my feet and listen to me. Those were wonderful moments, because then, with my elder brothers, I understood how difficult the art of reading in front of an audience really is. It needs that mix of cheerfulness and tears that must always be held in a miraculous balance, without going too far in one direction or the other. It's a sort of fragile but decisive happy medium, because too much war and too much fighting get tedious after a while, and sad stories are moving but... have you ever heard of anyone who feels like going to the café to hear such sad stories after spending ten hours at work? I haven't. Not here, at any rate, not in Damascus.

And then I realized almost immediately that the secret of storytelling is not the actual narrative but the interruptions. It means knowing how to create a second story imperceptibly, before the first one ends, and then building it up gradually, so that when the first one comes to an end, the audience doesn't even realize it and is already looking forward to the end of the next one.

Then there's the outline. It's not just a matter of recapping the things you said on previous evenings, but it's a sort of introduction you need in order to gradually draw the attention of the customers in the café towards you. And it's a way to slowly get into the life of the café and make sure that after a few minutes no one wants to do anything else except listen to you.

It's funny, sometimes I think back to my father. When he wanted to speak, and when he wanted people to speak to him, he would be silent, and the longer he was silent the more the people in his shop felt a kind of unease, until either my dad said what he wanted to say or those who he wanted to speak did so in turn.

But if I sit on the armchair and keep silent, nobody realizes I'm there and the café carries on its routine without anyone paying the slightest attention to me. If I had to wait for everything to go quiet around me before speaking, I would never get started. But if I begin my story when no one is listening to me, then what do I do afterwards? Do I have to repeat it? And that is where the importance of the outline and of all the preparations comes in.

I walk into the café and greet everyone with the utmost composure; they need to see me and realize I've arrived. Of course the H. brothers have already set up the room, but that isn't enough. People know that at a certain time all the chairs are turned towards my armchair and the tables are cleared, but this has become routine by now and doesn't really mean that everything has begun. And then you obviously need to give the waiters enough time to take the orders. They know perfectly well that a particular customer will order tea and a waterpipe, and that another customer will need his ashtray emptied and only drinks unsweetened coffee, but they still have to give the customers enough time to call them over. In the summer, with the café's lovely grapevine arbour outside, everything is even more difficult because the customers get lazy. They are already sitting outside and persuading them to get up and come inside the café is not an easy task. And then there are the foreign customers who stay till late and make a noise without realising what is happening. I'm not talking about the silent and solitary ones, who sit in the corner with a notebook watching and writing notes. They don't bother me at all, they only upset the H. brothers who sometimes complain that they just have some tea and sit for hours without ordering anything else. I'm talking about the ones with the black plastic shopping bags, who show each other the things they bought in the afternoon, talking loudly, laughing and making a racket. They don't even notice whether I've arrived or have started storytelling. After a while they don't even notice the other customers, it's as if they had the café all to themselves, but they are a nuisance, they make a noise and distract people's attention. So, during the summer, my preparations are slower and more drawn out. I pretend I can't find one thing, and then another. I light up a cigarette, even though I don't feel like smoking, just to waste a little more time, and then I pretend I can't find my sword or the book. It's a kind of ritual that the H. brothers know by heart by now. But I also do it for them. If I turned up and started reading straightaway it would be disastrous.

This is probably why I much prefer the winter to the summer, and January, one of the coldest months of the year, is my favourite month. When I walk into the café, there is already the right atmosphere and people really seem to be ready for me to start. Then, when I sit on the armchair and open the book of Antar, you can hear the chatter dying down immediately; some people stop talking, others nod to let me know they are ready to listen to me. So I ask people some questions, I pretend not to remember where we had left off, the usual things, until I open the book and begin to read.

The tale of Antar is obviously the best loved story, and virtually the only one I read in this café. The reason it's interesting is not because it's so old. Who knows whether it was written before the Quran or not anymore? These days the stories of Antar have been written about by so many authors and there are so many of them that we don't actually know anymore whether what we're reading was written yesterday, a hundred years ago or a thousand. Antar... Antar is me, he's my regular customers, my listeners. Because anyone of us who has ever suffered a defeat in life will naturally find pleasure in identifying themselves with the exploits of this warrior, the son of a king and a black slave, who would fight for years before fulfilling his dream of being recognised as a king's son. Antar is a victim, but he's also a warrior, a noble spirit, a pure man. The war he fights has no hate in it, he feels no pleasure in killing. He loves men as he loves horses, and women 'with teeth sparkling like the blades of India.'

I am not a learned man; I mean, I didn't study as I could have done. And my job at one of the ministries is fairly straightforward. But when I read the tales of Antar and I see the lights of the nearby Umayyad Mosque through the café windows, it seems to me as if the whole of Damascus is the shining city it once was. And that it is still full of gardens and water streams as it was back then. As the poet says: 'She is adorned with the flowers of sweet scented plants, displaying silk-brocaded garments in the form of gardens.'[4]

Sometimes I harbour the illusion that that it is exactly what the café's old-timers feel, those who often sit and listen to me while drawing in the smoke from their waterpipe in such deep silence that sometimes I think they've fallen asleep. Then I read more slowly, I separate the words, leaving longer pauses between them. I brandish the black sword as if it was Antar's and do 'not cease charging them with his throat and breast,' and I wait for someone – thinking perhaps that I have lost my thread – to add 'until he became covered with a shirt of blood.'

When that happens, it's a great joy to me. Sometimes I notice that the H. brothers are also standing still by the kitchen door listening to me. And although they know the stories almost as well as I do, I fancy that they, too, want to know how it's going to end.

Some days ago a boy walked into the café. That would have been impossible when I was young. But today, although the H. brothers have kept everything as it used to be in the old days, too many things have changed. Until seven or eight years ago, women weren't even allowed to come into the café. Now they spend hours here, chatting and smoking as if the place had always belonged to them. I'm not bothered by them; it's the ongoing exchange of text messages that disturbs my narrative. But this is not what I wanted to talk about. There was that boy, and I thought he had only come in to find shelter from the cold outside. But when he came back the next day, and then the next day again, I realized that he was coming because of me. I can tell from the fact that he almost inadvertently makes the same moves I make, and sometimes it almost seems as if he is silently repeating the words I utter.

I have never felt old, I still feel quite young, but when I saw that boy listening to me with his mouth open, it struck me that he is not very different from how I was at that age. And so, as I was reading, even though I actually know all the words I have to say by heart, I realized I was reminiscing about my father and his barber's shop. I was thinking about his art of making people speak not by saying things but by his measured silences. It brought back to my mind the bathroom, with those 'Hush, the children will hear us!' and the smells coming from the kitchen, and my brothers. I thought of the green Damascus that doesn't exist anymore, with its streams of clear water and its gardens.

Now I am wondering if he'll come back again this evening, with all this snow. Maybe his parents won't allow him to go out because of the bad weather, or maybe because they don't want him to go to the café and waste his time with the souk merchants, the artisans that make metal trays, and the grain traders.

But if I see him this evening, then I think I'll talk to him, I'll ask him if he too wants to become a hakawati like me, and like the famous Wahab, who told his stories in this café before me. Maybe I could take him home to see my wife and children and show him the two or three books I have. Or perhaps I could take him, along with my grandson, to Mount Qassioun, inside the Cave of Blood,[5] where they say that Abel was killed by Cain. Maybe I could read that passage to him and remind him of a time, not so long ago, when the fountains of Damascus flowed perennially, and its courtyards smelled of orange and jasmine blossoms. I won't talk to him about Antar and his stories straightaway. I'll wait for him to ask me about them.

Maybe one day I'll also be able to sit, on a beautiful snowy night like tonight, and listen to the stories of Antarah Ibn Shaddad al-Absi. Then I'll watch him opening the pages of my own book and, while smoking a waterpipe, I'll wait for him to speak the same words that I read now, the same old immortal words:

'Oh house of 'Ablah situated at Jiwaa,
talk with me about those who resided in you.
Good morning to you, O house of 'Ablah,
and be safe from ruin...
And verily you have occupied in my heart
the place of the honoured loved one,
so do not think otherwise than this,
that you are my beloved.'

Who knows? Maybe I'll be sad that day because I'm no longer seated on the high chair at the H. brothers' Fountain Café. Or maybe I'll do what old Wahab did with me: I'll nod approvingly while he reads the most celebrated pages. And, after looking at me, the customers at the café will whisper to themselves: 'That boy is good, he's got talent!'

2 - The Kurdish Weaver

I don't see why we had to talk about it today, of all days.

Newroz is Newroz. It's a holiday, a day for relaxing. Even in my home we didn't talk about work on days like these. We would get ready, dress, and maybe start bickering over something we couldn't find. But to talk about work and, what's more, in the morning after prayers... I could understand it if we had more days like this, but for our New Year we only celebrate on the day itself, the 21st of March. Was there any need to spoil it for me? Yes, okay, I'll see him today, and he probably knows she has already talked to me about it. But even if I didn't know, what of it? Even if she hadn't mentioned anything to me, what difference would that make? We can't do anything about it today. We can't talk about it just like that, as if it were a matter of no importance, a detail about something we've already spoken about many times before.

Then she looks at me and says: 'Why must you always get angry when we talk about work?' She says it casually, while I'm getting dressed, as if she didn't know that if there is one thing I find more annoying than anything else, it's this way of hers. And it isn't true that I was in a bad mood from the moment I got up, it's not true at all. While we were praying for all the Kurds scattered throughout the world, I was just thinking it was a nice clear day and even the temperature wasn't that bad. I thought we would go down to the same old open field, the one flanked by blossoming apple trees, and light our fires in ideal conditions, without the wind we had last year or the rain we had two years ago. There would surely be more of us there than last time, we would meet families we hadn't seen for a few years or that didn't usually celebrate Kurdish New Year with us.

That's right. I was expecting it to be a fairer and more peaceful day than many previous ones. And, at least this year, our celebrations wouldn't be starting with the usual list of those killed in Turkey, Iraq, Iran, and elsewhere.

And, with that look of false shyness of hers, she says to me: 'Merwan, remember that Aram wants to speak to you about his son Kildan. I promised you'd think about it.' How did she expect me to react? With a smile? As if we didn't both know that if we'd had a son she would never have spoken to me about him, let alone in this way.

Anyway, I must calm down. There's no point spoiling the day like this. I'll tell him what I can, then I may ask him to come around and see me another day, with the excuse of this din, the noise and the crowds. Aram will understand, perhaps he won't feel like talking about this today either. Of course, if I think about the five thousand Kurds living in Damascus, I wonder how many others like me have four children, all girls! And then, for one reason or another, the years go by you don't realize it. Then you find yourself without any male heirs, without anyone to leave your name or your profession to. It's not just the history of our family, Ferah knows that very well. The family is only one part of the problem; the other part concerns all the Kurds in Syria, all of us. I really don't think my father went into brocade for purely personal reasons, and even less because he thought that one day he would leave everything to Kildan, however good he might be. He, too, would have been sad if he had known that one day all the jackets and costumes we wear at Newroz would become "Kildan Karabulut". He used to say that with brocade we would restore the light and the joy that our family had deprived so many people of. That our company would become... No, perhaps he wouldn't have minded. It wasn't the name of the company he was concerned about but that the brocade tradition should carry on.

Dad... So different from me, and from Grandad. With his little grey suit, like a civil servant, and the white shirt he wore, even in the summer. How he stirred his tea with a teaspoon a thousand times in the glass until the sugar had completely dissolved and you could only see the red colour of the tea, and the gold rim with flower buds printed on the glass, almost completely rubbed off from so much use, from the age-old custom of tea drinking. Whom had he got that gentleness from? That ability never to be aggressive? As for myself, as soon as I move, I'm aggressive. As soon as I speak, whatever I say, I'm aggressive. Although no one has ever said it to me, and my father certainly never suggested the idea to me, I am sure I've inherited my grandfather's character – his terrible temper that left its mark on our whole family.

Was Dad different because he had reacted against it? Or would he have been just the same if he had had different parents or lived in different circumstances?

I remember the first time he took me to Newroz. The festive atmosphere was just the same, but the joy of a child for New Year's Day is so different from that of an adult. And Damascus was so much smaller and more family-friendly. There were far fewer of us then. But how magnificent those costumes were, and with all the families sitting on the ground eating and playing the buzuq and the tanbur. Then the women would get up and start dancing a sultana, a *govend* or a *shishaneh*. And the circle would form and break up in a matter of seconds, with new people joining in, while those who had already danced, with their foreheads beaded with sweat and that somewhat awkward look that adults have when they've just done something they used to do when they were young, would go back and sit under the blossoming apple trees. And even now I get emotional when I think about my first-born daughter – I, who supposedly got up in a bad mood! A few years ago, while I was trying to fix some apple blossoms in her hair, she said to me: 'Last year, Grandpa put them in my hair. Dad, I'm sorry that Grandpa isn't here anymore. He was so gentle.'

And the fires, those fires! The flames were so tall, and the crackling of the wood split by the heat; and in the distance, the Arabs from Damascus, who weren't sure whether they could get close to us or keep away. Until the day before we were just like them, and the next day we would be just like them again. But on that day we were Kurds! It was our day, no one else's. It's not that I'm bothered by the fact that the Syrian government has decided to celebrate Mother's Day on the same day as our New Year's Day – it doesn't change anything and doesn't create any problems. But it was different in the old days... the fact that we were celebrating while the city was going about its usual business made the holiday more of a holiday.

We felt different, that's what it was. And those fires, rising up in the plains outside the city, seemed so special to me, so unique. They weren't just fires: they were *our* fires – beautiful, crackling and tall. They had something in common with our clothes, the fabrics, crafted from the same brocade we now make at home. Everything has changed, of course, but at least the fires are still the same. When I was a kid there weren't so many radios in the background, and the sound of cracking wood was sharper and more distinctive then.

Today there is music all around, but the atmosphere is still the same. There is just a bit more bustle and noise, but it's not as if the fires are less beautiful because of that. Dad used to say that the fires, the brocade and the language were the three most precious things our people had. He said that as long as those were still alive then Kurdistan would be a reality that no one had the power to suppress. The day the fires were no longer lit at Newroz, that would be the beginning of the end.

I still remember very well when, as a teenager, I asked him why he thought that. I told him I didn't understand how a modern man like him could still believe in those things. He, who had taken part in founding the Kurdish Communist Party and had fought "alongside the people of Russia", as he used to say, for the emancipation of the working class and the peoples of the world. He, who had read Marx and wanted me to study in Russia, which I eventually did. And he would watch the fires as if they were magic, pure magic. I remember he was silent, and it was my other grandfather, my mum's dad, who answered for him.

He said we were Kurds, and that being Kurdish meant keeping up the tradition, the language and the history of our people. He said that those fires burning on New Year's Day were lit not just in Damascus but through the whole of Kurdistan. He said that if a man could fly high in the sky on a spaceship – I wonder why my grandad had a fixation with airships even though airplanes were already around at the time –, he would be able to see the entire Kurdish nation from the fires burning across the land. A vast region of the world would have appeared where people lit fires at Newroz, the Kurdish New Year's Day. That's why they were important, because each of those fires was like a message sent up to the sky at the beginning of the year.

My father had something else to add. 'Merwan, it's not just about that,' he said, 'there are some people who think that the fires are needed to warm the Earth or other such things… folk stories… but there's a deeper idea.'

Dad said that the fires were even more important; they were the memory of our Indo-European origin and of the ancient worship of fire, like in Iran and India. 'We,' he said, 'live amongst Jews and Arabs, we even speak their language, we are Muslims, we dress like them every day. But there's a huge difference between us and them. They are Semites and we are Indo-Europeans. Their brothers are the Bedouins from the desert, ours are the Armenians, the populations of India and Iran, and even Europe itself.'

'And what about the Turks?' I asked him.

I remember it as if it was yesterday, my dad didn't say anything. My mum linked arms with me, almost as if to defend me.

'The Turks,' said someone, 'come from East Asia. They are a landless people, without culture, without anything. They don't have their own religious faith or their own art. They take the best they can find and say it's theirs. Can you tell me,' he said, turning to the other men sitting by the fire, 'can you name anything that is really Turkish? Nothing, they are nothingness. The only thing they have is being Turkish, compact like a herd of sheep and proud like soldiers. But nothing else! Nothing else!'

Some men spat, some moved away from the fire and went back to join their families who were having their lunch close by. I remember very well that a sudden gust of wind lifted some petals from the nearby apple trees and some of them disappeared in the fire.

'It's not a good thing,' said Dad, 'to have such bad thoughts on the day of Newroz – to feel hate and resentment. You see, that's what fire is to us: it's purification, it's purity. It means beginning the new year as pure as these flames.'

I didn't ask why we had prayed to God in the morning, just like every other Muslim. I understood they were two different things, but ultimately did not contradict one another. There was the Quran and there was Allah. And we also had fires. We were different, we were something else!

I've asked myself many times how much of a role all this played in my dad's decision to become a communist, and whether reading Marx and Engels in Arabic or French didn't perhaps become a way for him to recall these common origins. And while during their mandate the French encouraged a relationship of greater trust between Christians and Europeans in a way that was unpleasant and wrong, my father responded by playing the same game, showing himself to be more European than the Europeans, choosing a model, Karl Marx, that every Frenchman feared and admired at the same time.

For a long time I didn't understand my father's choice to become a communist in Syria, to look towards Europe and end up with Lenin and the Russians, who were no less different from us than the Arabs or the Jews. But by the time he was born too many things had already happened. We had lived and breathed certain values ever since we were children. We assimilated them along with our mother's milk. Independence, equality, social justice. The world to the workers, the land to the people living on it, and culture to all, especially those most in need. I suppose that is the reason why my father – when political experience became less idealistic and more concrete (why didn't he ever talk to me about it in detail?) – left his job in the Party to start his own business, the first large brocade making company in Syria. He gathered together twenty or so artisans in our house in Damascus to produce brocade. I wonder if he thought he would set up an ideal factory, a sort of socialist commune. I was too young to understand, or at least I didn't understand many of the things I'd like to know today.

Everything seemed very natural to me. I knew we were Kurds and that we came from the mountains in Anatolia. As a matter of fact, I didn't know much about my family's past. Dad didn't talk about it very much and Mum avoided making any reference to anything that went beyond our immediate family as much as she could. I thought we had reached Syria much earlier than my grandfather Saman, perhaps a few centuries before. Today people say a lot of things about the Kurds, and sometimes it's hard even for me to know what is true and what is false. And besides, I've always worked in silk and brocade, that has been my job. Sometimes I hear people say that the Turks apparently sent us to Syria so that they could have greater control over it, relying on a population that was more loyal to them. It's all nonsense... We, friends of the Turks? Has anyone ever heard anything more absurd?

But all this silence on our origins at home made me feel uneasy. I realized I wasn't supposed to ask, but I wanted to know. If we came from Anatolia, I asked myself, then why were the Kurds already here a thousand years earlier? Saladin was Kurdish and his Army was mostly made up of Kurds. The Turks were still not around or would come later. If it was us who re-conquered Jerusalem and not the Arabs, and even less the Turks, then it means that we arrived in Syria long before then, but how long? Where did my family come from? When did they move south from Kurdistan into Syria? But while Dad never missed an opportunity, and indeed seemed happy, to talk about our traditions, about our culture, and about a general, and to me unfathomable, migration that over the centuries would take our people to Iran, Turkey, Armenia and Syria, while he talked about all this in the calm and reflective tone that was so habitual to him, the history of our family remained obscure. Throughout my childhood I tried in vain to find an answer to this question. I wasn't interested in the history of "our" people. I wanted to know where my family, my grandfather and my great grandfather came from. I wasn't interested in a general history of the human races; it was my history that I needed to know. And at school, when my classmates said they came from Diyarbakir, Malaya, Van, or any other city in Kurdistan, I would try to move away from them so that, if I was asked where my family comes from, I wouldn't have to answer: 'I don't know. My father has never told me.'

I was very curious, but my ideas were confused. Once, when I was already a teenager, probably during the Fifties, I read in a book that we had supposedly allied with the Turks against the Armenians, and we allegedly helped them carry out the genocide at the beginning of the 20th century. It seemed impossible to me, although we should ask the people who were in Turkey at the time about that. But my family was already here when those massacres took place in the early 1900s, and here we have always had good relations with everyone except the Turks. So how could any of us possibly have helped them? When we talked about them at home, Mum would always sigh, and Dad would become gloomy. Just like he did once, not such a long time ago, when a Frenchman came into a shop to buy some brocade and they started talking about these things. Then the Frenchman started saying that it was time to reassess the Ottoman Empire and its ability to keep together people who are so different from each other without them fighting one another. I think it was in the early '90s, when the war in Yugoslavia began. My dad was already very old at the time, but he got up from the back of the shop where he was sipping a cup of tea and came to the counter, something he hardly ever did. 'If you talk to me about the Turks,' he said, 'and tell me they are human beings just like us, if you tell me that they are twice our brothers, brothers in our faith and brothers in humanity, I would agree with you. But then there is what our parents have seen, sir, and that is not good at all. Nor as bright. Perhaps you are not aware of what they did here. But I think you might be able to understand what we feel. Name something Turkish that you like, anything at all.' The man looked puzzled. He didn't expect that kind of answer, and in such good French. But I know very well that it wasn't my father's words that were so disarming to people when they discussed things with him. It was his voice, which was always so calm, so gentle, and people would feel naturally inclined to think he was right. They discussed things for a while. The Frenchman kept insisting that the question was badly framed; if it came to that, he said, he wouldn't have been able to name one thing that was exclusively French. 'And yet I think you have a few thousand in front of you, but you would be hard put to find just one, even just one, that is actually Turkish. Whatever they are, sir, the Turks are not what they do and what they say, but what they hide. And only those of us who have lived under their rule for many centuries know just how terrible that is. Not in itself, but in terms of their relations with others. To a Turk you'll always be "someone else", do you understand? Is there anything more terrible in the world than dividing it into "us" on one side and "them" on the other?'

Poor Dad, with his worn-out copy of the *Manifesto of the Communist Party* in Arabic. And Lenin's pamphlets bought second-hand from the market. The way he would watch television in the days when the Berlin Wall came down, in silence and without commenting. The end of Russian communism. The joy he showed as he listened to me when I came back from Kiev, where he had sent me to study. And how he would ask me over and over again to tell his friends about the grand avenues and all the greenery, and about the order that reigned in the streets of Ukraine and across Ukrainian society back then. Today it's common to say bad things about the USSR and its conquests, but those people were not much richer than us. The road that they built in such a short space of time, who is to be credited with that if not Lenin or Stalin? Sometimes I think I would also like to go back and live in Kiev when I'm old. I'm not saying that Damascus is not a good place to live, but Kiev… Or maybe it's just hard to forget the places where you lived when you were twenty years old.

But it's true that it was the Turks who pushed so many Kurdish families, including my own, to move to Syria. At home, people always said that the Turks had encouraged migration from Kurdistan to Damascus. Here in Damascus there was already a large Kurdish community, maybe even bigger than we have now. But my parents used to say that although there had always been Kurds in the city, the art of brocade had never spread outside our ethnic group. Brocade, people said at home, is not a Damascus specialty but a Kurdish one. That's why the Turks wanted us for their palaces and their residences in Damascus, they wanted our fabrics. I think that's why my family emigrated from a village not far from Diyarbakir and moved to the plains of Tartous near Latakia. Then we came directly to Damascus, which had the most important silk and brocade markets.

When did I find out the truth? When did my father finally decide to tell me about the things I had been asking him for so many years in vain? It was only then that everything became clear: the gentleness of my father and my uncles, the huge house in Damascus, Marx, communism and Russia. I remember I had lost my temper with my brothers over some trifle and, as young boys do, we started beating each other up, but I was so angry I couldn't stop. And when they shut themselves up in a room, I started kicking the door until I broke it at the bottom, a few centimetres from the floor. I remember my mum standing silently at the other end of the corridor, holding a piece of fabric in her hands. 'Now go to your room,' she said, 'and don't come out until your father gets home.' You didn't argue with Mum, especially when she spoke so softly.

I waited for hours, and the more time went by the more afraid I felt. Then the door opened, my father came in and sat down on a chair. He wasn't angry, but he looked at me with such a sad look on his face I would rather he had hit me. He told me it wasn't my fault if I had my grandfather Saman's character, but the fact that I wasn't able to control myself, that was my fault – and what a serious fault it was! He said that perhaps the time had come to tell me what I had always wanted to know, and he had never revealed to me because until then I had been too young.

Once, not so many years earlier, ours had been one of the richest families in Syria. We had lands, houses, olive groves, sheep and men. 'Yes, that's right, that's what I said. Olive groves, sheep and men. My father was an agha, which meant he didn't just own land, houses, things and animals, but also men. They were his property because that's how things worked back then. His farm workers couldn't get married or move to a new house, they basically couldn't do anything without his permission. He had enormous powers over them, such as you can't even imagine.' And he had my temper. He treated everyone harshly; he would switch from insult to physical violence in a matter of seconds. 'He may not have been wicked; if he had been, he wouldn't have married your grandmother and wouldn't have loved her for over seventy years.' But with other people his nastiness went beyond the boundaries of brutality and cynicism.

Once he got into an argument with one of the farm workers. That marked the beginning of a new chapter in the history of my family. My grandfather had told him to do something, and the farm worker said it couldn't be done. But my grandfather had insisted and the man, who couldn't answer back, had lowered his head and listened to his tirade without saying anything. The same anger I had felt when kicking the door took hold of him and he started beating the peasant, slapping his face once and then again and again. He carried on like that until the man collapsed on the floor. He didn't die but he lost his sight forever. These things were probably common at the time, but they weren't for my uncle Gazind. He was my grandfather's eldest son and had been working alongside him for some time. He was fifteen when he witnessed the scene. I knew my uncle, he was like my dad. And he was known for his very deep faith in God and from this faith he drew his strength to treat everyone with compassion, whether or not they were his farmer workers.

Nothing happened; nothing could have happened. My uncle Gazind didn't say anything. But this episode changed him forever. When my grandfather Saman died and my uncle became an agha in turn – and with the title he also acquired the family's properties and the responsibility of being a father to all his brothers who were still young at the time, he summoned all the family heads to his house. And he said that now that he was the agha he had to tell them that all the properties of his family were Haram, meaning that they had been gained through looting, exploitation, violence and abuse. And because these methods were illegal, he said, the properties were also illegal. In front of a crowd of incredulous peasant farmers and factory workers he took the titles to the properties and burnt them all. Although some of them offered to pay at least part of the redemption fees, he wanted nothing. In a stunned, eerie, silence – Dad could still remember it well, although he was only a boy at the time –, he said that from then on everyone was free. The land was free, the houses were free, the farm tools were free and so were the herds. Let everyone take what they were entitled to, and each was entitled to take the land he had worked and the tools he had worked with.

'I am no longer the agha,' he said, 'not because I don't want to be, but because neither I nor anyone in this family wants to share in the evil suffering and sin that produced this wealth.'

Dad was speaking calmly, and the room was dark by then. 'None of us,' he said to me, 'has ever regretted any of this. We would have done more if we could. Now you'll understand why we have this big house in Damascus. It's the only thing we kept for ourselves because it was the only one we lived in and to which we were entitled. Men are not guilty before God for what they inherit or for their character. But they are accountable for how they use it and how they control it, always remember that. You have many virtues, but anger is only good when it becomes tenacity, and it's bad when, like in your grandfather's case, it becomes wickedness towards others.'

It took me a long time to understand how deeply and how heartfelt this decision had been. I understood firstly the sense of deep respect that surrounded my family and which I used to take for granted, but now had acquired a depth that... I perhaps don't deserve. I don't have the same level of culture as my father and my uncle did. Or maybe I still haven't had time to develop it. And then, after that day everything started to become clearer. Of course, when my father suggested to all the men who weaved brocade that they could get together and start a small factory, they all accepted enthusiastically! And it was also clear that in a family such as my parents' this form of religious and moral commitment could turn into something bigger. And so my uncle, who lived in a different era, found his path in religious faith, and my dad, who was twenty years younger than him, combined this with the socialist idea, and with Marx, Revolution and Russia. And also brocade... It was not just to do with fighting for an ideal but it also what my parents were most knowledgeable about. As a wealthy family, they used it, produced it and exported it. Many of their lands had mulberry plantations on them because mulberry leaves provide the food for the silkworms, which is where silk comes from.

And this too is something that there is a great deal of misunderstanding about. Since Aleppo and Damascus are on the Silk Road, many people think we work, or worked, with Chinese silk. Of course it used to be like that once, but that was many centuries ago. But this doesn't mean that brocade weaving in Syria was done using Chinese silk. Our silk had a unique shine, just like Italian silk. It was magnificent silk, of superior quality. Heaven knows how many times we tried to use Chinese silk. I don't even remember how many times, but it has no personality, no life in it, it's dull.

And my wife Ferah wonders why I get angry when I talk about work. I don't get angry; it has nothing to do with anger. It's anxiety that comes over me. Ours is a wonderful silk, it's unique in the world for its shine. And here they do everything, really everything they can to ruin production, to make it fail. Other people are proud of their skills, why do we have to feel almost ashamed of them in this country?

Only the French understood this. My father used to say that during the mandate a lot was done for silk and brocade production, partly because the French are connoisseurs, or because it was cheaper than producing it in France. So, in those days, mulberry cultivation along the coast became more intensive and factories like my dad's benefited from that.

It was during that period that Dad bought some Swiss mechanical looms of what seemed to be unrivalled precision and quality. We lived on the floor above the workshop, and we boys would go down to the factory to learn, to have a look around and also to have a bit of fun.

Dad was in charge of everything: he had to buy the silk, hire the workers and teach them all the technical weaving skills. It has always been a very difficult job; you can't say that you need two or ten years in order to learn to weave brocade. There are some weavers who learn everything within three months and immediately begin to make suggestions about how to improve things. They enjoy themselves; they are happy to produce one of the richest textiles in the world, and it's as if they were actually rich themselves. With these workers there are never any problems. We talk, we discuss things, and we make improvements, slowly but steadily. Then there are the others, the ones who sit at the loom and, while they weave, they are thinking about things at home, about their own affairs, and they never learn anything unless they have to. And they constantly complain about this, that, and the other. Obviously these are the ones who always talk about rights. They have a right to all kinds of things. And perhaps just two of the good ones – the ones who don't ask for anything and work hard and with satisfaction – could do ten times the work of the others. I wonder what Dad thought when he came up against this kind of problem and realized that not all workers deserve trust, and that some seem to have been created deliberately to kill off any hope for socialism.

I don't know… I wish he was here with me today. I'd like to ask him what I should do. Perhaps if he was here he would tell me to take on Kildan, maybe we would find a way for our family name to continue. Or maybe he would be even sadder than I am.

The patterns he had collected, the weaving techniques with three, five or seven colours… What would he think now if he saw that we don't have a domestic market anymore, that there are fewer and fewer of us and that I am on my own now? Would he tell me to carry on? Even if I have millions of pounds worth of unsold silk stocks? Exports now make up a hundred percent of our market. Here in Syria too, the culture of brocade has been lost. Sometimes I hear shopkeepers telling tourists about Islamic patterns and Christian patterns, showing that they haven't got a clue about brocade and don't even know how to recognize it anymore.

Does it make any sense at all to carry on with a business that doesn't bring in any earnings and doesn't provide jobs just because it belonged to my family, to our people? How can Ferah fail to understand this? Sometimes I think my misfortune was to be the last. If I had been the second last, today I would shut up shop and give everything away to someone else like myself.

This world doesn't appreciate what we produce anymore; it doesn't know how to interpret it and can't even understand it. In the old days brocade wasn't just for palaces and mansions. It was also used in places of prayer, like Christian churches. And here in Syria brocade was used in mosques or to cover sacred or devotional objects. Sometimes it featured in costumes for festive occasions, just like the ones I'm going to see in a little while at the Newroz festival… But nowadays, who uses fabrics with gold and silver threads anymore? A brocade tablecloth: who can afford it? And even those who can, wouldn't use it anyway. It's an old-fashioned taste.

Do Kildan and his father, old Aram, realize that there is no money to be made in this business anymore? Do I have to tell them myself?

The world I live in is a world I don't love. People don't love beauty anymore; there is no longer any love of quality. Customers walk into the shop and don't even realize what they're holding in their hands. They say – at the souk – that people come in to have a look at my brocade and then they leave having bought some cheap printed fabric in fake batik. And maybe they're even happy with the fake Indonesian rubbish they bought.

Sometimes I think the problem has nothing to do with wealth, but with the mind and culture. It has to do with ideals. To my father, and to me, brocade has never been just a product; it's a world and an idea, a value.

Yes, that's just what I'll do. We'll sit by a fire, old Aram, Kildan and I. I'll tell them what I learnt as a child. Do they know, they who are skilled with computers and know how to make new brocade patterns, do they actually know where it comes from? Dad used to say that brocade is a corner of heaven on earth. And that those who wear it share a tiny corner of heaven. And that tiny corner can be the light of heaven, the light of those fires at Newroz, or maybe even the light of the revolution that purifies and from which a new world will be born, a new humanity, a new faith in other men.

Yes that's exactly what I'll tell him – that when we weave brocade, God takes possession of our hands. And the decorations we make are neither Kurdish nor Christian or Islamic, but they are for everyone, they belong to the whole of humanity. And to weave in the seven colours you don't need skills, you don't need technique, but love. Love for men, love for nature, love for the family. Love for justice.

I wonder if he'll understand. I wonder whether I'll be able to make him understand that in mechanical weaving the Chinese will always be ahead of us, they will always produce more cheaply than us. But in our minds we are unique, because what grows out our factories is not a human art, but a divine art.

I suppose he, too, knows that story. But I'll tell it to him again anyway. It doesn't have anything to do with family, family name or silk. I'll tell him what people have been saying for generations, about all the meanings encapsulated in the word "brocade". 'You know Kildan, besides all the economic problems I'm going to have, and that we are going to have, do you know what brocade means in Kurdish?' And before Aram can say anything I'll tell him myself: 'It means the work of Abraham,[6] Kildan, it means the work of Abraham. Now do you understand what it means to make brocade? Do you understand what it means to weave silk with gold and silver threads?'

Then I'll decide, when I see his face and his eyes. If they light up, even just for a second, if they light up and have a sparkle in them just like my dad's did, if they remind me of something of the joy or the pride I felt when my father talked to me about it for the first time, then I'll take him on and he can come and work with me. Even though he's not my son.

I wonder how it feels to watch all your friends dancing and playing the buzuq next to the burning fires – watching them and knowing that there is someone who will carry on, and that it's not the end of the tradition. Perhaps that day I won't be so angry, I'll be able to feel more at peace. I'll also be able to enjoy the apple blossoms and the green fields of sprouting wheat. I'll smoke by the fires and feel more serene. The world will not end with me, it will carry on. There will still be brocade when the Kurds throughout the earth are together in their own nation, an independent and socialist nation. When humanity will somehow be more just.

3 - The Shiite Sheikh

Yes, I also know that story, the one about the three merchants who talk about God. But they weren't from Isfahan; they were three traders from here, from the souk in Damascus. One of them was talking about Judgment Day, when Jesus will appear on the minaret of the Umayyad Mosque to separate the righteous from those who have sinned. It's a popular legend here in Damascus, that's why the minaret is called "Minaret of Jesus". 'I've made too many mistakes,' one of them said, 'God won't forgive me for it. I did the wrong thing knowing that it was wrong, and I kept on doing it. I've done so many stupid things in my life.' The old man was troubled and could find no peace in his distress, he was really afraid. One of the other men tried to comfort him by saying: 'God is first and foremost a Father. He couldn't condemn his own child, even if he wanted to. He'll be angry, he'll be enraged, but in the end he will forgive us all. No father in the world would be able to condemn his own son for all eternity.' And yes, in the story I knew, there was also a third man who said: 'I think on that day, the Lord will come to me with the attitude of a painter, and He'll say to me: "What you saw, I made for you. I created the flowers and the women, the mountains and the desert, the rivers and the sky. Did you enjoy yourself? Did you like all that? Did you love the women, the roses, the silk, the dawn, the family and work?"'

Except that in the version I know, a sheikh walks past the three men as they are having this conversation, and when the third man stops talking, he clears his throat to draw the attention of the small group of friends and says: 'If you'll allow me, I'd like to tell you what I think. We live in the kingdom of goodness, which is the fruit of an act of love by God towards men. Everything we see and do is part of that. Even though we see terrible things every day, and although we do everything to act against it, the world we live in is the kingdom of love and peace – nothing more and nothing less. God's mercy and love towards men are infinite. Blessed be the Almighty and His mercy!'

'Blessed be the Lord!' the three men replied.

I suppose this is a very natural ending for me, isn't it? I too sometimes ask myself whether I heard it and simply added these reflections of mine to the story of the three souk merchants in Damascus. It seems so fitting, so natural. But there again, that's how I've always seen God, and that's how He was portrayed to me by my parents, ever since I was a child, when I lived in a valley in Lebanon with my family.

I suppose we might say that mine was quite an important family, partly because of the name we carry and partly because it has always been quite wealthy, but most of all because it has dedicated its whole life to God and to the knowledge of God for many generations. There are not many Shia Muslims in Lebanon, and they all live mainly in the south of the country, spread across seven villages located quite close to the border with Palestine, which Israel occupied in 1948, and in other villages that Israel occupied when it invaded Lebanon. It wasn't a particularly large community, but it was an important one. There are millions of Shia Muslims throughout the Islamic world, and the Lebanese among them are a minute portion of this vast crowd of believers. Yet, a great many sheikhs, or *ulamas*, are from Lebanon: almost one in five is actually Lebanese.

My father was a scholar of the scriptures and he too studied at the university in the holy city of Najaf in Iraq, as I eventually did. I was one of seven siblings, four boys and three girls. When I was a child, I went to elementary school in Habboush, not far from Nabatieh.

Of course, Mum and Dad were the first people who talked to us about God but, quite honestly, I don't think anything has been as important to me as the feeling I've had since I was a very young boy. I remember I kept thinking that I hadn't created myself on my own and that someone must have done it for me, and that not even my father and mother had created themselves on their own, that's what I felt. Obviously I must have picked up something at home, I probably felt the spiritual atmosphere permeating our home, but I also think it was something that came from me and that I felt inside me ever since I was very little. Dad was very supportive and encouraged me to go on with it. He gave me books and information that helped my development. Naturally they included the Quran, the Sunnah and the Hadith,[7] and then, when I was a little older, he also gave me the first philosophy texts. That may be why when I was twelve years old, soon after the end of the war, I was sent to school in Najaf, in Iraq. I wasn't afraid to be going so far away from home: after all, my father had also studied in Najaf, and that school felt a bit like "our" school. There were also a lot of Lebanese teachers there, and some of them were my father's friends or remembered him when he had been a student there in his youth.

That was when I saw Damascus for the first time. Or maybe it wasn't actually the first time because my family used to come here often. In those days, Damascus was a quiet little city where people went to rest and relax. The water was wonderful and there were lots of vegetable gardens all around the old town. There was not much more to it then. It was a small and peaceful city, graceful and simple. In the evenings, even in June when it was very hot during the daytime, you had to put on something warm after sunset as it was always cool. And then there was this friendliness between neighbours and people who knew each other. Everything was very simple and very dignified, sometimes poor, but very dignified. There was a lot of respect for old people; neighbours were important, and one never did anything that might disturb them. It was a peaceful society, perhaps more peaceful and simpler than Lebanese society. To us, coming here was a joyful event, we relaxed, and it was like going on holiday.

Then, one day, the Shiite Sheikh of Damascus died. I remember his name was Mohseh al Amin – a holy man – and my father was appointed to replace him. He became the Great Sheikh of Syria's Shiites, as I eventually became myself and as my son might perhaps become one day. So my family moved to Damascus, and that became our home and our city.

But none of that had taken place yet when, as a young boy, I travelled through the desert to the holy city of Karbala, on the Euphrates River, in Iraq. Although the sunlight was blinding and the road was long, a great experience was awaiting me, and I was proud to be part of that world. I remember we came across several coaches along the way and we spent a while with some of the people travelling on them at one of those refreshment areas you find near the filling stations. There was a group of religious women who took me under their wing. They thought I was on my own and asked me if I needed anything. There was a great sense of brotherhood between us and it was a very good feeling. Then, of course, my parents appeared and when the devout women realized that my father was an important religious figure they immediately fell silent and almost stepped aside. I remember it as a small yet highly significant episode.

I came from Lebanon, and my family enjoyed the sort of respect that is normally accorded to important religious families. And although there was a sociable and brotherly atmosphere around us, we were always a bit more equal than others. There, in the Syrian Desert, on the road to Karbala, I felt both grownup and protected. It was not the holiness of the city that made me feel protected, but the religious and god-fearing spirit of all the travellers, which I could easily identify with because it was the same spirit that dwelled within my home and in the heart of everyone we knew. Yet, the sincere and very direct religious faith of some of these women made me feel somewhat ill at ease. Eventually, I would get to know them and also to appreciate their instinctive faith in God. But at the time, as a young boy who had grown up in a family where God was not only a revelation and a prophet but also embodied doctrine, justice and mercy, I remember being surprised to hear that these women were going to Karbala to ask for this, that and the other. There was a time, a few years later, when I became very rigid towards these kinds of attitudes. The more I studied, the more I realized that the act of creation is in itself an act of love, and that it will not necessarily be confirmed by other divine interventions based on daily or individual appeals. So, these devout women who had embarked on a journey in order to ask for a son or a grandson, or for a sick relative to be cured, seemed to me, for a brief moment of my life, something too concrete and too simplistic. It has taken me years to realize how important this kind of faith is too, especially for us and for people like myself. It's a religious faith that knows how to be humble and modest, and which presents itself before God with full awareness of one's own insignificance. The important thing is not what one is asking for, whether it is for someone to become pregnant or for a quarrel between siblings to be resolved. It is to surrender to God: where this is concerned, those who study only have to learn. Sometimes surrendering to God is not easy, especially if one is young and wealthy, and if one is grappling with complex philosophical problems. But it is surrendering to God, trusting in Him and in His mercy that will save human beings, not the arrogance that comes from culture and from thinking that one knows. It is humility: this is what God asks of us and has given to all men, as long as they know how to nurture it.

I remember that when we got back into the car I felt proud not so much because of my Lebanese origins but for the fact that I belonged to a community. And this community suddenly became richer when, a few hours later, we saw some Bedouin tents in the desert, far away from the road, with their flocks and their camels. Dad said to me that the life they lived was not very different from the life that Abraham had led, and that the men in the tents were much closer to him than we ourselves were. 'And Abraham,' he said, 'was not only the father of us all, but the one who answered God's call unquestioningly. And he obeyed Him as one obeys one's father, trusting totally in His words and His will. Abraham was the model for Man, with his pure faith. "He rendered thanks to Allah for His bounties so that Allah chose him (for His favours) and directed him to the Right Way."'[8] 'Oh Lord,' said my father, 'whatever my abilities are, they rest on You.' My mother added nothing to these words, but I knew that the low whisper coming from her lips was praising God and His wisdom ('O Lord, Your name embodies the essence of all creation'), and then I felt as if I was enveloped by something that didn't concern just myself and my own learning, but also my family and all the people I knew. And so, to me, Karbala was becoming an appointment with God, and I too, like many others, had been summoned to go and meet Him and to serve Him. I know I was deeply aware of my own importance and of the path that lay before of me. I felt weak and strong at the same time, as if my path, and the one my parents had set out for me, was the same as that of the people in the tents, or of the women we met along the road.

Although of course, there was everything else as well. It isn't as if these devout women were the only people going to Karbala, and among those I met there were clearly some who were less honest than others or whose purposes were not exactly upright. Many of them were merchants, and although they spoke the right words and the sentences they repeated were those of true believers, it was clear that in Karbala they would be spending more time doing business and meeting with other merchants like themselves rather than praying. They went around in groups, often in silence, and when we met them on the road they always stood a little aside. But when they saw a group of men like themselves, either in a rest area or along the road, they would immediately strike up a conversation which could sometimes become very lively.

Eventually the desert became less harsh and the roads started getting busier, and even the light was no longer as crisp and clear as it was in Syria but became humid and the vegetation grew more luxuriant, until my father said we were now approaching the Euphrates River. That is where the two holy cities of Karbala and Najaf had been built. In actual fact, there was also a third city, Kufa, where Ali was beaten and made into a martyr. But that city is damned by all Shiites and nobody wants to go there. And the mosque where Ali was killed was dilapidated at the time and no one took care of it. But Karbala and Najaf, with their golden domes and their great mosques, then as now, were not just holy cities but major centres of culture for Shiites and Sunnis alike.

I saw something of that myself, of course. But I remember being told that the two cities had been much more impressive a few years before then. There used to be huge processions coming in from very far away, from places like Samarqand, Iran, Afghanistan and Syria itself, transporting the bodies of the deceased shrouded in cotton cloth and rolled inside a modest carpet. In the old days these caravans were looked after by Indians who came all the way from India. Sometimes there were plague outbreaks, and the processions would be stopped before reaching Karbala and Najaf to prevent them from bringing the disease with them. But to avoid being discovered the caravans would bypass the cities along the way and continue their journey as far as the holy cities. Although I don't recall experiencing it personally, I was told that the smell from these processions of death was so obnoxious that you could tell they were coming long before they arrived: you still hadn't seen their faces, but you could already perceive that terrible stench. There were thousands of them every year. The dead bodies were first taken to Karbala, where they would be placed inside the great mosque, and then to Najaf to be buried beside Ali.

That's what Najaf was like back then. People would bring their dead to be buried. The faithful would come, even from great distances, and teachers, the ulamas, came here from across the Islamic world. Sheikhs from Persia, Bukhara, Herat and Syria would all gather here. And many of them were from Lebanon, like my own family. Of course, there were merchants too, as always when there are large gatherings of people. There were traders from Basra with Indian goods, and merchants from Persia, who did business in Persia and Samarqand or Afghanistan. Many came from Aleppo in Syria, and some, though not as many, from Damascus. So Najaf was not an unknown city to me. As well as the framed picture of it we had on the wall at home, it was a place I had always heard people talk about, more so than many other cities in Turkey or Palestine. Najaf was near, I might say, it was our world. So in my mind, I wasn't going to study abroad, or to a challenging, faraway place; it meant moving somewhere not too far from home.

And then, once we got there to study, it wasn't as if we were allowed a great deal of freedom. As with all cities where there are lots of people flocking in from other places, for religious reasons or otherwise, there were places where a twelve-year-old couldn't, although he wanted to. Discipline was very strict at university and you did exactly as you were told. That's still more or less what happens in our religion today, where the opinion of the Great Sheikh has to be observed by everyone, whether or not they agree with it. To us, he is a kind of descendant of Ali, the one who interprets his role on earth. His wisdom and competence to decide command a great deal of respect. That is why we obey even though we may disagree. Doesn't having religious faith mean understanding when one has to obey? Trusting one's superiors and accepting what they say is not just obedience but humility. There is no faith, and perhaps there is no religion either, without the humility that accepts one's inadequacy and submits to the opinion and the advice of those who know better – or those of God.

I studied in Najaf, and that was a great experience for me on a personal level, thanks to the people I met, but also on a religious and educational level. Everything was highly codified and precise. It couldn't be otherwise since it has been a centre of study for over a thousand years (I believe it will be one thousand two hundred soon), so by now there is a very well-established approach to studying and to its rules and methods. Obviously the Quran was the most important subject, but it wasn't the only one. They taught us the history of the various religions in the word, the sayings and commandments of the Prophet, the history of the world, and the Arab world in particular, along with a vast amount of Arabic literature and grammar. You couldn't leave that school without being learned in Arabic and grammar. Besides, we didn't study a particular science or doctrine but the path of a believer in this world. And so it was important to understand what was passed down not in a literal sense but in terms of its deep meaning, so that we would eventually be able to apply all this to our world and interpret it.

Then there was this ongoing, almost daily, bustle which we boys loved very much, with teachers coming and going all the time, holding classes in one school, then in another, then in another one again. There were also visiting professors who ran short and very intensive courses then left for somewhere else. It was a very lively environment when I went there as a boy. You would meet men from far-flung worlds, with different life stories, professionally and culturally, but all of them helped us to develop, to learn, and to one day become skilled at interpreting the doctrine and pronouncing judgments.

Of course, there were Sunnis and Shias, together. And this too was a great merit of those holy places. There, you learned to understand that these schools of thought are not divided by doctrine. There were obviously differences, but we also had a great deal in common, and the fact of living daily side by side, sometimes praying in the same places, or simply studying and listening made me realize just how artificial this division running through our religion really is. Since then I have always firmly believed that there are only tiny differences between Sunnis and Shias, but they are exacerbated by politics, by men and by power for purposes that have nothing to do with spiritual issues. This division is exploited by some men in order to boost their standing or impose their power, but it has nothing to do with Islam. So, after living in Najaf for a few years, you felt you belonged to group of people that may have enjoyed some privileges but also gave you a different way of seeing the divisions that exist between nations, between schools of thought, and between political regimes and politicians.

This perspective was definitely linked to my personal history. After all, I was born in Lebanon to a Lebanese family, my family had moved to Damascus, in Syria, soon after I was born, and in my teens I grew up studying alongside Iraqi, Persian and Central Asian youths. But it wasn't just this personal history that enabled me to see events with a sense of perspective; it may have contributed to it, but only up to a point. I believe that by far the most formative part of my background was this community of purposes and shared study that one lived and breathed in Najaf. After a while, you felt part of a religious community that had no boundaries, either geographical or related to superiority or inferiority. Together we studied the life of the Prophet and Arabic, grammar and literature; and this bond grew day after day until it became so strong that it was almost natural. Then, you would turn around and look at your country, with its many small divisions and wonder how it was possible for us to live together for years in Najaf, studying and developing the same beliefs, while people out there could become divided over a trifle, like a river or a mountain boundary, or over a mere word. The divisions in our world were not born in Najaf or Karbala.

It is not that there weren't any differences between us, but they were not so strong on a doctrinal or religious level. Shias and Sunnis are two banks of the same river: there are differences between them but without politics and tangible human interests they are not rivals. So, in Najaf we all studied together, Sunnis and Shias and, to make sure that this place of faith and culture remained outside of worldly matters, the university was effectively independent from all forms of state subsidy. Our governing body guarded, and still guards, this independence jealously. Education, learning and science should be free from any kind of influence: money, buildings or any other help from the state should not be accepted because we all know how these things turn out in the end. No one gives anything for nothing.

So, those who could afford to, gave one fifth of their earnings and those who couldn't gave nothing. And the sum collected was allocated in such a way that part of it would go to the areas where a Shiite sheikh was needed, and maybe useful, but there weren't enough believers to provide a living for him. And part of the sum, of course, went to charities in Najaf and other cities in Iraq, as well as to universities and education. This independence of our institutions has always been at the root of the diffidence shown towards them by states, and, at the same time, it a source of pride to those who entrust us with their money because they know how it is used and where it goes. That way, they feel part of the great mission carried out by a university of huge standing and are proud of it. Maybe they'll boast about it a little with their friends, but in the end, they feel part of it and maybe they'll remember it for many years afterwards, when their children graduate or when their experience in Najaf is only a memory.

Najaf was not just a holy city; it wasn't merely the place where Sunnis and Shias could meet and discover that 'men are brothers in faith and equals in humanity' – how beautiful are these words pronounced by Ali! Najaf was a university for all of us, and from there we were sent back out into the world as adults, each with their own ideas and personal beliefs, but all of which were to some extent part of one and the same religious and human experience, of the same educational path. The brotherly solidarity that grew between us who studied there was the same as that which developed among our sponsors, wherever they were and whatever land they trod.

It was important that this should be so because, once we went back to our homelands and to our families, we would eventually be called upon to interpret the law and express our opinions. It was obviously essential that what was said in Damascus was not the opposite of what was said in Isfahan, or that the words spoken in Yemen were not the opposite of those spoken in Baghdad. But it was also important for each of us to attain a status which, in the eyes of the world where we would eventually go and work, set us above the issues of that particular place and moment in time. The soundness, and the very credibility of certain answers, depends on this general sense of equidistance, so that I am no longer my father's son or the first born to a Lebanese family, with its own history and its own past, but I am part of a higher community which by virtue of this is accepted by all, because it is and must be above all the parties, nations and individuals concerned.

How else would I have managed in the perhaps minor yet quite dramatic situation I had to deal with a few days ago? There was this woman, a worthy woman. And there was her husband, who had seemed to me to be a good person. Their love story had been more difficult than many others, and perhaps for that reason too, it appeared to me to be blessed by God. Their family history was very different, and their personal background was different too. Yet the love that bound them together was so strong, so true, that she – who was born a Christian – had agreed to become a Muslim. And her husband had welcomed her renunciation with the devotion with which a man in love receives a gift. Yet, it is so difficult for anyone to abandon their original faith, even though Christianity is not so distant from ours, indeed, it finds wide scope in ours. But the study of God and His will is one thing, and the way families react is quite another. And this married couple had agreed to meet on a level that was everyone's and no one's at the same time. Of course, things were easier for him. But this didn't mean that his family was less upset about it. As to her family, especially her father, the daughter's choice had become a source of great sorrow. Of course he understood; of course he realized that the ways of the Almighty follow paths which men are incapable of understanding. But understanding and accepting something are two different things. Sometimes, the love for one's child doesn't stretch far enough to accept all this. And so, the couple had started a new family, divided in sorrow – though not in affection – from her family, and to some extent also from his so as to counterbalance her separation. That way, the scales wouldn't tip too much on one side or the other, and neither of them would one day feel they had given too much or received too little.

Of course, word gets around; when you raise your voice your neighbours hear you. Some people keep it to themselves while others can't wait to tell everyone. But until she came to me herself I didn't want to believe it – I preferred not to believe it. She started telling me about the beatings and the battering, and about her husband's aggressiveness towards her. In a case like this it's easy to listen, but it's so hard to give advice, and there is a danger of getting it wrong! How can you intervene in such a difficult situation? And knowing so little about it?

There she was, asking me the same question over and over again: can I separate what God has joined together? And, at first, I wondered whether this was part of her past upbringing. Initially I thought the reflections she was expressing to me were part of something that didn't belong to me. It took me some time to realize that that wasn't the case. Her conversion had not been instrumental, merely for the sake of love or a husband. It had led her – perhaps driven by love, this may have been part of it too – to think in ways she had not considered before. The new dimension of faith she had attained was as close to her heart as her former faith, because she had suffered for it and had chosen it. But I also think it was because she had come to realize that there is a strong human element in all these divisions invented by man. And she understood that God belongs to everyone, and somehow manifests Himself to and is part of us all. So, at some point, I think I understood what she was trying to tell me: she was not concerned about the beatings or the distress that comes with married life. She wanted to know, with my help, whether this too was one of God's trials. And just as the first painful trial had brought her a new inner life that she cherished, she wondered if the beatings and a husband who didn't deserve that name was somehow a new test, a call for a renewed commitment to religious faith and knowledge.

She sat there, not very far from me, beside a basket of fruit, and I wished I could have shared her faith, or her trust rather than her faith. And what I wanted to say to her became clearer and clearer to me, but I didn't know how to say it to her, because this woman had clung to that hope with all her power and the only response she expected from me was to confirm that she was right. If she felt she was being called upon to fulfil that duty, she had to obey herself and do what she felt was right at that moment.

I also wondered what a Christian priest would have said in that situation. And of course I knew that there were also others waiting to hear my answer. Not that other people were important to me or to her, but what I said to her would carry significant weight with all of them.

Is that what inspired my words? I am still not sure what the answer to that is. I tried not to let myself be influenced, I tried to think in solitude, without attaching any importance to everything that happens in this city and in this neighbourhood of Damascus, where people live side by side with everyone else without taking much notice of the faith of those they meet. Instead, I focused on honesty, sincerity and the things that matter.

So I said to her: 'Sometimes God joins together, sometimes He separates. His will is not tied to a choice but changes according to each case, though its substance does not change.' At these words, she started crying and sobbing. It was a very emotional moment for both of us, and then I understood that my words had been a release for her. At first I felt almost happy, but then I wondered if I had done the right thing and whether I had a right to use such weighty words in a situation I knew so little about.

It was important for me to have studied in Najaf, and to have all those years of study behind me at a level that was well above what was required of me in ordinary life. Whenever I have to make difficult choices, some of course far more difficult than the one I faced with this woman battered by her husband, Najaf is a point of reference. When I feel unsure, I ask myself what my teachers would have said and how they would have answered if I could have put the question to them. We belong to a community of faith and knowledge that continues through time, even though you may no longer be in touch with its members – and even though when you go back to Karbala and visit the madrasah where you were taught so many things you don't see them anymore, and maybe there is only an old caretaker left who tells you about a teacher who got sick and died, or about another who was sent to Tabriz or Tehran. But you perceive around you the same enthusiasm of the old days; the only difference is that the teachers are all younger than yourself. Then you realize you are getting old and it won't be long before someone will say in turn: 'Ah! The great Sheikh of Damascus! He was here only a few weeks ago! Who would ever have thought?'

The second source of learning for me was my father. Sitting there where my son sometimes sits, I would listen to my father talking to people who came to ask for his advice, without distinctions between Sunnis and Shias, but also without barriers between languages and nations. There was a French diplomat who spent many afternoons with my father and would stay until late at night. He came not just for pleasure, but to learn about our world. This is Europe's great advantage, something that we need ourselves. Europe may be weak; it may be divided, and it may be of no account. But it knows how to listen to our voice, and it doesn't matter whether ultimately all this produces nothing. In the long run something will happen. Others don't listen: they get here and have solutions for this, that and the other. They may be in good faith. They may genuinely trust men and their goodness. But what good can you do in this country, and in this region, if you forget to listen to people? And so, that Frenchman loved talking to my father and would discuss religious doctrine, the law and international law with him. And I remember my father would walk him to the front door late into the night, when the roads leading to our house were dark and deserted, and ask him whether he would go back to his country and tell people about everything they had discussed. And the diplomat, betraying his personal feelings, replied affectionately: 'When that day comes, I shall miss your big turban, and sitting with you for hours talking about God as well as your great moderation and wisdom.' And Dad would smile and say: 'We are all human beings. We try to do our best for the good of humanity.'

When he came back indoors, my father would look at me and I couldn't tell whether or not he wanted to hear my views. He'd ask for a hot drink before going to bed and while I prepared it for him he would stroke his beard. As I brought him his chamomile tea, he would say with a dreamy look: 'He is a good man, he's a good man.' Sometimes I would lie awake all night, trying to understand what the Frenchman had said and work out the strengths and weaknesses in his knowledge of the scriptures. But, in my sleepy state, the doctrinal differences between us would lose their significance and all that was left was my father stroking his beard, repeating to me: 'He's a good man.'

Even nowadays, when I have trouble getting to sleep, I still think about those evenings and my days in Najaf, and about the people of this neighbourhood of Damascus where I live. I think about the Christian family living opposite and their idle son, who has nevertheless managed to get a degree in English, to his grandfather's great joy. And I think about the other Sunni family, on the opposite side of the road, which runs a wholesale florist's business, and about the woman who washes the pavement outside our house in the morning. One day I said to my son, loudly enough for her to hear me, that we should wash our own entrance, and she peeped out of a window and said to me: 'Your Grace, let me do this humble job, it's the only one I know how to do. You can take care of us all and of all the ills and adversities afflicting humanity.'

And then I think about this understanding that reigns among us, something that is neither forced nor imposed by anyone. We are neighbours who try to love and get along with one other because we are human beings and see each other as human beings. In our everyday lives, religious differences or differences in the way we interpret the faith don't matter, they are not important. Being brothers in religious faith or bothers in humanity, what is the difference? When the person near us becomes someone we know, we can no longer be afraid of them and see them as an enemy. If men can talk to each other, even about small and simple things, they cannot fail to see their own humanity reflected in the face of the other. Then, the great questions of principle disappear before this powerful sensation that we are all humans, we are all brothers in this world.

This is what I learned in Najaf and from listening to my father when men in charge of the national law came to discuss things with him and would ask him how to interpret certain passages and to confirm or otherwise whether a particular interpretation was right or "less wrong". This is what Islam is, it is this too. It is a very flexible religion that does not put forward fixed, unchanging solutions. Just as in the episode I mentioned. Sometimes good is achieved by separating what is joined together, other times by joining together what is separated. And this simple and practical approach always forces you to find a human and acceptable solution, but it somehow also ends up being harsh and intransigent when you are trying to deliver a practicable solution. And also, confession doesn't absolve from sin, as is the case in the West. No man on earth has this power, not even in the name and on behalf of God. Man is alone before God, before His infinite mercy and love: but this mercy requires repentance to be deep and sincere and to be followed by a real change, and not just words to that effect. Sinning belongs to the world of human beings, but to carry on or to persist in sinning shows lack of repentance or that one is merely seeking an instrumental and temporary forgiveness. Confession may be a good thing. But Christians are aware that it often becomes a tool to avoid changing and to carry everything on as before. Of course this is not in the spirit of confession but in the use that men make of it. But this is precisely why I think the simplicity of a faith that offers no excuses is somehow more useful. There is no sin that is not human, but there are no excuses, there are no attenuating circumstances for continuing to sin when one is alone before God. There is no remedy for behaving wrongly except by correcting one's behaviour.

So it seems to me that everything is perhaps much simpler in our faith, or very clear, if I can put it that way. We don't have secret books for the initiated, whose interpretation is the preserve of a few with superior knowledge. In Islam there are no books whose reading is prescribed for those with the ability to understand and grasp things. Everything takes place out in the open: the scriptures are what they are, and so are the sacred texts; anyone can open them and read them; anyone can get an idea of what they are about. It is precisely this flexibility within our faith that places men before themselves and offers them no excuses. Anything is possible, and perhaps anything may be right, as long as a man's spirit is honest and righteous before God – as long as he doesn't try to shrink from this encounter that involves righteousness, honesty and mercy.

Then there are men, their history, their disputes and their interests, politics and parties. And these things certainly change the course of events and therefore also change the course of history. But though unrelated to religion, they are nevertheless in some way part of it. Because there is no religion, there is no faith without men. Men are not separate from all of this. Faith, what is faith?

There was a professor in Najaf who once said something that impressed us all. At the end of the lesson, almost as he was closing his books and waiting for us to leave his classroom, he said: 'No matter how much wrong and how many dreadful things man can do, however much he can stain himself with terrible misdeeds before God, faith is not something that lives outside of man. It is within man; it is man himself. Faith is our relationship with God: it is not just God and it is not just man. It is the path that leads us to Him and that leads Him to us. Faith can lift us up to God's heart and can lift our lives. But it is nothing other than what we are and how we live.'

The other day, a group of boys asked me what globalization is, and whether it is a good or a bad thing. I asked them to come back to me the next day, not because I didn't know what to say but because I realized there was something I knew that was struggling to come out, it was as if I had forgotten it.

I sat there in silence for a few hours. I talked about it with my son and we said a lot of sound things that I could have said to those boys. But when I retired to my bedroom, that something still escaped me. I don't know whether I fell asleep or was just dozing. Then I heard the muezzin's call to the first daily prayer.[9] Maybe that reminded me of when I used to get up with my parents as a boy, or of the university in Najaf, who knows? But while I was praying, the words of that old professor came back to me and I realized what I wanted to say. When the students came back in the afternoon with their teacher and sat very respectfully around me in my room, I told them about that sentence, about how faith can be nothing other than human nature, and how in the religious person the one and the other must proceed in unison.

'I can't talk about globalization in the abstract,' I said, 'for nothing exists in the abstract. If faith doesn't exist without men, then neither does globalization exist without men. So, I can't merely consider what globalization says about itself and about its nature. If I did that, I would have to tell you that it uses wonderful concepts and opens a new era for mankind. It puts peoples in touch with one another; it forces them to open themselves to each other, to speak the same language and also to exchange views on the many differences that divide them about God and the earth. How could I tell you that all this is negative? These are beautiful concepts that belong not only to our religion but also to all religions across the world: it is a good thing that these values stop being confined to the religious sphere and become part of the everyday life of human beings. But, do you think the kind of globalization I have just described actually exists? If we look around us, we can see that globalization says one thing and does another. And this other globalization, the one we see every day, day in day out, affecting people, our lives and our world, bears no connection whatsoever to all the values that globalization supposedly brings with it.

Many years ago – shortly after my father died and I had become head of the Shia community in Syria – I was invited to a European city. And the welcome and kind assistance I received, along with people's deep desire to learn which I perceived during my lessons, made me say, on my return to Damascus, that although I had spoken with Christians, I had met the spirit of Islam. I also said that this clearly went beyond the words and the definitions found in books and applied to all religions, indeed became part of them. It was a great joy for me to go there and come back enriched by this experience. So, when I was invited to go back there again a few months ago, I accepted eagerly, thinking we would pick up the conversation from where we had left off. Some people were the same, others were new, but everything else had changed! There was less openness and less interest. And all the people I met seemed poorer inside and, less profound, more shabbily dressed, more selfish in their family relationships, more arid. Thirty years ago, they didn't keep talking about freedom, democracy and progress because they didn't need to. Each of these values was pivotal to their existence, but there was no need to say it because it emerged from everything.

What I was seeing now was a façade, embellished with beautiful words but with nothing behind it anymore. I saw a cynical and calculating vacuum that frightened me. And so I said to myself that if globalization is the capacity to transform an open and God-fearing society – or at least a society in awe of everything that God represents even though He is not mentioned by name – into what I was seeing, then it was an evil force. It was a cancer to be eradicated. It is cloaked in fine words, but it is a poison that kills, that sets wife against husband and father against son. But it is even more dangerous because in order to do all this it disguises itself behind noble concepts and words that no one dares to challenge. It was much better years ago, when the young people I met knew nothing about the Shi'a and the Quran but came to me with passages from the Gospel that they knew and asked me to comment on them in light of our doctrine.

Today, they came to me with some research they had done on the Internet. From the words they spoke they seemed to know everything, but in actual fact they hadn't the least idea not only of what the Shi'a and Islam are about, but also the Gospel. I think many of them wouldn't even have been able to recite a prayer without stopping and waiting for their teacher's cue. So, if globalization is what I see, and what we are seeing, this culture of which television is the symbol and the conveyer, then I say it is an evil and that we should fight against it.'

I don't feel old because of this, and I don't even feel distant from our times. I just think that those who still haven't been contaminated by this poison – which makes our consciences shallower and leads us into a world of set phrases empty of meaning and value, lacking a deep identity in terms of what we find and what we experience – have a duty to say so. And they have a duty to stop this avalanche that leaves nothing to build on as it passes through. So I ask myself whether I am lucky to live in this city

in Syria, which has changed and has grown bigger — too big actually
— but where words still have a meaning that people can understand
and where men are men first and foremost. And while here too a
great deal has changed, and your neighbours are less important and
families are not quite as close as they were in the past, the society I
live in is not split — as it seems to me to be in the West — between
words and the substance to which they refer. That is because
freedom, globalization, exchange and knowledge are wonderful
words, but not if they coincide — as was my, perhaps mistaken,
impression — with a great deal of superficiality and shallowness, and
with such a deep and hopeless selfishness that the woman who lives
opposite me, the one who washes the pavement outside my house
every morning, can't even imagine could possibly exist.

4 - The Palestinian Builder

I was born in a village just outside Safad, in Palestine. My parents had a small, 250 acre property: it was a plot like many others, neither too fertile nor too arid. On the whole, my family enjoyed a good standard of living. When we talk about those days, we always say those were happy times. We had sheep and olive trees; we had all we needed to live a decent life. My father was very determined that I should go to school, so I went to primary school and I didn't start helping around the house, in the fields and with the sheep until seven years later. Everything was very simple back then; we worked our land and took our flocks out to graze. Sometimes, when the farm work became more demanding, some families would come and lend us a hand, and sometimes we would go and lend them a hand. Working your own land is a great joy, you feel free and independent, even though you may spend too much time alone. In later years, when I looked back on that time I often wondered whether it was harder to work your own land, on your own or working with other people as an employee... Yes, you get to know more people, and the atmosphere around you may be more cheerful. But I would never have wanted to change things. You were happy, you did what you wanted, and what you wanted was what the land needed. And if the loneliness of the countryside got to you in the evening when you went back to the village, you could spend time with your family or go and see someone.

Yes, it's probably as you say. Since it's all over and it will never come back, it's only natural to think that it was wonderful and perfect. But I can remember it being really like that, as something I experienced myself. I don't think it comes from being exiled.

It all began on 15 May 1948. I was a teenager and I still remember that day very well. The British had told our village authorities that they would be leaving their public posts, the police stations and the municipal offices at 4 p.m. We did what we could to organize ourselves in order to be ready, but it was all in vain. The British had actually left two hours before, at 2 p.m., and had told the Jews that. When we got there just after 4 p.m. all the positions had been occupied, the barracks, the fire brigade headquarters, the school – they had occupied everything... I don't know if they had any weapons. Some of our people said the British would also leave their weapons and ammunitions behind in the barracks, so the Jews were armed as well. But looking back on that now, it seems unlikely to me. I don't know, you don't leave weapons around just like that, for anyone to help themselves, even if they were Jews and their relations with the British were different from ours. So that's how we left.

All of us, I mean all of us... Did we talk about it? Of course we talked about it, but there wasn't much to discuss. The Jews had everything; people said that they also had weapons. In the weeks before there had been some terrible massacres on both sides. There was nothing to talk about. Those who stayed behind were in danger of getting killed, and in some places that's actually what happened. Who would want to stay in that kind of situation?

Some elderly people decided to stay on, but there weren't many of them. I don't know if my parents understood things better than I did, although I was already grown up and they were getting old by then. When I left the village I didn't think it would be forever.

Around forty thousand of us left from the Safad area, but I don't think any of us thought it was anything other than a prudent and temporary departure. Or, at least, that's what I thought, otherwise I wouldn't have left. They were armed and there had already been clashes with massacres. It was natural to get away from the region. You didn't trust anyone anymore, even though some of them had been our neighbours. Now there was war, you see. Only soldiers can stay on the war front, not farmers and ordinary people. That's why we left. We had 250 acres of fertile land, a house, and everything we held dear. If we had thought it would be forever, I would never have left my home, I would rather have taken up arms.

It wasn't until a few days later that the truth began to dawn on us. We were living in camps near the Syrian border. The large mass of refugees was beginning to divide. The townsfolk, those who were used to living in Safad, were thinking of going to settle in Damascus. The farmers like ourselves only thought about looking for a plot of land to farm... What would we do in a city? There was talk that the Syrian government was prepared to give us some land on the Golan Heights. So, some went one way, others went another way, it was a harrowing scene. Families were splitting up, each going their own way. One child went to one place and one to another. Then we had to decide who would stay with the grandparents, the elderly and the children. There was despair, but it was still contained. Mothers would say to their daughters: 'It won't be for long.' Old people said they could stay and wait where they had stopped because the situation would be sorted out in a few weeks. There was a lot of sadness, but not dismay. We would be going back before long. Then some people started shouting that we were crazy and had no idea of what was really going on. We were going back and forth within that crowd, without knowing who to listen to, where to go or what to do. Just then, a car that had fled from Safad suddenly approached us. It was driven by a middle aged man wearing a European suit. I don't know why but I thought he was a doctor or an optician. I remember he got out of the car and walked into the midst of the crowd. He was crying and raising his arms to the sky and bringing them down on his head, like this... And people crowded around him to find out what happened. Some thought there had been a massacre, others were thinking about an armed conflict. No one imagined... No one could have thought...

... No, no. I want to carry on. It happened sixty years ago but it still seems like yesterday to me. My life is different now, it has changed forever. The man told us that as soon as we had left, on the very same day, without even waiting for an hour an hour the bulldozers had gone and razed the whole village to the ground: the houses, the shops, everything. Everything had been torn down by bulldozers. The houses were gone, and so were the roads, the mosque and the burial ground. Everything had disappeared, you see. There were scenes, you can imagine what happened. Many were crying, some said we should go back to Safad and take back our land. Most of us thought our situation was so absurd that sooner or later something was bound to happen to bring everything back to normal. There was no reason for it, or at least we didn't think there was. Perhaps because I was young, or perhaps just by intuition, or maybe someone told me, but I know I realized then that we had lost everything, and we would never be going back. And that's how it was...

... No, nothing at all. Not a letter, not a photo or a note, we've never had any news, neither about the village nor about those who stayed on. It's as if our village had moved to an imaginary place from which we get no news, no images or anything else. It's as if we had only dreamt about it. Sometimes I say to myself that I'd like to see the place again even just for an instant. I would be prepared to stay in a tent, even just for an hour, like a tourist. But my son disagrees, and it's impossible anyway. I'll never be able to go back to my land.

You heard him, didn't you? There you have it, that's my son. But there are many like him. He wouldn't hurt a fly, but ever since the Berlin Wall came down he just keeps repeating these words: 'Would you ever have believed it, Dad? Would you have thought it possible?' He has hopes, he keeps hoping. He says that if the Soviet Union collapsed then here too anything can happen...

I know you don't want to talk about politics. We won't talk about it anymore, but you see, I, we, have this hope in our hearts. It's like a hope that salvation will suddenly come and bring our ordeal to an end, return our land to us and enable us to go back to our old life, without hurting anyone. I'd like to tell you... some people have talked about giving money as compensation to those who have lost their land. I want you to know that there is no possible compensation. Would you ever accept compensation in exchange for your mother or father, even if you were offered a great deal of money? There are some things that money can't buy: we're Palestinians and nothing else. Once you have given me money, do you really hope I will become something else? Could you ever become anything other than Italian? If they can't become anything other than Jews, why should we become anything other than Palestinian?

Yes, we stayed in a refugee camp for a few days and then we left for the Golan. And each of us was eventually given a plot of land. That's where my eldest son was born, the one who told you about the Soviet Union. Slowly, bit by bit, life seemed set to return to normal. We were living in tents to begin with, then we were housed in barracks, and then there was also talk about the possibility of having houses, some small properties. It's not that I don't want to talk about it; quite honestly, the Syrians did all they could to make us feel at home. I've never felt I was treated differently because I was Palestinian. What little they were able to give they gave us, and it might even have been enough. But I find it impossible to talk about it now, after what happened.

We used to come to Damascus a few times over the course of the year to do our shopping and buy what we needed. It was a small town back then, small and charming. And there too, our family members and acquaintances were well received. Those who came from Safad and didn't have a clue about working the land were welcomed. Everyone was able to pursue their own line of work. There was a lot of greenery in Damascus at the time, it was a small town surrounded by greenery and water: it was very different from what it has become in recent years. I looked at it and didn't look at it. I still had a faint hope that sooner or later we would be able to go back to Safad. We were living in this new situation in the Golan, and although it was very different from what we had left behind, it was nevertheless acceptable. Life was harder. There wasn't a major town like Safad nearby, and the soil was much less fertile. But our life could have been okay.

Then a new war broke out, and we had to flee once again. There were no alternatives left; we had to take refuge in Damascus. We have been living here ever since and, in actual fact, the people of Damascus have never made us feel like refugees. We are treated as if we were born in the city and really belong here. But we are farmers; we were used to working the land and had nothing left anymore. We didn't have the money to buy a plot, and we used our savings to buy the land in this Damascus suburb where we built our house. I built it myself, a bit at a time, but we couldn't afford to buy some fertile land in the outskirts of Damascus, you needed too much money. Even if we had been able to sell our land outside Safad we might not have made enough to buy a plot here in Damascus.

I remember we reached the city just after the end of the school year. We lived in the school buildings for a few months while we waited for a refugee camp to be ready. We were also given a little money and some food and clothing. We had lost everything for the second time. When the schools reopened we were offered the chance of living in the refugee camp, but as to that... We discussed it at home, and we all agreed that if we stayed in the camps we would be living in an absurd and impossible situation forever. We needed to work and earn money. In order to do that, you couldn't stay in the camp and take the food and the daily allowance that the Syrian government gave you. And so, with the little money we managed to scrape together, we rented an old house in the centre of Damascus and from there I would set off every morning to look for work. No, I don't remember anything about Damascus in those days. I was desperate. And I was obsessed with the idea of finding work. If I couldn't get a job, we would have had to go back to the refugee camp. And that would have been the most disastrous situation of all. And, besides, all of us had always worked... What would we do in the refugee camp? What would we be waiting for?

I found a job as a builder. There was this man who took me on to cut limestone and build dry stone walls. He was looking for someone who knew how to make dry stone walls and that's something I had learned to do in Safad, and I was quite good at it. When I started, my job was to cut the stone, which may seem easy, but it isn't at all. That's because limestone is like meat, it has streaks and weak points. There are some pieces of stone that are made to become quadrangular blocks, and others that naturally become wedges. But making wedges with the former is incredibly hard and making blocks with wedge-shaped ones... They keep crumbling and also don't last over time. I can't remember who taught me these things in Safad. It was a neighbour, a good and very hardworking man. He used to say that the stone already knows where it wants to go and that a good stonemason adapts himself to the stone; he doesn't force the stone to go where its nature doesn't want to. He had a lot of experience. He needed the dry stone walls to support the terraced fields where his family had planted olive trees many generations before. No matter how well-made the walls were, all it took was an unusually heavy storm or a blizzard to damage them, so there was always something that needed repairing. So, that's how I started working as a stonemason for this man in Damascus, and after a while he realized I was faster than the others and began to think highly of me. He once said to me that I shouldn't worry anymore and that for as long as he was alive I would always have a job and would always work for him. We were together for twelve years – twelve years of extremely hard but also satisfying work. Not long after I started, he got me to teach the other stonemasons how to cut the stone. Then he asked me if I knew how to put the stones together and, when he saw that I was quite skilled at it, I started working on the actual construction of the walls. The stones were brought to me and I would choose them according to the cut, the colour and the density of the stone. So I built walls, and my boss said he was happy and that I was doing a fine job. But the most beautiful things I made were not the new houses, even though I built lots of them. I was asked to restore the mosque and that was the most beautiful thing I made here in Damascus.

My wife worked with an association run by the mosque in the nearby village. It had been set up to help Palestinians, like many others that were around at the time and like the ones that are still around today. Their aim was to collect money for the most needy, provide care for the old, the sick, and so on, the usual things. But the Palestinians in need of help were really too many and the association needed a place where they could manage all this. There was a small, very dilapidated Ottoman mosque nearby; or rather, the mosque itself was open and quite a lot of people used it even though it was small, but the rooms around the courtyard, just a few square metres in size, had been used as stables for many years and were in a terrible state. So the association asked the *Awqaf*[10] for permission to occupy them, which we were granted for a few pounds. I used to go there after work and I enjoyed putting all the stones back into place so that the walls would be solid, but also to preserve the beauty of the work. They were not made of limestone but of two different kinds of marble, pink and black, like the ones you see in many other Ottoman mosques here in Damascus. At the beginning they all looked the same, pink with pink and black with black, but then, if you looked carefully, you realized that certain pinks were lighter and others darker. So the stones had to be matched and arranged in such a way as to achieve a uniform overall effect.

My boss suddenly showed up one Friday evening. I remember very well that I was discussing with the other men in the team how we could replace some of the missing parts of the wall. There were some women standing by who were getting a bit impatient with us because the work was proceeding too slowly, we were enjoying ourselves while they needed the place quickly. But if we had listened to them and put concrete where the stones were missing it would have looked awful! My boss looked at me and said: 'So you still feel like working after hours? Isn't the work I give you enough?' He was a strong and very generous man, with an impressive paunch. But like us, he enjoyed it too. So he told us that an Ottoman house has just been demolished not too far from there, and that it wouldn't be a problem to reclaim a couple of stone bricks from the site. When the work was completed it really looked beautiful. Our wives were happy. The sheikh came and said a prayer for the association and our room eventually became one of the meeting places for the Palestinians living in the neighbourhood, and I think it still is now. But I don't go there anymore. I know I've given you a different impression, but I don't like crying over the past. I forget nothing, and the pain and suffering don't go away. But you can't spend your life only thinking about your pain and suffering. And this getting together with other Palestinians, sometimes it's good, but other times it's too much. Life goes on. My boss then said to me: 'So, you would be able to do restoration work as well, would you?' I think I told him that if he needed the sort of work I had just done, then maybe I could help.

That was a good period of my life. I was with him for twelve years. They were twelve tough years, of hard work but also of some satisfaction. We worked together on a few mosques, a couple of caravanserais, and also on some restaurants near the Umayyad Mosque that had to look beautiful and in keeping with the old architecture. But that's not the sort of work I like. Restoring and preserving an old wall is not the same as building a new wall that looks old. The stone has a different light. Maybe it would be different if we could always do what we did with that old stable, but you can't tear down historic buildings to turn them into quaint restaurants.

Sometimes I think I understand what Damascus must have been like in the old days, even before we got here, it has to be said... No, I have no idea. I think I've heard that there are over 300,000 Palestinian refugees in Damascus alone, but I think that's far less than the actual number. Maybe it only takes into account those who are still in the refugee camps, or who are somehow involved with international humanitarian organizations. We don't call ourselves refugees. Or perhaps just my wife and I might be considered as such. But, between them, our four children now have more than twelve children of their own. I don't think the Palestinian population in Damascus is much below one million. It may actually be a bit more. I don't know for sure, it's not my job. But when we went to work on the houses in the old city of Damascus where builders were needed, you felt that the world opening before you must have been good to live in. The streets were narrow, and the doors were small, almost poor. But once you walked into a house in the old city you immediately realized that there was quality around you, and that there was a lot of smart thinking behind the way they were built. Whatever the location of a Damascene house, the light exposure was always right. Whether or not there was a garden, the windows were always in the right places, capturing the light yet also avoiding the cold in winter and the dust in summer. Also, the houses were large; they were built for more than one family, like our house in Safad. Families all lived together back then, the grandparents, parents, children and grandchildren. Sometimes the individual family units had their own small apartment overlooking a courtyard, which was also overlooked by those of the other relatives. It was a way of being together and having one's own space at the same time.

And then there was the water: a great city of water! What you see now is not even a shadow of what Damascus used to be. The water flowing down from Mount Qassioun and from the Barada River was made to run underneath the city, and it broke up into many different streams that were channelled under the various neighbourhoods of Damascus. You can imagine my reaction when I – who had never seen so much water since my time in Safad – realized that every old house in Damascus actually had running water to use in the kitchen, bathroom and garden. Today the water is gone; it is collected and sent to the water network that supplies the whole city. It may have been wasteful, with all that unused water eventually being lost in the desert. But when, as a builder, I had to repair these pipes or go upstream to remove any obstructions, I saw some highly sophisticated works. There are underground canals lined in marble, and others with ingenious systems that allow the water to settle so that it loses at least some of the lime scale and becomes lighter. Especially in the areas around the *hammams*[11] or the cafés, where there is greater water usage, you can't imagine what sophisticated contrivances have been put in place in order to clean or filter the water. And so, in some cases, when we were able to fix the old water pipes and get them working again – as we did in some of the restaurants we worked on – the inner garden would be completely transformed. I don't know what it is about the soil here in Damascus – I've never been able to buy even a small patch of land for a vegetable garden – but, whatever it is, it gives the plants and the flowers a special brightness that you don't see anywhere else. A rose from Damascus is not like a rose from Safad, or from where you live. The colour of the petals almost lights up, and you can smell the scent across the whole garden, it becomes the fragrance of the house. When the jasmine or the lemon trees bloom, some courtyards in Damascus seem almost like enchanted spots, the scent spreads to all things and makes everything incredibly sweet.

I can't say I'm happy to have been a builder: I was born to be a farmer and to work my land, in Safad. Yet I realize that this job gave me the opportunity to see things that I would never have seen otherwise. When I came home from work in the evenings – not today as we are both too old now – I'd tell my wife we should go and visit the building site together on Sundays. I wanted to show her all kinds of things there. When my boss saw me there on public holidays he would laugh and say: 'Don't work too fast, otherwise we won't get paid because we finished the job sooner than we said we would!' But I think she too got a feeling of satisfaction from some of the things she saw. Our house is comfortable. I built it with my sons. It's a nice house, if you consider what things were like for us forty years ago. But the houses in the old city of Damascus are something else. There is really a taste for living a good and simple life there, with gardens and flowers around you. Every now and then some property owner would come over to the building site. At the beginning I didn't understand what they came for. Then I gradually learnt to recognize them. And they all said the same things, that selling and moving to the new Damascus had been a mistake, in those estates with fifty blocks of flats, where it's hot when the weather is hot and cold when it's cold. The only advantage is that they can park their car, but as for everything else... and what did they need a car for when they lived here? Some of them even try to buy them back, but they usually can't. The Damascus city centre has become extremely expensive now: those who have a house next to the Umayyad Mosque won't sell, and if they do they want a lot of money for it. And besides, everyone has learnt the game.

Next to the Fountain Café there was a group of families living in a traditional Damascene house, a wonderful old house. They have all moved to the suburbs. They set up a company and converted that group of apartments around the garden into a big restaurant. It's always crowded, at all hours of the day. Maybe the families haven't got rich as a result, but when the renovation work is done I think they'll be able to look forward to a very bright future. Also, that way, they've provided work for their children and kept the families together, just like in the old days. Sometimes things carry on as they did in the past, but by changing everything! The restaurant's opening night was a great event, I wasn't there but the owner told me about it. They filled the alleys leading up to the restaurant with rose petals, and the closer you got the thicker they became. It was one of the young men who had the idea, he had a degree in Arabic literature and had read about it in the *One Thousand and One Nights*. It seems it was a tradition during the time of Sinbad the Sailor or Harun ar-Rashid. I was told the fragrance was so intense that people naturally followed it as overpowered everything else, including the smell of spices, of coffee and of the smog. It was great idea, and cheap too. Everyone is still talking about it, and the restaurant is very successful.

Yes, there were a lot of us here in Damascus. And a great many ended up working as builders, as I did. It was natural to talk about Palestine on the building site. But it was the same for all of us: none of us knew anything about it anymore. It was as if our land had been covered with quick lime. Later on, when the Palestinian refugees came here from the West Bank,[12] we noticed that things were different for them. They went through the same military occupation and suffered the same violence, but their relationships weren't torn apart forever. Even now, there are some Palestinians from Nablus living next door to us. They haven't lost touch with those who stayed behind. They phone each other and send each other presents.

No, that isn't possible. We don't have a passport. We have a document that is recognized in Europe and many other countries around the world, but it's not a passport. As Palestinians, we can't go to Jordan, or Lebanon or Egypt. If we travel outside Syria we can go to France, and to Italy where I have a relative who has a pizzeria in a town in Central Italy. We can also go to Spain, but not to other Arab countries. I don't know why. Maybe it's because they already have enough Palestinians there.

No, not even if they offered it to me. No, under no condition would I want a Syrian passport, and if you ask my son, or your interpreter… You see? He says the same thing. We regret that we can't vote. We regret that we can't travel to other Arab countries. But I don't want, and will never want, a Syrian or a Jordanian or a

Lebanese passport. I am grateful to the Syrians, for the way they've treated us and for the simple way they did it. When I am among them, I am not a refugee. Well, I am so old now that I am not so involved anymore, but you know what I mean. No one has ever said to me: 'You've taken jobs away from the Syrians,' or, 'Go back to your country; this is not your home.' My children have had the same education as everyone else here – for free. It may not be wonderful but still, you're now looking at my son who was born in a refugee camp in the Golan Heights and now teaches English in a middle school. And, I take it, your interpreter is also a Palestinian who learnt English in a Syrian school, is that right?

Exactly! And that's what happened with all of us. We have been welcomed in Syria not just as if we were Syrian, but as true Syrians. I don't know how things would have been in Jordan, in Lebanon or in Egypt. But that's how it was here. Yet, although I feel very grateful towards the country that hosted me, I am still Palestinian: the only passport I want is a Palestinian one, not that of any other country.

5 - The Young Armenian Woman

I know I'm married and have children. But I meant to say something different, without any of this ambiguity or innuendo. I love my wife and I wouldn't change her with anyone else in the world, but that's not what I meant when I talked about Agnes and her family. To me, she is something I shouldn't even be talking about. It's so easy to misconstrue things and get the wrong idea. Is it love? No, I would never call it that. And as for worship, that's far from being what I feel for her. It's as if I were seeing myself reflected in her, or maybe in her family, or in her culture. Perhaps by protecting her, as I would like to do every single day of the week, I feel as if I were protecting myself, or my past. Yes that's exactly what I mean: she and I are two different people, with very different backgrounds, but there is something that she and I share. It's as if within the overall picture of these events, all altered and all different, there were some constant factors that are greater than our own individual characteristics, and which ultimately become our story – mine and hers.

No, I don't expect anyone would understand me. My wife may be the only one who knows, because I've talked to her about it so many times, what a deep boundary protects her from everything that I feel for Agnes. I think she too would be able to explain this something, which is not merely affection yet can't be mistaken for love.

I still remember when I saw Agnes for the first time. How she glided over things with that firm yet sweet gaze of hers, allowing everyone to admire her without letting it distract her from her work. Her hair was slightly dyed with an auburn hue, and she wore a light silk scarf around her neck that moved with her body and added a breezier, more cheerful and changeable note to her still and serious face. I too sometimes ask myself what would have happened to Agnes and me, I mean to what I feel for her and which she knows very well by now, without my first vision of her as she walked among the machinery at the building site, surrounded by workers in tank tops, cement mixers, shovels and bricks.

It was one of the many periods of unemployment in my life as an English literature graduate in Damascus – one of those periods which I've come to realize will be part of my life for years, maybe forever. So I started helping a cousin of mine who had a business trading in electrical materials. As my English was good and I was educated, I acted as a kind of company representative for him. He would send me to speak with the agents and start off his major business negotiations. Once he even sent me to China, and now I am his partner in a profitable company that imports electrical materials. Of course, Chinese goods are very low quality, nothing like the materials we used to import from Italy, from a company based in Novara. But they are so cheap that even our top customers have decided to try them, and if a part needs to be replaced after a few months, it's so cheap that it's always worthwhile. But this is something that concerns Europe and how it will manage to survive Chinese competition, not Agnes and me. And so, I had gone with my cousin to a building site near Aleppo, where our electricians were installing the electric system in a small residential building. The material had just arrived, so we decided to pick it up from the customs office in Damascus and take it to the building site in Aleppo ourselves. While the workers were unloading the van, my cousin and I wandered around the site and noticed that this wasn't the usual rushed construction job but a high quality building. I remember my cousin saying to me: 'Perhaps we should have brought some Italian supplies here; they have the money to be able to afford them.' And indeed there was something beautiful and sophisticated about the building. There was a professional touch to it. That's how I met her, and before I even saw her I realized her worth from the quality of her work and her drawings.

Then we saw her coming over, with this flimsy scarf fluttering around her neck and her auburn hair. Standing around her was one of the site managers to whom she was explaining – with a very sweet manner accompanied by a look of steely determination – what she wanted, what had to be taken down and done all over again, and what they had got wrong. And he listened to her with the kind of look that workers have when what they are really thinking is: 'Now she'll go back to her architecture studio and we'll just carry on with what we were doing before.' But Agnes, who understood it all, called over a workman and told him to get a pickaxe and take down a badly constructed false ceiling there and then. And so the man looked at the site manager then looked at Agnes, and at that point the site manager, without uttering a word, grabbed the pickaxe from his hands and dealt two powerful blows in the middle of ceiling with it, tearing it open. He then looked at her and Agnes smiled and said: 'That's it; it's exactly what I wanted.' With that, a smile appeared on her face which I really wouldn't know how to define. It was sweet, incredibly sweet. But it seemed to me to conceal something irreversibly sad: as if everything that happens in daily life helps to alleviate a deep pain that no one and nothing will ever be able to take away. I know that smile, I recognized it because it's the same as mine – as my wife says. She thinks it's something I've had inside me since before I was even born, since my family fled from Nablus when it was occupied by the Israelis and we, like many others, became a family of refugees, without a nation, without a state, without anything.

But in Agnes's case, where did that smile come from? I remember very well when she came towards us and introduced herself to my cousin, with her white teeth, dark green eyes and her simple but clean-cut, elegant features. When she held out her hand to me and said: 'I'm Demerdjian, the architect,' I thought I had never seen a woman of such elegant beauty. She held the drawings of the building's electric system close to her chest, as if she was cold. I heard my cousin say: 'This is Hassan, he's an English teacher.' And while he spoke I wanted to say something that would take me far away from the truck, from the electric cables and from that building site yet I could do nothing but keep silent and look at her while my cousin joked and said to me: 'Have you lost your tongue?' And Agnes went off. She gently moved a wheelbarrow full of concrete out of the way, walked into the building with the site manager and, after a while, I could hear her voice coming from inside asking for other changes to be made and for more partition walls to be taken down.

We've seen each other many times since then. I've taken her to my house and introduced her to my wife and children. We have become friends, even though no one would actually be able to say what our friendship is based on. Nor have I ever wished to go beyond this general feeling that we still share today: we've both fled our homes. We have both lost our homeland and are both guests in Syria, even though we were born in this country. I lost Palestine and Agnes lost Armenia. All the differences between us that set us apart, and there are a great many of them, are nothing compared to this wound. It may not be bleeding anymore, but it reminds me of certain trees struck by lightning that I saw in

Lebanon. They often survive, even for many centuries, they have a sturdy trunk and a beautiful top, but the wound from the lightning is always visible. It never goes away, never.

Many years ago, by which time we were already part of each other's lives, Agnes invited me to have dinner at her house, where she lives with her mother. It was June, and I remember it had been a terribly hot day and even after sunset the streets of Aleppo were slow in getting back to life. When the sun goes down, our cities usually come alive and are bustling with people who go out to do their shopping, take a walk or dine out. But that was one of those evenings when people still didn't dare to leave the house, as if they were asking themselves: 'Is it really over?' I remember I went to a florist's so that I wouldn't get there empty-handed. He was spraying water on the flowers, telling me they were really beautiful, while I said: 'No, look, they've already wilted and gone yellow. Not this one, not that one.' After a while, he smiled and asked me where I had been that day. He said the flowers were really fresh and had been picked that very day, but that in Aleppo June is June. 'After twelve hours in this heat,' he said to me, 'what do you expect any flower to look like?' But of course I insisted; the flowers I had to show up with had to be absolutely fresh. So the man picked up a flower, discarded it and threw it on the floor, then he would choose another one, with the patience of someone who knew it was the end of the working day and anything he couldn't sell me would be thrown out anyway.

It was peaceful evening, as peaceful as Agnes herself is, and as is her mother. They were talking about the employment situation, about other members of the family who were now living in France or Lebanon, and so, without even my asking about it, they started talking about their great tragedy. It was something I had heard about in very general terms and of which I had never known the full details.

It wasn't a sad story, on the contrary. There was this wonderful love story between Agnes's grandmother and grandfather. But it had all taken place during terrible times, so similar and to what my family went through.

They were a wealthy family from Erzurum, in Turkey. I don't remember what they did, but Agnes's great grandfather must have practised a liberal profession, he might have been an engineer or a doctor. I know they were an affluent and educated family, one of the most important families in Erzurum's Armenian community. Then there was the genocide, such a huge and all-out tragedy that in comparison even what happened to my own city of Nablus pales into insignificance. First one person died, then another, until the dead were so many that you could no longer count them individually but by the dozens and then by the hundreds. The Turks had opened up the jails and given free rein to the country's worst criminals. There were gangs rampaging through the cities, going into the Armenian neighbourhoods and destroying everything, throwing children and women out of the windows, killing the men by the dozens after torturing and sometimes butchering them as no human being could even imagine. I remember asking them why, and who those people were. And Agnes and her mother, with that oddly tolerant attitude shown by people when they talk about events that happened in the distant past, told me that everyone was guilty and no one in particular. And even the Kurds, who these days are often accused of having committed the worst crimes against the Armenians, they said, 'were not really "Kurds", but ordinary criminals let out of jail. It wasn't the fact that they were Kurds that made them so vicious towards us, but the fact that they were criminals and were paid by the Turks to exterminate us.'

That was until the day when – I can just imagine with what harrowing pain – they finally fled. When the dead bodies laid piled up in the streets and nobody dared to protect them anymore, because it was clear to the whole of Erzurum that the massacre targeted not only the Armenians but also anyone who gave them protection, the decision to leave was finally taken. It was evening, and the women at home were sewing, hiding inside their skirts the gold coins that would ensure the family's survival, and whatever jewellery they could take with them. Every family in the neighbourhood was rushing to leave, going through the usual distressing process of choosing the things they would take with them, putting them by, then casting them aside, then picking them up once more, only to leave them behind yet again. 'It's no use, you will never be able to take everything with you. Leave it, leave it,' people said, amid the crying and despondency. Old people who knew they wouldn't be able to leave with them looked at everything with the distant gaze of those who know they only have a few hours left to live. The children didn't understand what was happening and carried on playing, electrified by the frenzied atmosphere of the evening. The men stood in silence, without even the strength to cry. And the women carried on sewing, hiding gold and money in their corsets, skirts and bras, sparing only the girls who knew the fate awaiting them if they were not far from the residential areas by the first light of dawn.

Then, when everything was ready, and this procession of tears and gold coins stitched into the women's skirts began to move, something happened that neither Agnes nor her mother ever knew about. Did the men already know about it beforehand? Had they pretended to be surprised? The Turks appeared, with the usual line of horses, their swords, and their sneering laughter. In the darkness of the night, Agnes's great-grandfather said: 'You go on ahead; go on and we'll catch up with you.' And the dark procession of women set off into the night, walking on as the shooting, the shouting and the screaming behind them became fainter and fainter until silence descended on the city. So Agnes's great-grandmother fled, a widow amongst widows and orphans, leading a procession of women devastated by grief but with a will to live, to honour the sacrifice of their brothers, their cousins, their fathers and their grandfathers, marching all the way to the Syrian border. They had a will to live, come what may; to live for the men too; to live for the Armenian nation, for the burnt down churches, for the girls who had been raped, for the priests who had been tortured; to live, at all costs, to keep alive those who had died, those who had sacrificed themselves for them. They travelled through the night for weeks. They slept during the day in sheltered corners, trying to go as unnoticed as possible. Once a girl left the group to go and fetch some water from a fountain they had just walked past: when they found her again, she had been raped and nailed to a tree. A three-year-old boy died of typhoid; a slightly older boy died of cholera. And Agnes's great-grandmother walked in front of them, immersed in the tragedy. 'I have another husband with me, girls,' she would say, 'don't worry.' And as she said this, her hand stroked the great black skirt where she had sewn the family fortune and whatever she has been able to take with her.

Occasionally a group of soldiers on horseback would appear, but they gradually became fewer and fewer and just stood on the mountain ridges watching this long procession of women walking on, without even trying to hide anymore, in the grip of a sort of desperate fatalism. Or maybe, to those last groups of Turkish horsemen, they seemed to be so hopeless, so destitute, so close to death by now, that they weren't even worth one last strike or one last bullet. They weren't worth the effort of lifting a sword and driving it through their flesh.

Until, one night, they saw the outline of the Citadel of Aleppo in the distance, and just then everything that had been held back and left unspoken for weeks now turned into crying and desperation. The city awaiting them meant safety, it meant life. But it was a foreign city, the beginning of an endless exile.

Agnes and her mother told the story, which took place at the beginning of the 20th century, and although I knew nothing about it, everything sounded familiar to me. In my mind, the grandmother's face became that of my own grandmother: this group of women standing on a hill looking down on the city of Aleppo in the twilight reminded me of my father's and my grandfather's description. They told me how, when they reached Damascus, the column stopped outside the city and what they saw – they too said the same thing – was not a more or less beautiful or welcoming city, but the symbol of a life sentence: the symbol of a departure with no return and no stopping. Exile is an endless journey that carries on through the generations. Is this what I had seen on Agnes's face the first time I saw her on that building site?

As they approached Aleppo their group was joined by others that were appearing all around them until, just outside the city, it was no longer Agnes's great-grandmother entering Aleppo, but a procession of people coming from the most disparate and faraway places. They hadn't even reached Aleppo when they were already talking about leaving, about going away. Nobody wanted to stop in Aleppo. Aleppo was too close to their pain, too close to their memories and to everything that had been burned down. Some people were talking about going to France, others to America, a few to Italy. But all of them talked about getting away from places that were too familiar, too close to their grief and their anguish.

'Do you know what it means to be a refugee, Hassan?' Agnes's mother spoke these words as to someone who knew nothing about it. Before I could say anything, Agnes answered for me: 'He's Palestinian, mum, he's from Nablus.' 'Oh, I'm sorry,' she said, 'I didn't mean to... Then, you know all about it.'

Yes, that's right. To be a refugee means being forced into perfection, into never putting a foot wrong, into absolute honesty, into cleanliness and into silence.

Aleppo back then, like Damascus now, was not hostile to them. But there were tens of thousands of Armenians, just as there were tens of thousands of Palestinians, and what happened to us was in no way Aleppo's or its citizens' fault. But still, bread, water and a place to sleep all had to be found. Yet, although the city was called upon to make an effort that it didn't have the resources to sustain, it was great, in its own way – just as the people of Damascus were great with us. No one asked them for anything, no one blamed them for anything. The people of Aleppo withdrew within their own circles, they protected themselves in the neighbourhoods where the Armenians couldn't afford to buy a house, but they didn't isolate the newly arrived refugees.

The presence of the French was helpful to the Armenians, but it wasn't just that. It was the city itself: it was cold but showed hospitality; it was distant yet also essentially open. No one asked for the tens of thousands of Armenians to be put straight on the boats in the port of Antioch. No one even thought about isolating them within a refugee camp. At the same time, no one gave them anything for free, but it couldn't have been otherwise. They suddenly found themselves alive, but at the bottom of the social ladder. They had been craftsmen, professionals and land owners: now they were nothing, their worth lay in what they could do, in their intrinsic honesty, in their skills and the reliability of their work. So they had to start from scratch, with nothing. And they had to do this knowing all the while that by welcoming them, Aleppo had already done the most it could: it wasn't possible to do any more. Now they had to roll up their sleeves, work hard, and earn the trust of the people and the city.

Agnes's great-grandmother had never worked. She had only done the sort of embroidery work that wealthy women typically did, and which lies somewhere between art and virtuosity for its own sake. She started darning and repairing clothes, and she eventually opened a modest dressmaking workshop where Aleppo's well-to-do women found that extra something that comes from having high-level technical skills and culture especially. Then the women started going to her house. As Agnes's mother often told us, a sentence she heard again and again at home was: 'When you take on a job it must be delivered an hour before the agreed time. We have to prove to our customers that we are totally reliable. When they order a dress or a hat from us, it's as if they were already wearing it.' Yes, hats: in those days everybody wore a hat, although the custom has died out. But a hat is something where the class of the person who designed it becomes a trademark, you either have it or you don't. There is nothing in-between. And the old woman who had fled from Erzurum had a great deal of class and culture, both of which she passed on to her daughter, Agnes's grandmother, her mother's mother.

Many of the people they knew left for Europe, hundreds of orphans were sent to France by the mandate authorities. But her great-grandmother and grandmother started benefiting from the new reputation they had built for themselves. Of course, they were well aware that the Arab women in Aleppo looked upon them as "poor little seamstresses", as Dickens would say, but the money was beginning to come in. It was very little, but every month there was always a bit more than in the previous month, until one day the great-grandmother and grandmother decided it was time to put it in a bank.

It was Agnes's grandmother who took care of that. They showed me some photos of her, and she is her splitting image. She is a young and very beautiful woman, with a much more mature expression than you would expect in a twenty-year-old woman. She has piercing black eyes that in the photo look sparkling and sad at the same time. Every week she would go to the bank to deposit what little money they had earned, and on this too – the great-grandmother had been very specific about it – you needed to be reliable and above all predictable. 'Bankers are not artists, she would say, they like regularity and predictability. To a banker, to be regular in your payments means to be reliable and credible!' She must have been an amazing woman, this great-grandmother who took the family from Erzurum to Aleppo. So Agnes's grandmother would go to the bank every week, at the same time and on the same day. When she had money to deposit, she would put it into the account, and when she didn't have any, she would go there and ask to be shown the balance on the account. If it was good she would say it was a fortunate coincidence, if it was low she explained that it was a peculiar and unfortunate circumstance. But she always went.

And he would look at her. He couldn't wait for her to come in to get up from his desk where he sat as branch manager. As soon as the bank door opened and the twenty-year-old Miss Demerdjian walked in, he would get up and go and greet her as if she was his most important customer. He would listen to her with an attentive and friendly manner. He showed he knew about her situation and offered helpful advice without being too "obliging", as we would say today. And naturally, as the weeks went by, he noticed that Miss Demerdjian was always dressed poorly but neatly, and he could see that, well yes, she made an effort to look presentable. And also, certain lingering gazes, perhaps lingering a little too long before she cast her eyes down modestly, couldn't be meant for the bank but were for him.

It was love at first sight. It was one of those wonderful, great and happy love stories – of the kind that defies everything and wins over everything with the sweetness of something irrepressible: his family to start with. 'You'll never marry an Armenian refugee!' his father said. And he obeyed, but added, 'I'll do as you say, but I won't marry anyone else!' And the tension grew at home and it also grew between them as they started seeing each other. But as it grew, the Armenian community also grew, having stabilized itself after the first mass migrations to the United States and Europe. It had its own schools, which were much more numerous and crowded than before, its own churches and its own neighbourhood, Midan. And the same thing that was happening throughout the world was also happening in Aleppo: a good engineer can work as a builder, but sooner or later he'll go back to working as an engineer. A good administrator can work as a labourer for a few years, but eventually he'll go back to doing what he's always been good at. And while Armenian mechanics may not have been the best, they were still good. The watchmakers were highly skilled, the jewellers were reliable and discreet, and the dressmakers were refined. The Armenian community started to recover, and the citizens of Aleppo – being wealthy and industrious people themselves – learned to appreciate them more and more.

Yet the divisions remained. You could go and see an Armenian doctor if he was really good, but not marry his daughter!

Agnes's grandfather was not the sort of man to give up. An Arab Christian, he held fast even though the church railed against mixed marriages. Then one day his father, a prominent entrepreneur in Aleppo's business community and from an Aleppo family that had been wealthy for generations, began to waver. Without saying a word, someone was sent to Erzurum to make enquiries, and her grandfather realized he had won the battle when his mum told him that they had both been highly impressed by what they had found out. They had heard that in Erzurum people still remembered them as a family of high standing, which – according to her grandmother – meant that the family was not only cultured and well-educated but also had the kind of skill in dealing with money that was typical of every well-to-do family. It was the sort of business acumen that is not lost in one generation, whatever ordeals or tragedies they had endured.

So they got married. Soon Agnes's mother was born, followed by her siblings, and their household was always permeated with the kind of warmth that is generated when love and respect are mutually reinforcing. Yet their life was not easy: everything seemed designed to make life difficult for them. The fact that they were from different ethnic backgrounds could be ignored, but everything else – and there was so much else! – was an uphill battle. To begin with, there was the language: neither of them particularly liked the

Turks, but Turkish was the only language they both knew and in which they could communicate with each other. And although there were two religions in the household (Armenian and Arab-Christian), there were three languages: the father spoke Arabic to the children and the mother Armenian, while the two of them spoke to each other in Turkish. Then, at that time, it was impossible to survive in Syria if you didn't speak French, so Agnes's mother grew up in a family where they initially spoke four languages, and later, when English took over, they actually spoke five.

Then there was the grandmother, the legendary lady who had led the women in the household on the journey from Erzurum to Aleppo. They obviously took her to live with them, but a woman like her, with everything she had been through and everything she had done, was not a reserved sort of person or reticent to speak her mind. So, while of course they held her in high esteem and loved her very much, she was a very strong presence and got in the way.

Then there was his family. Although they had given in and accepted their love and were full of praise, it didn't go any further than that. His two brothers kept saying: 'You've been so lucky in your marriage! Can't you find a good Armenian woman for us as well?' Of course for the young couple this was praise indeed. But it changed nothing as far as the inheritance was concerned. The father had not been disinherited but had effectively been cut out of the estate. I think many things changed as time went by and, on her deathbed, the grandmother said she wanted to reinstate her son in her will, but everyone knows what happens in these situation, those who die don't speak and those who live do more or less what they like.

There were just as many problems at school, as Agnes's mum and her sisters were sent to a school run by Catholic nuns. It was a very good French school but obviously there was catechism and they had to attend mass. And the women would keep looking at Agnes's mother as if she was born in sin, because marriage between an Armenian and a Christian was not accepted or recognized. So, while they approved of the fact that the daughter of such a scandalous marriage was Catholic, there was always a shadow hanging over her, not necessarily amounting to sin but something very close to it. They were French, and we know how the French think: they have extraordinary qualities, but they also have their faults. And these nuns, who had come over from France to spread the Christian message, couldn't accept this situation and had many opportunities to point it out.

And then there was Christmas, which is obviously of paramount importance to a Christian. I remember that Agnes's mum started to laugh when she mentioned it, and even the handkerchief she had held through most of the story disappeared. 'We were lucky,' she said. 'To make sure that everyone was treated equally, we had two Christmas celebrations, Catholic Christmas on the 25th of December and Armenian Christmas on the 6th of January. But to us this meant two lots of presents and two Christmas parties!'

Agnes's grandfather must have been an extraordinary man, not just because he had fallen in love with an Armenian refugee but also for this open-mindedness that permeated their home, and which was of course typical of Aleppo but was also peculiarly his own. At home he always said that God had much more important things to do than worry about the dates of the calendar, and that Muslims, Christians and Armenians were just the different faces of one and the same God. He would say that God was everyone's father and it certainly wasn't an issue for Him whether Christmas was celebrated on one date rather than another. So with her mind thus set at rest,

Agnes's mum – still a child at the time – would go back to school and tell everyone what her father had said, on hearing which the horrified nuns would all start making the sign of the cross as if it was blasphemy. They would then get the whole class to stand up and recite the Lord's Prayer as if to blot out what Agnes's father had said. 'Hush, hush, we are not interested in what your father says! Girls!' They would promptly clap their hands, saying: 'Stand up girls! Let's recite the Our Father and Hail Mary!' And the whole class would recite the prayers in Latin.

And Agnes listened to her mother telling the story, enjoying it and with the somewhat dreamy look that girls have when listening to a love story with a good beginning and an even better ending. I am hoping she'll turn around and look at me, but I know she won't. She can feel my gaze on her back, she may even be blushing, she never will.

Sometimes I ask myself what's left of that world now, whether behind the walls of this city, which they say has changed so much in recent years, there are other stories like this. What are open-minded men like Agnes's grandfather doing today? Are they still here, behind these doors, or have they moved elsewhere, maybe to Europe or America?

One evening I invited them to have dinner with me in a restaurant in the Armenian district, not far from their house. It belonged to a friend of mine and was set inside the renovated underground cellars and shelters that many Armenians had built underneath their houses to escape persecution. Agnes's mum had not been happy with the choice and initially said she didn't want to go to a place that she felt was imbued with memories too closely associated with the genocide. 'There were persecutions in Aleppo too,' she said, 'even though they ended many, many years before we got here.'

So, in the atmosphere of that gloomy place, which I now also felt was an inappropriate location for a restaurant, she told us about a brutal event that happened a long way back and is still remembered by some people in Aleppo. It was a blood-curdling and mysterious story centred on a Jewish family from Aleppo, the Hararis. It concerned a Christian priest called Father Toma who went missing in Aleppo's Jewish neighbourhood one day. Following the involvement of the French consulate, investigations were carried out, and it was discovered – allegedly discovered, rather – that a gruesome criminal event had taken place, probably made-up but very real to the extent that it was a dramatic illustration of anti-Jewish prejudice. Poor Father Toma had apparently been captured and taken to the house of the Harari family, where the brothers David, Isaac and Aaron supposedly cut his throat. It took them almost forty minutes to collect the blood, which they then presented to the Chief Rabbi to use for making the Jewish Passover bread, the Matzah.

The story about Jews murdering Christians and young men in order to make Matzah epitomized one of the many anti-Jewish prejudices that existed in the old days, and I don't know if it still lives on in the minds of some people, or whether others still talk about it. But that old story, evoked inside that restaurant by a woman whose family had directly experienced the trauma of genocide, seemed absurd yet real at the same time. Not in terms of the facts – who would ever believe such a thing? –, but for all it said to us about the past: the diffidence between communities, the fear of diversity and of a different religion that keeps itself apart from the others.

In this macabre scenario, more replete with violent prejudices than with grisly events, Agnes's mum kept shaking her head and remembering when, somewhat apprehensively, she had gone to her father to tell him she was going to marry an Armenian man.

'He looked at me, hugged me and asked me if I was happy. And when I said I was, his only remark was, "I've deprived the Armenian community of a woman, it's only right that I should now return one to it."'

And so another Armenian family was created, the family to which Agnes and her brother were born. But it was actually the same family since, in those days, when girls got married they didn't leave home. And the grandfather, now an old man, saw his house becoming once again what it had been when he had married the young Armenian woman and the old woman from Erzurum had gone to live with them. Agnes listened, in the dim light of the restaurant; she looked at her mum not as gripped as she had been while listening to her grandmother's vicissitudes, but still moved and full of admiration.

'And what about the nuns? What did they say?' she asked. Her mother started laughing: 'Oh they were desperate! I was summoned by the Mother Superior who told me I would be out of the Church and would never be able to take the sacraments. Poor women! They believed in this. They truly believed in all this. It was only with the Second Vatican Council and Pope Paul VI that I was allowed to take the sacraments again.' 'So you never went to church until then?' 'Oh yes, I did go, and everyone saw me there. And I respected their wish that I shouldn't take Holy Communion as they regarded me as being in a state of sin. But I never missed a single mass. They saw me every Sunday for almost ten years, and I'm sure that all this meant something to them.'

I look at Agnes, and I know that she is now also part of the picture. Her mother's story is now her story, or it could be. But everything around them has changed. The Armenians here are no longer the bedraggled exiles "condemned to absolute honesty", who came here from Erzurum with coins sewn into their skirts.

They have their own schools, the best in Aleppo, their own doctors and their own lawyers, the best in town. And although Agnes doesn't tell me this in so many words, from the many little things she has told me over the years, I have gathered that the somewhat closed, small-town world that had received them with diffidence in the early twentieth century has now become their world. They have their own social clubs and cultural centres. They have their own churches – I remember that Agnes once insisted on taking me there – and the choirs during the mass were so silvery and solemn that even I felt as if they were the transposition of Heaven on earth, whatever Heaven and whoever its Lord may be. And when the women's singing and these powerful male voices reached a pitch, I was sometimes stirred and moved by an indefinable feeling. Not because it was the service of a religion that wasn't my own, or because it might have all seemed like a pagan ritual to me, but because it made me wonder whether it's fair that music should catch you unawares and make you feel so defenceless, in front of everyone. And when hearing certain tunes resonating through the air, even if they are sung by a people whose ideas are different from mine and whose faith is different from that of my family, I have often asked myself what it is that allows man to lift himself to such heights when celebrating God.

But then, in this intertwining of emotions aroused by the music and the choirs, I sometimes found myself wondering whether my people too, the Palestinians, will follow the same path, and whether the day will come when someone in my family will look at the streets of Damascus and feel that they are truly theirs and not a place in which they are condemned to live in permanent exile. For the sense one gets from the vicissitudes of the Demerdjian family is that their homeland no longer exists – or rather, it exists but is so distant and so abstract that it has become a sort of mental frame of reference lacking any tangible form. Armenia, to them, is nothing more than the place they come from. It is not like my Palestine, so physical, so earthly and so "photographically recognizable".

Once, the three of us – Agnes, her mother and I – talked about it. It was her mother once again who told me a story that changed forever their perception of their faraway homeland. It happened when the Soviet Union urged the Armenians to return to the newly established Republic of Armenia, to which Stalin had promised real independence if they managed to reach a population of two million, and hundreds of them agreed to go.

'Many people left. My mother too would have left if it hadn't been for my dad and for us. It was a very emotional time for those who left: they sold everything, absolutely everything they had, so that they could give their contribution to the nation that was being reborn from a past of death and genocide. Amid their enthusiasm, they promised they would write and let us know what life was like in the new nation. They promised they would tell us the whole truth, so that everyone would know what to do. For a few months we had no news, until the first letters started to arrive, all invariable enthusiastic and very positive. But in each of those letters there was a sign, a hint of something that only we could understand. "I met the Aghassian family, they are happy too," said one of these letters. But hadn't they all been massacred in Malatya? Wasn't that the family in which no one had survived? "Yesterday I met old Shakarian in the library and he told me he is now much happier than he was before." But didn't he die in Aleppo a few weeks before they left? So, through a list of impossible encounters with dead people, we discovered what we should have guessed, and what it took the West far longer to realize, namely that in the new republic not only was life bad but also the censorship was so strict that no was able to write what things were really like. It was then that, for the first time since the genocide, Aleppo became our new homeland to us. It was then that something broke off between us and our Armenian homeland, so that even today, when it is a free nation and anyone who wants to can go there, no one actually does. It's still our homeland, it's still the place we came from, but it's not Aleppo and never will be.'

Sometimes I wonder how Agnes and her mother felt in the early Nineties when Aleppo became a city of refugees fleeing from genocide once again. In the early twentieth century it had happened to them and also to the Greeks on the Aegean coast; now the same has happened to the Kurds. Everything may be less conspicuous compared to back then. But not a day goes by without more people arriving from Turkey, bringing all-too-familiar stories about night-time raids, persecutions and killings. At the time of the Armenian genocide, there was no need for lies: the persecution was talked about openly, without any distortions. Today, everything that happened eighty years ago is being repeated, but you can't talk about genocide. The Turks talk about fighting terrorism, putting down the Kurdish guerrilla war and combating separatism. But these villages razed to the ground by bulldozers, covered in concrete to make sure no one can go back and live there again, or with the dead bodies lying in the streets killed during 'anti-banditry operations' don't fool anyone here in Aleppo, not when Ankara regards even the Kurdish New Year celebrations as a revolt against the nation-state. What more needs to be said?

Sometimes I look at Agnes and her mother and search for something from the past, a shadow hinting at the memory of when the Turks used the Kurds themselves against the Armenians. But never, not even once, have I heard them speak a word of bitterness, of the hidden anger of those who don't forget.

So I find myself thinking that in this land, which has many faults and is certainly not perfect, Aleppo and Damascus are to some extent an exception. Perhaps it's because no one is Syrian and everyone comes from someplace else, or maybe because there have been so many persecutions around here in the past that nowadays nobody feels like repeating them. Possibly because everyone is weak and we are all basically minorities, it's almost as if, in the end, a conscious acceptance always prevails. First the Armenians came, then it was us Palestinians, today it's the Kurds, and who knows whose turn it will be tomorrow. Syria and Syrian cities are thrown off-balance for a while, and then they reorganize and seemingly change. Then, after a few decades, what remains is the memory of a past journey, of coming to this land from a lost nation. Yet it's no longer something painful, as it is for me today, but a diluted and almost sweet memory.

Perhaps it's only partly tinged with a deep vein of sadness that never visibly comes to the surface. While it is not manifest, it casts a dim shadow on a smile like Agnes's and reminds me that although there is much that sets us apart and that our people have a completely different history, culture and conception of the world, we share something we have both lost. It is something that will never be returned to us and is gone forever – something that now only lives in the memory of our families, in this being Syrian and not being Syrian, in being here and thinking about somewhere else.

Or, perhaps, it's not even about that, but about the perception that the land that took us in, the cities that hosted us, are all like us. They are fragments of histories that started elsewhere and have shifted to Syria because of events, because of men and the madness of the human race. Perhaps it also has to do with the injustice that many of us have endured. We are families without a homeland, together with other families without a homeland, landless people together with other landless people.

Maybe there is no such thing as being "Syrian", just as there is no such thing as "Syria". Perhaps it is neither a nation nor a people but the condensed heritage of a continent, of centuries of history – a sort of mindset and attitude that people have here, which has created this real yet at the same time impossible miracle.

I once told Agnes this in a restaurant in the outskirts of the city. It was one of those summer evenings when a slight breeze blows down on the city of Aleppo bringing with it a pleasantly cool, dry air. She smiled, wrapped her shawl around her shoulders and said: 'Hassan, you should have studied philosophy, not English. Deep down you are a philosopher, and maybe that's exactly why I like talking with you.'

There was a glowing light coming from candles protected by the glass covers and we could hear the wind blowing through the Aleppo pine trees. In the distance, the Citadel was lit up, shining with a familiar light. Agnes was resting her face on her hands, with her elbows on the table. In her smile, I seemed to notice, there wasn't a trace of sadness.

6 - The Souk Merchant

You see, what did I tell you? I haven't even started yet and... That's what boys are like. They've heard something at home, and they think they understand. The truth is that they don't understand anything... But they haven't lived the life I have. "What did you say? Would it still be adventurous if I didn't make it all up? You're an insolent boy, you know? I don't think your dad ever taught you certain things. Go and get us some tea, off you go. If you stick around here you'll make me lose my temper!"

You mustn't take any notice of him. In the summer, when he's out of school, he spends his time here at the souk with me. "Hashem! Get the barber to come over here! My beard is getting so long that in a couple of days I'll look like a sheikh." So, yes, as I was saying, he hangs around here at the souk and gets bored because nothing has been happening around here in the last few years. He wanders about, so maybe he hears all these stories from the other boys and believes them. But then, wasn't I just the same when I was his age? Of course he's like me, he's my grandson! I was a smart young lad when I was a boy, very smart. But when I came over to Aleppo to live with my uncle: that was scary, very scary!

He was a huge man, with two flashing black eyes. He looked just like a warrior. And when I got here, I saw him standing by the door of the house looking at me without uttering a word, and my aunt said to me: 'Come, my poor boy. We are your family now!' Then the door opened, and I found myself inside the courtyard, and all the families were looking out of the balcony to check out the new boy. Of course I was afraid, who wouldn't have been without their mum and dad? But I felt that this uncle of mine, as big as a warrior, would protect me from everyone.

And that's actually how it was in the old days. Being a merchant meant defying the desert and marauders, and many of them were Bedouin... I'm sure you've heard about all the people that were robbed and killed in the desert. That's why people travelled in caravans, so they wouldn't be alone. But, even though so much has changed since then, the Bedouins still have a great sense of honour... "Oh, Hashem, good boy! There, put it down here. Did you find the barber? What do you mean he came by earlier? Where was I then? ... Oh yes, I went out for a second. Well, I can't go home looking like this, like a hedgehog. You may laugh, but even at my great age you're not completely dead. And today is Thursday, you don't expect me to go back home looking like a shepherd, do you?" They're funny aren't they? It's always like this: when I start telling my stories they all stop at my shop because they have fun. They listen to me for hours and then they say I'm a chatterbox and make up a thousand stories. But I don't need to make up my stories! Ah, they laugh! "Hashem, come on! Go and call him over." Yes, I'm sorry, so, yes, as I was saying...

The Bedouins, sure they were dangerous! When they crossed the desert and you'd suddenly see them appearing behind a rock or in the distance, the first thing you did was always to reach for your weapons to defend yourself. But when a merchant goes for his rifle or his gun I think he's already lost the game, he's already dead. The Bedouins are much more skilled and experienced, and they know what they're doing. Ever since I was a young boy I'd ask everyone what you had to do to stop them from robbing you. A few people kept their flocks near some Bedouin families, and every now and then they would see each other and do business. So, obviously, when the merchant had to go through their area, the shepherd would come and protect him. Also, everyone said that friendship is hugely important to Bedouins. So, if you ask a Bedouin for hospitality, he can't refuse. That's just the way they are. But after three days you have to leave and, I was told, after someone has left a Bedouin tent, he only has three days to get away. If they catch him again after three days, they kill him.[13] And then, there was only one way to stop a Bedouin from robbing you, and that was to appeal for his protection before he pointed a gun at you. All my friends would be shaking in their shoes, weapons in hand. But the fact is that back then, when I was a boy – I'm sorry but there's no point going on with the story if you don't know certain things –, we went around with our money in our belts or sewn into our jackets. The coins were really heavy, so these men, all dressed up in their travelling gear, moved about clumsily. What could they hope to achieve with their guns? And the others turned out in large numbers but, most of all, they knew exactly how to attack and rob us. They didn't need to fall upon us like that, at the break of dawn. Anyway, as I was saying, once I remembered this and, when the leader of the party of Bedouins who were about to rob us got close to me, I grabbed his belt and shouted at the top of my voice: 'I appeal for your protection! Please protect me and my friends!' You could see he was angry because I was only a boy and he didn't expect me to know about these things, which is also why he had come so close to me, because he was sure I wouldn't try anything on. So, he turned towards the other Bedouins – who, by the way, are not all marauders, there are also some gentlemen among them... There was one who came to my uncle once... oh, yes of course, later, later – and he said to me: 'Where are you heading to?' The eldest in our caravan shouted: 'To Najaf.' And the Bedouin replied: 'We'll follow you up to Deir ez-Zor; after that you're on your own. Be thankful to this boy and for Bedouin hospitality.' So we were all safe, and the robbers didn't steal anything at all from us.

"What? Have you been listening or not? I said they left us alone. You're getting mixed up! I never said they robbed us of everything we had, not even when I told my grandson the story, you're the ones who are getting it wrong. Now, that's enough! Let me speak to this gentleman, you can carry on afterwards, whenever and whatever way you like." It's too late to do anything about it now, they're convinced I make up all these stories and, you know, once you have that reputation you can't do anything to change it. No, it doesn't bother me at all, they are just fooling around. At the end of the day, I know what happened in my life, don't I? And besides, do you think they would all sit around us like this if they thought I was making it all up? "Isn't that right Hashem? Your grandfather doesn't tell lies. Do you understand?" Well, of course, maybe sometimes when I talk to my grandson... we all know what boys are like, don't we? When you tell them a story, it has to be told in a certain way, otherwise they don't listen to you, or maybe they do but then they don't remember anything about it.

Were there any other dangerous areas? No! No! You know, back then the world was poorer and happier, and it was safe to travel. There was more faith in God and more trust in human beings! There was more friendship between people. "Tripoli? Oh! How did that old story get into your head? And is there any need to tell it right here, to a foreigner?" He wants me to tell you what happened to me on the road to Jounieh, in Lebanon. "How on earth do you remember that? Oh, what a cheeky boy you are!" Did you hear him? He says that I repeat myself all the time and tell the same stories over and over again but enjoy changing the ending. "Well, my boy, this is not the right time. When we get back home I'll be telling your father a thing or two." You know, I had more respect for my uncle and the old folks at home. It's all to do with these school holidays, he gets bored and spends hours wandering around the souk and listening to what people say. People were more respectful in the old days! "So, is this barber coming or not? What's the matter with everyone today?"

Still, what happened on the road to Jounieh is true, I remember it very well and so does everyone else. The fact is that the road to Tripoli,[14] which ran along the coast and was very busy, was quite safe. But then, from Tripoli to Jounieh, the road was terrible and there were a number of spots were it really wasn't safe to stop. If you had to travel to Beirut you had to go through Damascus, cross the mountains between Damascus and the Beqaa Valley, and then make your way down to Beirut. If you had to buy or deliver goods in Tripoli you'd take the road running along the coastline. But it was really unusual for people to take their goods from Tripoli to Beirut and, maybe because of that, or maybe for other reasons, it was a dangerous area and merchants weren't keen on taking that route. And, of course, I would never have taken it either, but we were a party of merchants, and when we got to the souk in Tripoli the price we were offered for our goods was really low. It was hardly enough to cover our travel costs. The elders in my caravan said they would accept whatever they got: they would sell everything in Tripoli and go back to Aleppo. But I told them I wouldn't go along with that, and while we were busy arguing, we were approached by a fellow who asked us how much we wanted for our goods. There were fifty or so carpets from Turkmenistan, you know, the ones they call Bukhara, even though Bukhara has nothing to do with it because they are not made in Bukhara but by some very skilled tribes from Turkmenistan, except that today's Turkmenistan has no connection whatever to Bukhara. Yes, to go back to what I was saying...

So, the fellow asked us to unroll some of the carpets and said he had a relative who had a carpet shop not far from the centre of Beirut, and that last time he had bought some he had paid a lot more for them. The older merchants in our group then asked around, tried to get information, but no one knew the name of this Beirut merchant who had supposedly paid a higher price for Bukhara carpets than they were being offered in Tripoli. And so, after a while, one merchant said he would sell in Tripoli anyway and go back; another said he didn't believe the man, that it was a long way to Beirut, and we couldn't be sure we'd get a better price; and so on an so forth. They were basically saying the usual things that merchants say when they aren't interested in doing business. But if they had told me what they knew, I would never have gone either. Instead, they started asking about the Beirut merchant, how much he paid, and so on, when the real issue was that none of them wanted to travel on the road to Jounieh. Wouldn't it have been easier if they had just said that?

So I started looking at them in the way that youths sometimes look at old people. And, actually, I think if they had thought that way when they were young, none of them would have made as much money as they did in the end, and maybe a few years earlier they would have been more enterprising and willing to take a risk. One old man, who was a friend of my uncle's, after listening to my arguments, said to me: 'Forget it, boy, you are with me and you'll go back with me. The road to Beirut is not for us.' So I started saying that they were rich, while I still wasn't and couldn't afford the luxury of earning so little. And then, what would my uncle say once I got back to Aleppo, and he found out that I had gone all that way for a meagre fifteen percent profit? He would never let me go off again. I was so insistent about it that they eventually let me have two donkeys and my share of the merchandise, and the next morning I set off for Beirut.

No, I wasn't afraid. I was young and had a gun with me, and the goods I was carrying weren't valuable enough for anyone to go to the trouble of trying to rob me – at least that's what I thought. But now that I'm old, I realize that robbing someone who's travelling with just two bearers isn't so hard and even a second-rate thief will probably give it a go if he sees someone travelling on his own loaded with goods. Anyway, we left Tripoli, and for two whole days everything seemed to be going well. Then, the road suddenly turned sharply because of a river flowing down from a mountain, and a man on horseback appeared on the other side of the bend. My bearers said: 'Here we go, Sir! We told you.' So I grabbed the two donkeys and turned around as fast as I could to try to escape but found myself facing another man with his gun pointed at me. It was almost a robbery between gentlemen. They asked me where I came from, how much my goods were worth and how much money I was carrying. I told them I had to sell the goods and use the money to get back home, and that my father was only a few minutes' away with a group of soldiers. So I warned them to get away quickly before there was trouble. One of the men said to the other: 'Let him go, can't you see he's only a boy?' But the other man looked at me and said: 'So, your father is coming to rescue you? Well, how about that!' And he laughed at me, clearly enjoying himself. At that point, I began to feel really scared. 'So,' he said, 'the only thing to do is cut your throat and get away so you'll never be able to tell anyone you saw us!' But the other man, who looked tough and had no time for fooling around, said: 'Come on, let's go. He's just a boy. Forget it.' So the one who was making fun of me said: 'Take your clothes off and we'll go.' So I found myself totally cleaned out, and they took the donkeys as well to stop us going after them, and the bearers were angry with me because now I had nothing to pay them with. So I walked all day and all night, and when I got to Tripoli the merchants in my caravan were still there, resting after their journey. No one said a word to me: they lent me some money and let me go back with them. And that's how I discovered that the road along the coast of Lebanon is dangerous and it's best not to take it. But they could have told me that before!

No, my uncle didn't really get angry with me. He knew my situation and also knew he could hardly shout at me. The fact is that my mother died when I was still a boy... I don't remember what she died of, maybe from the flu. I know it was something that killed swathes of people in those days. Maybe it's what they call SARS nowadays, or whatever. Back then it didn't have a name, yet many more people died of it, not like SARS, where it isn't clear whether it's a real epidemic or just a fantasy. After she died I lived on with my father, but he worked in the countryside, and although he did all he could to spend time with me, he often left in the morning and didn't get back until the evening. So, when he remarried, he said to me: 'This is your mother's inheritance. She wanted me to keep it for you until you became of age and give it to you then. But now there is another woman and I don't know how she's going to treat you when I'm not at home. So, I've spoken to my brother in Aleppo and he says they are all happy for you to live with them because they don't have any sons of their own.' The only problem was money, because they lived on trade, and my uncle couldn't take someone as a business partner who didn't have his own capital, however small.

So, my father sold off my mother's belongings, and with the money he got he sent me to live with his brother. This event changed my life forever, because instead of staying on in the country and working as a farmer I became a merchant and travelled a great deal, more than I ever imagined I would.

Of course I was sorry. But at eight or nine years old I had neither the spirit nor the inclination to become lost in nostalgia. I didn't see much of my dad anyway because he'd leave the house in the morning and come back in the evening every day. And then, when my new mum came to live with us, she immediately started complaining about the things I did. She said I was naughty and misbehaved, so, as it was, everything turned out for the best for everyone concerned. But my dad came to see me almost every month and we spent time together, so he never made me feel that I was left on my own. Come to think of it, the only time I felt wistful back then was when we walked past an abandoned house about which people told a weird story that scared the wits out of us country boys. It had supposedly belonged to a libertine, or I should say, a dirty old man, who enjoyed throwing parties and having grand dinners. He invited men with beautiful wives to the house and entertained them lavishly. But the wine he gave the husband to drink was drugged, so he would fall asleep leaving his wife to the mercy of the man, who would take her whether she liked it or not. And when the husband woke up she would never say anything about it because she was scared he would kill her if he found out what happened.

And in the neighbourhood – this is not a folk story; it really did happen – there lived a farmer who was married to a very beautiful woman. When the libertine saw her, he fell in love with her and decided he absolutely had to have her. So, of course, they got their invitation to dinner, which they couldn't refuse as the man was an agha and such an invitation was impossible to turn down. But the farmer pretended to be ill, and on the evening of the dinner he sent a message to apologize for not being able to attend himself, but saying that since he felt so honoured by such an invitation, and was aware that the agha was doing his family a great honour, he would send his wife along with her sister, who had recently come to stay with them from Aleppo, escorted by a servant who would bring them back home after the meal.

Obviously there was no such sister but only the farmer himself dressed up as a woman, armed and covered with a veil so that you couldn't even see his eyes. The agha didn't suspect anything and, when the dinner was over – by which time the servant who was supposed to take the women home was drugged and fast asleep –, he got close to the women and started telling them about the wonderful things he had in his house and how worried he was about the state of health of his neighbour, whom he said he regarded as a brother. He said he was thinking of taking them home himself to make sure his friend was okay. And he went on talking like this to get the women to believe there was a great friendship between him and the farmer who "sadly" hadn't been able to come. He then told the women they could make themselves at home and take off their veil because he was a friend of the family. The farmer's wife, who knew what was about to happen, tried to say she was tired and wanted to go home, but the man, blinded by passion started saying the kinds of things you don't say to another man's wife – that she smelled sweeter than Aleppo jasmine, that her skin was like a peach, and so on – until he went up to her, took the veil off her face and tried to embrace her. At that point, her husband jumped up and cut his arm right off, and while the man was screaming and crying betrayal, he grabbed his wife and they ran home.

They fled and fled! No one ever knew where they found refuge. The agha bled to death from the wound. His family had the whole countryside around Aleppo searched, but never found the farmer. Sometime later, however, they found out what had been happening again and again inside that house. Although they never said anything, they felt ashamed of their family member who had done such harm to so many women. They eventually let the house fall into decay and went to live elsewhere. My dad warned me never to go into that house because the ghost of the libertine was still there, trying to catch women or young boys and girls, and so it was best to steer clear of those walls. So, that house, which we would never have noticed otherwise, became a sort of field of honour for all of us teenagers in the village, where we dared each other in tests of courage. Once we had proved we were brave enough to enter the house in the daytime, we started daring each other to go inside during the night. Once, with a group of other kids, we made up a game in which, in order to prove that we weren't afraid, we had to go inside the house at night carrying a lit candle and wearing a black cape, a sort of shepherd's cloak that one of us had found at home. The idea of the candle was to stop you from running. As you approached the place everything was fine, but when you came back, that's when fear usually kicked in, and it's where the candle prevented you from running!

Well, we were all standing not far from the house, on higher ground where we had a good view of it, but we were all too scared to go in. Then, the eldest boy in our group, after telling us were all babies and had no idea what it was to be brave, grabbed the black cape and slowly walked up to the agha's house in the gloom of the night. We watched him approaching the house, all utterly transfixed, when suddenly something eerie happened, which we only understood afterwards. When the young man got inside the house and shook the candle as agreed, he turned around to come back. Then, probably a bramble – or one of those thorny shrubs that grow in abandoned places – got caught in the cape and he felt something pulling him backwards! We heard a ghastly scream, so chilling that I can still remember it. Then the candle went out and he started running like a boy possessed, screaming: 'I saw him! I saw him!' It was years before we worked out what could have happened, but that night brought our experiments in bravery to an end. We never went back to the house, and nobody else went there for years; that's why it's totally dilapidated now. Yet, when I walked past it back then, it reminded me of many boys I would never see again and made me feel a bit wistful.

So, I went to live with my uncle, in Aleppo. It was a beautiful house, but his family wasn't like all the others. There were flats laid out all around the garden of the house, and each was the home of a single family, all merchants and business associates. I didn't become part of a family as we would understand it today, but of a true community, a rich community even though each individual family may not have been particularly wealthy. The life we led wasn't... I mean, I wasn't just with my uncle but with around forty people, you see.

At the beginning, I remember thinking that it all had to do with being in the city, and that anyone living in the city had to live with others... It took me some time to realize it wasn't like that. They needed that kind of arrangement because of their trade, their line of work. That way, when the men went away, and travelled perhaps for six or eight months, and sometimes even for a whole year, the women could help each other. The children played and grew up together and never felt lonely. It was also a perfect way to protect the house and each of the families' savings. Of course, they also used all the old tricks, like double-base tins where you'd put the flour at the top and the money at the bottom, or hiding the family jewels inside the hollow of a beam, and so on. But all this wasn't important because each one of these merchants knew exactly how much the others earned. They lived together, they were business partners, their children married each other – this was Aleppo's traders' community. If you weren't born in it, or if you didn't somehow become part of it as I did, it was impossible to belong to it. It wasn't a closed community, but it was a system that affected everything: your work, your everyday life and everything else. I remember once – I was grown up by then – when we came back after being away for several months on a trip to Basra.[15] A widow in our household had died, and her daughter, who had married a teacher in Damascus, had sold her house to the first person who offered to buy it. We came back and found some new faces around, some new people. We walked into the courtyard and there were strangers around! We, who had been used to thinking about our courtyard as our safe area. To give you an idea of how safe we felt in our yard, sometimes we even got dressed there! So, when this happened, we all got together and decided what to do. We worked out how much we could afford to spend and went to see the new family. They had paid 'one hundred' for the house, and we asked them how much they wanted in order to leave. They didn't understand what we meant, so the eldest among us threw a sum of money on the table and said: 'Is that enough?' He had to increase it quite a bit before the new house owner eventually said: 'Okay, we'll go. We'll leave tomorrow.' The old man smiled and said: 'No, our offer only stands if you leave now!'

They complained a bit, but they had gone within less than an hour, and all the servants and the women in the house had put all their belongings out in the street. That wasn't a good deal. We get rich by investing in goods that we resell, not in houses. But when it comes to your house, your own house, I mean... Anything can happen when you're travelling. But those you leave behind at home must feel safe and protected. You can't have strangers in the house.

And so I started travelling with my uncle. He had my money. He had shown it to the other merchants in his party and everyone knew how much capital I had to spend and which goods I could or couldn't afford to buy. I went along with them, basically from the age of fourteen, and I realized that until I was eighteen years old they were all attentive towards me and took care of my money – and the money of that widow... the one whose husband's death led to such unexpected consequences. When there was a particularly good deal to be made, they made sure that my money, along with the widow's, was invested in it. And so the little capital I started out with grew very rapidly, and when I reached the age when I could go it alone, I found I had what amounted to a small fortune. The only thing they said to me when they gave me back my capital – making me officially free to go where I wanted – was to remind me that our trade was a system of interconnected values... of crosscutting values? ... Yes, you could say that. And, while not everything might have seemed useful or profitable, everything contributed to what was useful and profitable. They had protected me because it was right not to squander the small sum of money I had; they would expect the same thing for their own sons, one day.

But, of course, I didn't go off anywhere. The speech was just a formality to acknowledge that I was now a grownup man. I liked being with them too much, and – to tell the truth – I enjoyed too many advantages to give all that up so easily. What sorts of advantages? You have no idea! At the time there weren't any banks, it was my uncle and his associates who acted as "the bank". And, you know, the principle behind it was extremely simple. First, always keep your word. Second, give back when you can and give when you have to. Third, only do business with people who are as respectable as yourself. Everything else – believe me, everything else – is just drivel. That's why my uncle and his friends and associates had a worldwide reputation. People said: 'He's a trader from Aleppo,' which meant: 'He's someone who never goes back on his word.'

I still remember once – I was still a boy then – when an Arab officer came to our shop and told my uncle he had to go away and had some savings he didn't want to take with him as he was sure he'd be robbed. He simply asked him to deal with the money as if it was his own: if he lost money, it would be lost, if he made money, it would grow. But, whatever happened, he trusted him, and his money couldn't be in better hands. I remember my uncle giving him a receipt, but the officer said he didn't want it. He signed it and told my uncle to keep it as he trusted him fully.

I don't know how much time went by, maybe two or three years. We never heard anything more from this man, but no one asked, no one said anything, no one spoke about him. Yet, when we talked about business, the "officer's" share always appeared alongside ours, and the boys at home didn't know what the men were talking about and who this officer might be. Then, one day, a beautiful woman dressed in mourning clothes showed up at the souk. She was Armenian, with auburn hair, but she spoke our language perfectly and her face showed all the signs of someone who has been through a whole lot of things she would gladly have done without. She had married this officer from Aleppo then had gone with him to southern Syria, on the border with Palestine. There had been some troubles and he had died. She had previously fled from Armenia without a penny and had lost all the men in her family. She had come over here, and for a couple of years she thought she would become rich by marrying this man. He was much older than her, but he loved her. And then he died!

So, through the tears, she told us she had decided to go to America, because life, she said, gives you clear messages about what you should do, if only you are willing to understand them. And she had lost everything, first in Armenia then in Syria, so she realized that her destiny wasn't here, and now she was leaving. She had come to get whatever might be claimed out of her husband's money. I saw my uncle getting up, going to fetch some merchants from our group, and reappearing before the widow after a while with a little book that even I had never seen before. Everything had been noted down in it: every transaction, what they had bought, what the officer's share was and how much profit had been made on it. In the end, they called over the treasurer and he appeared with a sack of gold coins – it was this big! The woman thanked them, sat down and waited while they worked out how much she was entitled to take, as the others stood silently in front of her. So, a few minutes went by, sipping tea and talking about the French and the British, and the war that seemed likely to break out in Germany. The woman then said that was the reason why she was leaving, and, well, if it wasn't too much trouble, she would like to take her share and let us get on with our business.

My uncle looked at her and said: 'But your share is everything that's in that sack, the whole lot!' She looked at him, got up from the chair and tried to lift it, and... plunk! She fainted! It took a while to get her to come around; she couldn't understand whether it was true or just a joke. In the end, she decided to leave anyway, but she wanted my uncle to look after the money and said she would ask for it once she had sorted herself out and was settled in America. We gave it to her ten years later, and paid it into a bank in Los Angeles, in California. It was a fortune: for Syria and for Aleppo, it was a real fortune. It was the result of fifteen years of trade investments without ever drawing anything for living expenses, clothing, nothing! Fifteen years of moving money around to buy goods with, you see. My uncle never even knew what the 1930s financial crisis was: we never kept any cash, only what was strictly necessary – and never in banknotes but in gold.

... Yes, of course we were able to send the money. The French had opened a branch of one of their banks over here; it was very efficient and took care of everything. I know that after a while we received a telegram: the money had been received and the Armenian woman sent her thanks.

I know you won't believe me, but that's how it has always been Aleppo. I went to the bank just this morning and the cashier told me that a woman had come in earlier with a huge bag full of banknotes. It was the money her grandmother had been saving for years, stashing it under her mattress at home. The cashier told me she had come in by taxi, without taking any particular precautions, and wasn't at all worried about it. Yet she was carrying an awful lot of money!

But then, our whole world was like that, everything was based on trust, wherever you went. The journey we made most often with my uncle and the other merchants was for carpets: we would go to Mosul then to Urmia and Tabriz. From there, we almost always went on to Tehran. If we didn't find any high quality carpets in Tehran, we would push on to Mashhad or Ashkhabad. The communities in that region are still organized in tribal groups and carpet production is very good. They are called Bukhara... have I already told you? Okay, I won't go through that again. So, we would leave from Aleppo and sometimes we'd go to Lebanon, but less frequently. Sometimes we also went towards Damascus and would continue all the way down to Medina or Mecca. We always travelled together, sometimes joining the pilgrims' caravans and mixing in among them because the raiders knew very well that the pilgrims didn't have much while the merchants were rich, so they tried to single out the merchants in order to rob them.

We used all kinds of animals for transport, including donkeys, camels... I travelled many times to Najaf with camels. There you go, now they've started laughing again! "What now?" Oh yes, the camels, well maybe we didn't use them anymore because there were coaches by then and they were much quicker... But sometimes... I can't think why they're acting like this. As I told you, they've got it into their heads that I always make up these stories and they never believe me. "You lot have no idea of what I've seen! The fact is that you love making fun of an old man. What? I should tell the story about the wife I had in Najaf? Well, what's odd about that?" They say I must tell you what happened to me in Najaf...

What happened is, I had gone there with a group of merchants who weren't part of my uncle's group, and when I got to Najaf, you know how it is... I was a young man, so they said that after working so hard I should have a bit fun. I was actually married and didn't want to. But they said to me: 'What's the matter with you? We left three months ago and will be back in three months' time. You're not going to wait all this time, are you?' So we ended up in one of those places where you go in as a rich man and leave as a poor man. And while I was doing what everyone else did, all my money was stolen. "What is it now?" Why are they laughing? They claim I didn't go there once but for six months nonstop and spent all the money I had on women. "That's not true!" While I was with one of those girls, they went through my clothes and took everything I had. So, I found myself cleaned out and didn't know how to get back home. So I went to see a sheikh, a highly respected man, and he said I might be able to earn some money by taking groups of merchants like myself around the holy sites because, instead of praying, they often did business, had a good time and then went back home. It sounded like a good idea to me, but he said that in order to work as a guide in the holy places you had to be Shiite or have a Shiite wife. 'So, what should I do?' I asked him. He seemed to enjoy wasting my time, but he told me there was a penniless old widow near the mosque who I could marry and, that way, no one would be able to complain since she was Persian, so the various theologians in the mosques wouldn't stop me from doing that kind of work. I didn't think it was a very fair thing to do, but the sheikh kept on and on about it until he talked me into marrying her. And once we were married, she'd say to me: 'Will you be coming home tonight?' Can you imagine that? I was just under thirty years old, I was young and bursting with ideas, and every day this toothless old woman, who was over eighty years old, would ask me if I was coming home in the evening! She gave me the creeps, but she was a good cook and the house was clean. In the end, this went on a few months and I felt as if I had found a mother. Maybe I haven't told you, but I lost my mother when I was very young and I don't even remember her... Oh, have I told you already? I'm sorry.

Then one day, after I had been in Najaf for seven or eight months, a merchant from Damascus who I knew very well turned up in Najaf. He told me he'd heard that a ship had come into Basra from India with an important cargo of goods, and he was looking for someone to go with him to make a big business deal. So, I went back to my little old woman and told her about it. She insisted I should take all her savings and told me she was happy if I was happy, and that I must take as much as I needed. I was the apple of her eye, she said, and the pillow on her bed.

I promised I'd be back soon and that we would be very rich and went off to Basra with my friend. The cargo turned out to be very interesting indeed. There were guns and ammunitions, and those kinds of goods are easy to sell anywhere. But my friend fell ill so I decided to go straight back to Damascus, without passing through Najaf. So I never went back to see my old wife there. But another merchant told me she is in cahoots with the sheikh, dealing in some kind of trade. I don't know what it involves exactly... But it seems that whoever she marries always loses out, while the two of them get rich.

No! I've never stolen anything from anyone, it's just that I kept her company for almost a year and... I had earned that money. Anyway, it was she who insisted I take it. I would gladly have done without it. They should try spending a year with a toothless old woman who, every night when I got home, would start saying: 'It's so cold in my bed!' And, anyway, I had another wife and she was well aware of that. And I had to go back to Aleppo to see her again, to see my uncle and sort out my business affairs. It's true that my uncle and his associates were most respectable men, but it's also true that they didn't like the fact that I had gone off on my own and, after such a long time away, it was important for me to go back and sort out my family matters too. Yet I was sorry I never went back to Najaf, and so whenever I come across anyone who is going to Najaf, whether on business or to pray, I always tell them to go and see my little old woman and tell her I'm earning the money I owe her and that one day I'll go back and see her.

So, I decided not to come back via Najaf and headed directly for Damascus. And one day, on the road, I met a fellow who told me he was going to Yemen. "Hashem! Bring some more tea, the gentleman has finished his! Would you like some mint in it? Tell him to put some mint in the tea!"

There you go. So, I was telling you about the time when... Yes, the time when I went to Erzurum with my uncle and his friends, it was up north, in Turkey. I don't like Turkey, you know. As to the Turks, I don't know if they are good people or not, but I don't actually like them because that time, when we were travelling towards Erzurum... Oh, was I telling you about a journey to Yemen? Which one? The one I started on when I left Basra, after I bought some guns? Oh yes, that's it, I remember it very well. My poor old brain! This is what happens when you get old... Anyway, we were saying... Oh really? Surely you don't have to go just yet, do you? Let me tell you this story, the one about the woman who bewitched lorry drivers and then killed them off. This one ended up in the papers, you know. There was also a court trial... I'm not sure whether it was in Yemen or Arabia... But I remember it perfectly well... So, this woman had the most beautiful daughter...

7 - The Bedouin Schoolmaster

I am well aware of it, and even if I didn't know it, you only have to walk down the streets of Palmyra to see how it is, looking at these small groups of tourists with their sunburnt faces, in their shorts and cotton shirts, walking around with their backpacks and big water bottles. It's as if they still hadn't learnt anything about the sun even after being here for many days, and they still don't understand how important it is to protect themselves from it. They are often purple in the face, but even then, if they have to choose where to stand, at sunset like at dawn, they instinctively move into the sunlight, and if they are in the shade, they seek the sun with their eyes.

I think it's impossible to love the desert except for short periods of time. The tourists fall in love with a short-lived sensation… The sun, the spaces, the vast horizon, the silence and the nights around the camp fire… These are wonderful things and we, too, appreciate them. But life in the desert is something else, believe me, it's a nightmare. It's a nightmare that you might even love if it's part of your family and your history. You may even find some Bedouin who think they love it and would never consider living in ordinary concrete houses. I myself know many who are like that; my mother was one of them. If you could have spoken to her even just for a second – she died several years ago – my mother might have persuaded you that life in the desert is wonderful and impossible to give up, at least for us. And perhaps you might have gone back to your own country believing that Bedouin people can love the desert. But believe me, life in the desert is hell. Believe you me, I who am from a Bedouin family and have relatives still living in tents and have lived there myself can tell you, it's one of the hardest lives that God has ever offered to man. Some people may love its freedom, its community life in the tents and moving constantly from place to place, but all that isn't the desert, you know.

There is a doctor nearby who has managed to get an education and a degree, despite the fact that he comes from a Bedouin family. He's a dentist now and I think you could say he's still in love with his roots. Whenever he has time, he joins his family in the desert and stays there for days on end. When he's over there, he goes back to the old way of life and says he can't live without all that. And it's the same for his parents. When they come to Palmyra to see him and stay in the beautiful house he's built for himself, they seem to be almost in pain, deprived of the spaces of the desert, here in the city with its rules, its pace of life and its lights. Once, he and I were talking about the school children, and he said he had never seen so many rotten teeth. 'I can tell if the children's families are from the desert,' he told me, 'just by looking at their teeth, because they are strong, healthy and clean. The children from the city have terrible teeth, although they brush them once or even twice a day, while those from the desert never clean them at all. Milk, yoghurt, dates and a little meat is all you need in order to have good teeth. No toothbrush or toothpaste can possibly remedy the disastrous effects of sugar.'

Well, not even he – who seems to regret the loss of everything connected with the life he led when he used to take the goats out to graze as a boy – would go back to all that. And, although he'll never say it to you, I know that when he goes to see his parents he's always surprised that they still manage to hold out and by how staunchly they refuse to leave their tents and go and live with him, in his house, in the rooms he has already set up for them.

… No, I've never seen that film.[16] I don't think it's ever been shown in Syria. Maybe it's because the story of this Feisal and this Lawrence is so controversial… Or perhaps it's because of the way the British are portrayed the film… I don't know. But if at some point an actor says something like that, then it shows that the person who wrote the script knew the desert at least as well as we do. That's just how it is: we don't love the discomfort and hardship that comes from the blinding sun, the lack of water and the extreme cold and extreme heat of the desert. If I had the choice, I would go to Damascus, to be among its gardens, to listen to the water gushing from the fountains and smell its sweet-scented flowers. And if any Bedouin had the choice, they would do the same. They may well miss the desert and feel nostalgic about it, but they would stay on in Damascus...

Things have changed nowadays, at least partly. Many families now have a satellite dish so they can watch television. Some, like the doctor's family, have a car that they keep for emergencies... Everything is less hard now, far less hard than it was in the past. My father used to say to me that at the end of the day, everyone would be so shattered and exhausted that they didn't even have time to sit and have a chat. They would fall asleep in the tents just like that, sometimes not even getting ready for the night. They collapsed from sheer exhaustion.

Neither my grandfather nor my father could read. They were religious men, yet they wouldn't have been able to read a single prayer, or even a single word. Sometimes, a dervish or a sheik would come by where my family had pitched their tents. These men had chosen a life of hardship in order to bring the word of the Prophet to the people of the desert. Their arrival was always a cause for great celebration. We would listen to them with a mix of worship and respect, perhaps also due to the long journey they had made and their saintliness. But our reverence for them grew to new levels when they opened the book and we watched them reading from it. Then, when the prayers were over, our dad would look at us and say: 'You boys must learn to read. You won't be like your father and grandfather.' And in his voice there was none of the pride that people of the desert have? None whatsoever. There was humiliation. There were all sorts of feelings, but they all came together in a kind of despair about the world that was disappearing and passing us by without us even noticing, purely because we couldn't read and write. The despair came from this relationship of dependency that existed between us and those who read to us, which undid any other sense of freedom we might have felt and could have reason to be proud of. What kind of freedom can a man truly enjoy in life if he has to rely on someone else in order to find out what his own God said? And when he has to believe anything he is told because he is unable to develop his own ideas about God and judge for himself? I have seen humiliation, however dignified, written on my parents' faces and, believe me, it's something I'll never be able to forget. That's perhaps why I am a schoolmaster today and do the things I do.

Every so often, some travelling tradesmen would stop by. They were usually craftsmen who repaired our pots, sharpened our knives and sold us ammunition. And that, too, caused great excitement because they brought news from the outside world. They told us about other Bedouin families settled nearby and what the grazing land and the water springs were like in other areas of the desert. But they also told us what was happening in the city and in the world. Then, in the evening, when we boys had also returned to the tents, it was wonderful to sit and listen to them, with their fanciful and improbable stories, but which – at last! – were eventful and told of worlds where things actually happened. Because, we also shouldn't forget… Have you any idea what it's like tending the goats grazing in the desert? It means that "nothing" – literally nothing – happens for weeks and months on end! It brings a sense of solitude and boredom that runs so deep that, after a while, it takes hold of you and gradually, little by little, it switches you off.

Imagine our delight when we came back home to find these craftsmen just as they were beginning to tell all kinds of stories, which even at the time seemed outlandish to me but gave us exactly what we needed! The one they told most often was about a woman in a Syrian town who was tried and sentenced for poisoning her children and husband. And the tale always went into great detail about the supper she had prepared which ended in excruciating pain, and with the children shouting 'Mummy! Mummy!' while she was getting ready to meet her lover. I remember my mum and sisters sitting in the shadow of the tent holding their breath so that they wouldn't miss a single syllable of that ghastly story.

Then there was another one about a mysterious sect near Aleppo that cut people's throats for reasons that no one understood or which we later realized led directly to their death. So, the townspeople would wake up in the morning to find these corpses with their throats cut, and no one knew who had done it or where to search for the culprit. The storyteller greatly enjoyed scaring us (and we enjoyed being scared), and always started with an improbable but classic story that children love to hear. It tells of a boy walking in the streets of Aleppo at night on his way home, who hears footsteps behind him, and when he stops, the footsteps stop, too. And of course it always ended with a big black shadow looming over him, and the next morning the boy would be found with his throat cut.

There was also another story – it was the one that terrified my brothers and I the most. It was about a woman who had married a man with children from a previous marriage. When the husband left the house in the mornings, she would put bugs inside the children's nostrils 'so that they would eat their brains out.' Then she would hold their mouth closed while they cried, shaking their head. That way, they had to breathe through their nose and so – according to the story – the bugs would go straight up into their brain and slowly eat it! You see? These were the kinds of stories we sat and listened to. Eventually, 'with all those bugs inside their head eating their brains out', the children always had a headache, so their father realized that something was wrong and one day, after leaving for work, he went straight back home. I don't remember exactly how it ended, except that the children were eventually saved, and the woman was killed or thrown into jail.

When these travelling tradesmen came, we could sit for hours listening to these stories and it didn't matter that they were always the same or that we already knew them by heart. To us they seemed new each time around. And when the little girl cried and said to her stepmother 'Just one bug this morning! Please, just one bug!' we felt a shiver going down our spines and never bothered to ask ourselves how the bugs she put inside their noses managed to get into their brains.

Our relations with the other Bedouin groups were non-existent or very limited. We knew that if we moved our tents southward or eastward we would find those of another tribe. And if we came across another tribe it was never by chance. Sometimes our areas, the ones in which we traditionally moved, happened to be drier than usual or water would become scarce, or perhaps we knew that the climate was better further away. If we moved and happened to encroach on the territory of another tribe, no one tried to stop us, but the fact would be noted. There was neither a welcome nor a war, but people recorded in their memory that we had to give back what we had received. It could be in ten or twenty years' time, but just as we had moved into their land, they acquired the right to come and use our pastures one day. And all this took place in an area that seems vast if we see it on a map today, running from the Turkish mountains right up to Mecca or Medina. Distances could be great, but to us they didn't really exist in an abstract sense. It was a world we were familiar with, divided between different tribes or groups. Even if we didn't have any direct knowledge of it, it was still part of something that belonged to us.

So, we knew that the Syrian Desert was the northernmost part of this huge area, and to the north of us and our grazing lands were the Taurus Mountains and the beginning of another world, utterly unknown to us. That's why Syria and Damascus are also known as Cham. We are the north, the last section of the desert. To the west, there were obviously the cities of Aleppo, Homs and Damascus, to the east there was Najaf, Kerbala and Baghdad. Then, as I said, to the south there were sweeping deserts which took endless days to cross and extended beyond what we call Jordan today and even Arabia itself, reaching up to the mountains of Yemen. We knew there were Bedouin tribes in all of these areas, each with its own reputation, its own history and its own traditions. And each led its own separate life, without asking for anything or giving anything, isolated in its own desert, engaged in its own struggle for survival.

There were many stories circulating among us at the time, and we even started collecting some of them at school before they would be lost forever. People said that some tribes, which were poorer than others, regularly robbed the traders' caravans crossing the desert. Other, more ruthless tribes, perhaps in collusion with certain individuals, were said to have wiped out or attacked the great procession that set out from Damascus every year for the Hajj.[17] These were old stories by then because, partly due to the borders and partly to the railway and roads, the time for robbing caravans was already over. People said that one particular tribe, living not very far from us, had once attacked a neighbouring tribe in order to settle an old rivalry and had killed all the men and taken the women with them. But even when I was a boy, these were old stories that went way back in time. And then, as I was saying, life in the desert was extremely tough, so in every tribe there may have been some people who just couldn't take it and turned to banditry due to poverty and hardship. Such things happened just about everywhere back then, not just in Syria but all over the world.

Here in our region, the first major impact with the modern world and which essentially upset the balance of desert life came with the First World War. The Turks roamed the desert and picked up anyone they could, grownup men and young boys alike, to send to the front. My parents often told us about these convoys of trucks and men appearing in the desert, sometimes without any warning whatsoever, or coming in immediately after a similar one had left. In such cases, no sooner had the men who had gone into hiding returned to their tents thinking that the danger was over than another lot would turn up and take away any young men old enough to be enlisted. And if they couldn't find any, they would take the children or the elderly until the young man who was hiding to avoid being conscripted eventually came forward and enlisted. When they came to our tents, they took four or five of our men and left. That was before my father was born, but my grandfather told me several times about these trucks – with young men packed like sheep or goats bound for the market – that would disappear as quickly as they had appeared, taking with them anyone who hadn't been able to hide or was found hiding. Everyone who left for the front to fight for the Turks at that time died.

Our tribe didn't know anything about the Turks or the British, or about Feisal and the struggle to liberate Syria and Arabia from the Turks. Nor did we know very much about the Turkish or Ottoman Empire. Many in our tribe didn't even know who the Turks were until they came to our camps and took the men away to turn them into soldiers. They came across them in the cities where they went to trade, and maybe they even realized that they were our rulers, but their presence was essentially viewed as something that concerned the townsfolk, not the desert people. Not even the Turks came to the desert. My tribe never belonged to any Turkish Empire such as we see it on the maps in today's history books. It was on its own… And it went back and forth between the same places, the same pastures and water springs and the same towns where it sold its produce.

Obviously, people knew that they could buy dates in Najaf and Baghdad and get saddles and blankets in Aleppo, and that Damascus was a good place to buy gold… But as to everything else, I think they knew nothing about it, really nothing at all. They may not even have been aware of what was happening around us, or how exploited and even how feared we were. Although we lived our life alongside the other people of Syria, our paths never or hardly ever crossed. This is the kind of isolation I was telling you about. We grazed our livestock alone and were alone in the desert – alone because we were illiterate. We were cut off from everything, as if we didn't even exist.

I remember going to the souk in Aleppo with my grandfather and my father one day. It was autumn and we had to buy some covers and some thick woollen blankets for the winter. When we reached the entrance to the souk, I watched my grandfather delivering something to a merchant who in turn received it in a very dignified manner. I thus discovered that he owned almost half of our sheep and that for many years this sort of pilgrimage had been taking place twice a year, at the end of the summer and at the beginning of spring. My father and grandfather would go to the merchant and bring him the best things they had. They told him how many sheep they had, how many there were now in the herd – they basically reported to him. And he, our master, would sometimes say he wanted to sell some or would ask to have some himself, or he might say he would send a man to pick some of them up in order to resell them. But most of the time he didn't ask for anything. My father and grandfather would then go back to the desert, and everyone in our tribe knew that such and such a merchant owned fifty percent of my grandfather's sheep. He was a tolerant master and gave us Bedouin very good prices for our goods. So, to some extent, the merchant became part of our community, and whenever we heard that he was expected to cross our territory, perhaps to go and buy or sell something in Najaf or Baghdad, as a gesture of courtesy we would go and meet him just outside the city boundary and escort him during his entire journey across our lands.

I believe that some scholars who study the Bedouin world see all this as a kind of latent blackmail. By giving us sheep and trading with us, the merchants were seeking to protect themselves from robbery. These are the sorts of things people say, and maybe there is some truth in them. The desert is like a city, you don't know who is there and who isn't there, and so there may be robbers or thieves waiting to take advantage of the isolation that some people find themselves in when travelling through it. But the truth is that it wasn't all so adventurous and so romantic. The merchant from Aleppo gave us sheep, and in return he received yoghurt, wool and assistance from us when travelling through the desert, just as he gave land to the peasant farmers and got olives, oil, grain and pistachios in return. There was no real difference, and there is still none today. But, of course, although I was only a boy at the time, I clearly remember that when my brother and I realized that the sheep we tended every day of our lives were only fifty percent ours, we did ask ourselves some questions about our supposed freedom. And added to this was another feeling we experienced when walking into the Bedouin section of the souk in Aleppo, the one they call the Bedouin souk. It was a marvel of lights, noises and scents. I remember how amazed I was to see the richness and the abundance of goods on display. But, at the same time, I had the sensation that we were outsiders, and because of this I couldn't feel any pride. How much richer than us were the people of Aleppo! How poor my family was!

I was afraid of the city. I felt afraid about being without our animals, afraid of walking in the dark and enclosed arcades of the souk and of this sudden contact with people, of these crowds that suddenly materialized in a way I had never experienced before. But my amazement didn't prevent me from noticing that, although hugely diverse, the people there were all far richer than us. I wouldn't have been interested in wealth at all – just as many of the school children, thank goodness, aren't at all interested in riches – if it hadn't been for the accounting books that regularly appeared. I watched my grandfather as he talked with the merchant, who would open a register and show him the entries in the two columns with the records of the goods supplied and goods received, so that he could read what he was owed and what he owed. All I remember was the calm expression on his aristocratic looking and well-shaved face, and my grandfather's embarrassed silence as he stared at the writing in those columns, and the more he looked the less he understood. Then he would turn towards my father and us boys, pretending to be calm, to trust in his master and to have the situation in hand. Neither you nor I know how humiliating it is to open a register in which someone has kept your family's accounts, showing what you can give your women and children, what you are able or unable to spend, and understand nothing, nothing at all!

All he could do was look at the numbers and then judge – from the person's facial expression, his hand movements, the look in his eyes and tone of his voice, and any hint he could get – whether or not he was being robbed. Then my father would turn towards my elder brother and I and give us that look we knew so well. It was the same look he gave us when the dervishes came to our tents and read passages from the life of the Prophet to us, or when the travelling tradesmen read us articles from the old newspapers they wrapped the tools of their trade with. That look said: 'You boys will learn to read!'

And then, one day it happened. My brother hadn't turned six yet and it was springtime. Over the years, I've often wondered whether it was because the rains had been poorer than usual that winter, or because my grandfather was already ill and needed hospital treatment, or whatever the reason could be... These are all things I thought I would ask my father when I grew up, if he had lived. But my brother and I have often said to ourselves that, whatever the reason was, it was God who gave my father the strength to do it – it was God's will.

I remember all the men whispering in the tents. It was impossible not to notice the tension in the air. And the women were huddled in a corner crying. They wept silently, not as women cry in the city, where they sometimes seem to be performing in a theatre. My mother was crying, my aunt was crying, and my grandmother was crying. All the women were crying, but when the men called for more tea they looked composed and made up their faces so as to hide the fact that they had been crying and not let it show.

All I remember is that no one said anything. Nobody said to us 'We are moving to the city,' but we understood that very clearly. And although there were no discussions inside the tent, you could feel an almost violent tension between my father and grandfather on one side, who had decided to move, and my mother on the other, who didn't want to leave our desert life. Never again in my life have I witnessed such a fierce dispute, almost close to physical violence, yet so silent. The women moved about in the tent as if the men had lost all authority over them; they whispered while their husbands were talking, something they had never done before. The calls 'Tea, we want more tea!' were not requests but whiplashes. They were meant to break up the conversation, the grumbling and the constant rustling of dresses. Then, without a single word being spoken, the whispers turned into sobs, the dresses stopped moving about, and all that was left was the crying, my mother's and that of the women staying on in the desert. My father and grandfather stopped ordering tea. No one said a word anymore. When my brother and I came out of the tent, the men had started dividing up their goods and belongings. I don't remember ever hearing anything as heartrending as the words they exchanged: 'You are going to need this, I don't want it,' or 'Take this, you should get quite a good price for it at the market in Palmyra.'

I still recall some fragments of conversation, such as 'We are not going to another world, we'll only be a few kilometres away,' and 'You'll also decide to come when you see how we've set ourselves up,' and a feeling that was so… I don't even know how to describe it. Is that how children feel when their parents break up? Or is it how farmers feel when they move to the city? But – though I realize that our own ordeals always feel overwhelming to us while those of others always seem less so – this was all very, very traumatic indeed for us. The family was breaking up (not all the members of our family would be coming with us to Palmyra), our home would disappear, and the desert was reclaiming our days and our past. What would we do without our goats? How would we spend our days? How would we live in a real room, between four walls?

It was God who gave my father the strength to do all this. No human being can imagine he could have the strength and determination to face what he did without God's help. Being separated from his brothers, from his wife's family and from everything he knew how to do and had done until that day – alone, with his father and us children, with a wife who did nothing to conceal her disagreement and, I think I understood this later, with everyone's disapproval and condemnation, which only waited for him to fail before being openly and explicitly expressed.

I think my father was a hero. He was one of those unsung popular heroes that everyone forgets because the world is full of that kind of heroism, and after a while people don't notice it and don't pay any attention to it anymore. The world loves heroes who win battles, who fall as martyrs, fighting for a just cause – I think in Italy you are very fond of one called Garibaldi, aren't you? But that kind of heroism is fleeting, it only lasts for a second, a day or a year. Have you any idea what kind of strength it takes to give up all you have been until you are thirty years old and start everything from scratch? My father didn't even know how to sit at a table and had never seen a bathtub in his life before. He washed himself with sand and didn't even notice whether he had head lice anymore. Without his animals, his horse, his camel, his goats, his tent and his family, and without the desert, he was nothing. That's why I believe it was God's will that made him succeed. It was harder for him to move to Palmyra than for Columbus to discover America. My brother and I didn't understand very much about what was happening, but our father's strength was crystal clear to us. He and his father, who was just as strong-willed as him but was old and had nothing to lose, seemed larger than life to us. It was as if the courage and humility they demonstrated were not even measurable and couldn't be understood by anyone who hadn't gone with them to the souk in Aleppo to see the merchant in whose power they were. Only those who had witnessed with their own eyes the deep and hopeless humiliation they had had to endure, as my brother and I had, could understand.

So, we left, and perhaps today I would say that only my family unit left. But at the time I didn't even know what a family "unit" was or could be. The family as you might understand it didn't exist back then. We were all together, with three or even four generations, including aunts and uncles and cousins. Today, I realize that when I speak about my father and grandfather leaving for the city I have to use the term "my family", but at the time it wasn't so simple.

My brother and I stayed behind with the others without understanding exactly what was happening. Perhaps we thought that everything had ended on that tension-charged evening. But that expression on my mother's face was still there, and every time we looked at her we knew that my dad and grandad's absence was not the same as when they had gone away many times before. Something was about to happen to us.

Then one day, everything precipitated, and things suddenly moved very fast. My father came to pick us up in a car belonging to a gentleman we had never seen before and took us and our mother to Palmyra. We reached the outskirts of the city, not far from where my school is now. I don't remember very clearly what happened during the first few days, it was all very festive and new. The only detail I recall is the face of an old man selling dates on the road, in front of the house where we were staying. From the windows we could see a very modest house, with four walls and a roof and little else. During the daytime, my father and grandfather spent all their time unloading lime, mixing it with water and painting the house.

My brother and I thought it was fun. It was something we had never seen before. We lent them a hand and all worked at great speed to get our house ready. Yet my father and grandfather didn't seem very happy. They kept on working as usual but as time went by they started saying that something was wrong. It seemed as if someone was damaging or wrecking all the work they had done during the day. They went to work but didn't joke around anymore. Sometimes they would stand silently, looking at the work they had done the day before and wonder how it was that it had to be done all over again. For a while, they thought it might have had something to do with how overworked they were. Then they wondered whether it might be a jealous neighbour or a boy playing a prank.

It wasn't until many years later that I found out what had been happening. One evening my father and grandfather pretended to go to bed, just as they did every night. But they had decided they would get up during the night to go and see what was happening. They discovered my mother moving about like a big dark shadow, in a frantic state, and also crying I should imagine, hiding some things and getting rid of others, dirtying the newly painted walls and scratching the fresh concrete. It turned out that when my dad and grandad collapsed into bed with exhaustion in the evenings, she would go over to the house and hide a shovel or a bag of concrete and spoil some of the work before it set. What my dad did during the day, my mother undid during the night. She wanted to go back to the desert. She just didn't want to stay there.

It took a lot of determination for my father to hold out, as my mother was not a docile woman and wouldn't easily go along with things that she didn't agree with. Yet, deep in my heart, I feel happy that my dad managed to do it. And even though I still remember to this day many things about our life in the tents with something you might call nostalgia, I am happy to be here. The improvement he brought to all our lives was important, for everyone.

Of course we went to school, while my dad took odd jobs here in town. When we came home from school, Dad wanted to know what the teachers had told us and what we had learnt. In the evening, I watched him several times falling asleep on our exercise books with a feeling of admiration, even though he didn't understand anything that was written in them. When my elder brother managed to read a sentence that was not in a school book, I remember that even my mother smiled and there was joy in the house, or something like joy.

I don't think it's any wonder that right from the start I knew very clearly what I wanted to be when I grew up. After a few childish fantasies, I told myself I wanted to be a schoolmaster. And that's what I became. My father started earning enough money to be able to pay for my education, and both my brother and I made quick progress. We knew we couldn't waste any time.

Then I spent years teaching schoolchildren and wanted to make myself useful. I was also aware that there was one place where I could be more useful than elsewhere, among the people of my tribe. I still had many relatives among them, people who hadn't had the same strength as my father. They didn't lead a bad life, and even today their life isn't bad. But when I go and see them, they look at me with great admiration. And it makes me wonder whether they, my cousins at least, are thinking about how lucky I've been.

That's how it all began, when I went back to see my relatives in the tents during the summer holidays, and in the evening, since I was around, they would ask me if I could teach the children something. You know, the children who live in the desert don't just have healthy teeth. It would be interesting to understand how and why they are like that, but they are more alert. They seem to understand the meaning of things more easily and to grasp more quickly than the others where they have to get to. Perhaps it's because they don't listen to too many words or don't get drowned in them, as kids do in all cities. Or maybe it's simply because they have a greater thirst for knowledge and don't want to miss any opportunity that comes their way. The fact is that, at the end of the summer, I had to go back and teach in the city and had to leave them. It was very sad for me. I've been teaching for years and I know that this desire to learn, this curiosity about the complex world outside doesn't go on forever. It's a fleeting moment. If you grasp it, the children's curiosity grows and their culture grows with it; if you let it slip by, it can be lost forever.

That was how I become entangled in my past, driven by a desire to be useful, and by a sense of guilt… Yes, a sense of guilt! Because when you leave your uncles and aunts and cousins in the desert and see them struggling on, grappling with the harsh life that you yourself have left behind, it's as if they had been stronger than those of us who went away. So, sometimes you feel a bit of a coward and tell yourself that your place is still there, with those goats, those tents and that desert.

I promised I would send them a teacher as soon as I had one available in the school, which by then I was running. But obviously there were bureaucratic issues to deal with and it wasn't as if you could just get a teacher and send him off to teach in the desert. So, when I had a teacher young enough to do it, I would ask him to go and live in the tents of my tribe or the neighbouring ones for a few weeks and hold classes for the children. And while he was out there, I stood in for him and taught his classes as well as my own.

The project slowly grew until I managed to persuade my superiors to give me a couple of teachers a year who would move to the Bedouin camps and teach the children in the evenings when they came home after taking the flocks out to graze or in the morning before they set out. It took years to accept the idea that this system wasn't working. In the beginning I did find some teachers who were enthusiastic about the experience. They applied all their skills and somehow managed to keep the thing going. But, in the end, even though the teachers were competent and good at their job, there was always the issue of the children's families and all the people around them. There is a good reason why school is a separate place from the one where the family lives! At home, children are constantly distracted, and there's also the fact that they don't understand who is more important, the parents or the teacher. Not to mention the fact that the parents don't understand that they have to be quiet and mustn't intervene. Once, a teacher came to see me in a state of despair. He told me that during his lesson he would be offered refreshments every ten minutes. And, obviously, every interruption meant an additional effort as the children would become unfocused and think about other things, so he would have to start the lesson all over again as if they had hardly done anything up to then.

We had few results for our efforts, especially considering the commitment we were asking of these young teachers. It meant going to live in a Bedouin tent for a year, in camps that are never in one place for very long and move five, six or even seven times a year. You never know when you'll be going back home and see your family. If you have a girlfriend, you simply won't see her again. So the volunteers became fewer and fewer. And this is not something you can impose on just any kind of person. If you are not enthusiastic and committed to making it work, you won't get anywhere. It's true that teaching is a mission, but even so, there aren't many teachers who are prepared to sleep in a tent together with everyone else, without a toilet or bathroom, freezing in the winter and having to cope with the summer heat. And so I was eventually summoned by the education department and was told that the project had to be reviewed. It was a good and right thing to do, they said, but we couldn't ask anyone to put themselves through such an ordeal. We had to find a way to give the scheme a more permanent and solid foundation and make it less dependent on the teacher's individual skills. It had to be more intensive and more focused.

So there I was, addressing the points being raised one by one, offering to change some things and to consider any adjustments that could be made… when the department official looked me in the face, snapped shut the folder which he had seemed to be analysing in detail and said to me: 'Don't you realize I can't find anyone to send to you anymore? They don't want to go; they'd rather change job.'

I did realize it, of course I did. I talked to the teachers, listened to them and was well aware of their thoughts and reflections. But it was nevertheless a blow. It felt as if everything had come crashing down on me. I felt betrayed by the school, by my friends and even by the very Bedouin tribes who had hosted the teachers. But I wasn't going to give up, I never considered it for one moment. I went back to the desert, back to my tribe. I consulted with the families to find out what had failed and what had worked. So, after a few weeks of sometimes heated discussions and a great deal of reflection, I went back to the ministry with what seemed to me to be a revolutionary idea.

'A school tent? You'd like to get a tent and turn it into a school?'

'Yes, that's what we need to do.'

'And where would we pitch this tent?'

It was all decided. I knew where the summer and spring pastures were, and where the Bedouin spent the winter and the autumn. If we could find a place in each camp where a tent could be positioned in such a way as not to interfere with the grazing, we would be able to set it up with the proper equipment and facilities. The school would also double as the schoolmasters' living quarters, so we could have two or three teachers in the same tent running classes in the mornings and afternoons.

We began all over again – with renewed enthusiasm and also with a degree of financial independence. Some families in Palmyra, who also remembered the hard times and the illiteracy, offered us money to buy a power generator, and some people even thought about getting us a blackboard. Obviously, having a blackboard might be a good idea, but who was going to carry it when the tent had to be moved to follow the Bedouin to a new camp? Still, you see, there was enthusiasm. And a renewed will to succeed.

But it didn't work this time around either. One day, a group of teachers came to see me in the school in Palmyra. They had lost their students. 'What do you mean lost?' I asked. 'Lost,' they said, 'gone, they've disappeared.' What had happened was the most natural thing in the world for my people and for all the Bedouin tribes in Arabia and Syria. On the hills not far from the camp there had been some light rainfall or more morning frost than usual... Naturally, as soon as the headmen realized it, they had the camp moved, just like that, in no time at all and without saying a word to anyone, as they've always done and always will do. So, in the morning, when the school teachers looked out of their tent the camp was gone! There was nobody around, everyone had left. 'They won't come here,' they said to me, 'and we can't go to them. For as long as they are nomadic, they will always be illiterate. You have to resign yourself to the idea, Sir, nothing can be done about it.'

So a new school year began without any plans, or, at least, I prepared myself for a new school year without an education programme for the Bedouin tribes. I know that some people at the time suggested that the schoolchildren should put on a play which they would perform in the various Bedouin encampments during the summer. It wasn't a bad or a wrong idea but reading and writing is a different matter. And television, which is found in every tent nowadays, doesn't solve the problem. On the contrary, television itself is the problem!

Just as I was beginning to think I would devote myself to the more traditional kind of teaching, we were suddenly told that we would be given a new primary school in Palmyra. And one morning I found myself standing before a modest but large two-storey building with a good playground. Someone was telling me that it had been something else before, an army barracks, perhaps, and even it if wasn't perfect as a school it was still bigger than the facility we had been using until then. That's when the idea suddenly struck me.

'So now you want to set up a barracks for Bedouin children?'

'A boarding school, not a barracks, it's a different thing.'

'And do you think you'll be able to explain to your people the difference between the two?'

'I think so.'

'I don't think they'll give you a single child. Who is going to take the goats out to graze? If there aren't any children, the elderly and the adults will have to take care of that. And what's more, the Bedouin are extremely attached to their children; they'll never let them go.'

'I think it's worth trying,' I said to him. He didn't believe me; he really didn't believe me. He was getting more and more impatient as he listened to me, until he eventually began to wonder whether there might be a chance that my idea could work.

We refurbished the building. While the workmen whitewashed the walls and the army trucks brought in camp beds, mattresses and blankets from a nearby barracks, I went around all the local markets leaving leaflets announcing that the new Bedouin boarding school had opened and that all families were invited to send their children there for nine months of the year from the 15th of September to mid-June. I remember that although no one laughed in my face, many people thought it was the most ridiculous thing they had ever heard. Some of my friends said to me: 'What are you doing? Nobody will come, don't expose yourself like this.' Of course, I knew it was a very risky thing to do, and if it turned out to be a failure then every project would probably be abandoned as a result. But I knew my people; I knew what I had to do.

We were expecting two to three hundred children. On the first day of school about thirty turned up. I remember the school caretaker standing by the door and saying to me: 'There's another one coming, and another,' almost as if to encourage me. I think that morning I felt just like an actor must feel when performing in an empty theatre. Still, we did everything the proper way, as if there were hundreds of children. The first thing we did was give them a hot shower; then we got them to put on a school uniform which may look basic today but seemed very smart at the time. Then we showed them the various rooms where they would have their classes, where they would sleep and where they would play. We gave them their school books after lunch so they wouldn't get them dirty. Then we sent them back home so they could tell their parents how things were organized at the school and say good-bye to them before the school year began.

Well, what happened the next day is something I'll remember for as long as I live. You know that indescribable and unique din you hear outside every school on the first day of school? The thing I used to envy Damascus, Aleppo, Homs and basically all the big cities for? Well! I heard it rising up from the street leading up to the school, and it reached me like a wave while I was shaving in the bathroom. So, I went downstairs trying to look composed, opened the school door with the school caretaker, and was faced with two hundred and forty kids, no less, all saucer-eyed, pushing and shoving as they tried to look behind me to get a glimpse of the school that they had heard so much about. And the caretaker, standing behind me, saying: 'Where are we going to put them? Where are we going to put them all? Who is going to keep them quiet tonight?'

At the bottom of the road there were a few parents, some driving a truck, but many more sitting on donkeys, horses and even camels. I looked at them, and they looked at me, and it was clear that they had come to check whether we would really be able to keep our word.

They were still there almost four hours later when we sent the children home, dressed, fed and washed, with a pen, a school book and an exercise book. And as they filed past us on the way out, every single one of them said: 'We'll be back tomorrow, we'll be back tomorrow!' Some of them didn't want to leave and were already rolling on the camp beds, and we realized that this was going to be our biggest headache, our next challenge.

So, there it is. Now I'm retired and a government official has just come to see me, and they've just said to me: 'Please don't go, the school and these kids need you.' But the idea of leaving has never even crossed my mind. I still wander around the school rooms waiting for the next 15th of September, even though I could just stay at home as I am supposed to be retired. In fact, when you've finished recording, I'd like to take you out to the school yard and show you the new block we're building. We are going to more or less double the number of children and teachers. The dormitories are so packed at the moment that if the kids need to go to the bathroom during the night they have to step over the others. But it's worth it, you know. It's truly worth it. Bedouin children are smart, they are alert. They know very quickly, more quickly than the others, where they want to get to... And if you go to the market today, you'll come across some fathers doing business alongside their sons. When I saw that for the first time, I said to myself that I am a happy man. I'm a poor schoolmaster from a poor town in a country that isn't rich, but I've never wished for anything more in life than this.

8 - The Singer's Son

I think it's quite difficult to talk about myself, or about my life. It isn't even a question of privacy. The few things I can tell you are quite straightforward and not even particularly personal. I don't mind telling you about them. I have a very normal life: that's what it was like in my youth and that's what it's like now. When I was a teenager, my parents insisted I should go to agricultural college, so when I finished school I ended up working in that big farming company just outside Aleppo, the one you can see before you get to the city. It used to be quite a rundown farm that belonged to a souk merchant, and then it was bought by an international organization that turned it into a sort of research centre for agriculture in semi-arid areas. I worked there for many years. I was in charge of their crop irrigation studies and had to determine the limit between the dry weather and the onset of aridity. I had to note down the air temperature and any rainfall, check that the crops were sprayed regularly, and try to lower the amount of water more and more until I could see that things were about to reach the threshold level of moisture stress. I then had to record all the data in a book. That's basically the kind of thing I did, nothing particularly interesting. Then, one day, a fellow turned up, an Englishman. I had no idea who he was, but he asked to speak to me. 'What about?' I asked him. And again, I explained that my life was quite ordinary. But then I started talking about my father, and, to tell you the truth, he seemed quite bored. It was a conversation like many others, the kind of thing you soon forget about. Then a few years later, I got a phone call from someone in Canada one evening. It was a schoolteacher who said she wanted to visit Syria, along with four friends, and asked me if I was willing to take them around Aleppo. For a while I thought it was a joke. What made them think of calling me? Where did they get my phone number? They said I was a celebrity because my name, along with my address, appears as one of the most knowledgeable tourist guides in Aleppo! It turns out that the man I had spoken to was one of those people who write travel guides for that publisher in Australia or New Zealand, the ones that everyone has, and he had penned me in as a tour guide for Aleppo! My immediate reaction was to say they had made a mistake and that I didn't know anything. But then I said to myself that a bit of extra cash wouldn't hurt. So from then on I started working as a guide as well. I'm not a professional, of course, but at the end of the day, if they ask me, and want me to do it, I can take a few days off work and, that way, the company will pay me less, and in four days I'll earn what the company pays me in four months. And the customers are happy, so, basically that's how it works.

I don't know where or who the idea came from that I should study to become an agricultural meteorologist. In my family it was my parents who decided that sort of thing, and it didn't sound like a bad idea to me. Also, it's not as if I had a great passion for the countryside. I like to think it was my mother who decided because of something that happened when I was a child. My father... Here I go again; people ask me to talk about myself and I end up talking about him. But what can you do when you're lucky enough to have such a famous father, so popular throughout the whole of Syria? Anyway, going back to my story (we'll get back to my father anyway because he wasn't just famous in Syria but right across the Middle East, he was a national – in fact an international – celebrity, but I'll tell you about Paris and his concerts there later on)... So, my father had a plot of land where he used to go quite often when he wasn't busy working for radio or television. As performers often do, he often brought home people for the weekend that he had met but didn't know particularly well, and as he was a great conversationalist, he'd say: 'You must come and be my guests in the country.' My mother would get angry because he would turn up with ten or fifteen people without prior warning, and the beds had to be made up and the food and shopping all had to be done in a great rush. My father didn't worry about these things at all. 'Oh, we'll manage,' he'd say. And my mother didn't say a word; she'd be furious but kept silent. I probably take after her: if I have a choice, I also prefer to keep quiet. But my doctor says that if I could let myself go a bit more, my ulcer wouldn't be so bad, and I'd also sleep better. But then, that's what I'm like, I only speak if I have to and prefer to hold everything inside. Also, with the kind of father I had – who was too impulsive, too strong, too…. everything – the only thing to do was to lie low and attract as little attention as possible. It was a way of protecting myself from his overpowering love, and from his constant need to give me advice about everything, and always saying that he too when he was a boy… So, we would start by talking about me and end up only talking about him. And Mum too, who maybe wasn't all that happy, was troubled by this. But when you have such an exceptional person in the house, what are you supposed to do? And people would say to me: 'You're so lucky to have a father like that!' So, I would smile and say I was very lucky indeed. But don't people realize that the bigger the tree, the fewer the things that grow underneath it? How could you thrive in the shadow of such a personality? Also, I had a different character; I was like my mum, more fragile and softer. Now that I'm almost old, I can look back and say that my parents each did their best to be happy and to make us happy. But, of course, when my dad wasn't around, and we were alone at home with my mum there was a different atmosphere. Obviously I was sorry he was away, and I missed him, of course. But at least during mealtimes you could speak, or you could also be silent, without all your spaces – and I mean all of them, from dawn to dusk – being filled by this huge and overwhelming dad.

I'm not criticizing him. I've never done that in my life and still wouldn't do that now. But I'll always remember an interview I watched on French television once, when I had gone along with him and his orchestra on a concert tour. They were interviewing John Lennon's wife on French TV, his first wife, not the Japanese one that nobody likes. I thought she seemed a very nice woman, and also a simple sort of person. She said a lot of things that have nothing to do with this, but I was struck by one of the things she said because it described my situation exactly. 'I was the first person,' she said, 'to be ruined by the Beatles' success. Regardless of everything and everyone else, I had a man I loved and who was my husband. That was more than enough for me. But then, what happens? He becomes John Lennon! I'm not talking about being famous or successful – those are all things one could have coped with, but John Lennon! How could I stop him from being what he could be? But what was the good of having a partner who was more famous than Jesus Christ or the Queen of England?'

That was exactly my situation, you see. He was sought after from far and wide, by every radio station and every nation. Who was I to tell him about my homework, my girlfriends, or any of the ordinary things that happened in everyday life? He would call and say: 'I'll be home late. I have to sing for the President! I'll be home late because President Nasser is in Damascus and they've asked me to be there.'

And we'd be home waiting for him, and our maths homework and all our little things paled into insignificance.

Anyway, I was in our house in the country and some friends of my dad's came over with their families. I don't know what they did for a living or how long they stayed with us. I remember they had a little girl with them who was about my age and had auburn hair; she was probably Circassian. We spent the whole evening together chatting (at the table there was only room for my dad and his friends) and I think I fell in love with her, in the sort of simple and instinctive way you fall in love when you are ten years old. We then went for a walk in the fields and ended up in a pistachio grove. There was a full moon that night and my parents had always told me that when there's a full moon you can hear the pistachios popping open after the intense heat of the day. The seeds grow until the shells can't hold them in anymore so they burst open and you can hear clicking all around you. That night there was clicking everywhere and we were happily chatting about this and that – about games and toys and the kinds of things that children talk about – when we suddenly heard a meowing sound, then a sigh, then a little scream and after a while it wasn't a little scream anymore but a woman actually crying for help. We were really frightened and ran straight home. 'Dad, Dad, there's a woman crying for help in the pistachio grove!' I shouted, but he pretended not to hear me. But my mum blushed up to her ears and dragged us away, pretending she had some things to take into the kitchen. Once we were in the kitchen, she asked us what we were doing in the pistachio grove and told us it wasn't a place for young children to go, especially in the summer when there's a full moon.

I didn't understand what she meant at all, and neither did my friend. But later, when I grew up, I realized that there were two musicians from among my dad's guests who had gone there to make love. And it's also customary for young people in Aleppo to say, 'we're going to the pistachio grove,' when they mean 'we're going to make love.'

Anyway, my father was greatly amused by that episode. From then on I was the boy who 'took girls to the pistachio grove when I was only ten years old.' Every now and then when sitting at the table, I'd see Dad watching me and chuckling to himself, and then he would invariably add: 'Who would have thought... You have a way with girls, with those big eyes of yours. Good boy. Good boy!' And my mother always blushed and scolded him, telling him that I was only a child and I would never think about certain things if he didn't put them into my head. Yet it's true that from then on I realized, partly because of what my dad said and partly because of what I was like, that girls quite liked me. And even though I've never taken anyone to the pistachio grove, except my daughter, since that episode the reputation of someone who has a way with girls and loves nature has stuck to me. So, when the time came to think about what kind of work I would go into, it was natural for them to consider something connected with the countryside. Maybe it wasn't just that, but it also had to do with my dad wanting someone with the knowledge and skills to look after the farm while he was away. I guess these are the many things that happen in life because that's the way they are supposed to happen.

So, all in all, I've had quite a good life, especially after the Englishman put me in the guidebook. After a few years I resigned from the farming company and worked as a guide for a couple years. But my wife was right about that when she urged me not to give up my regular job and to push things as far as I could at the company but to stop short of quitting, as that was a secure job whereas tourism is not. But where tourism is concerned, although I really I loved the work, who would have thought that one day Sharon would go and take a walk on the esplanade of the Dome of the Rock causing all that havoc? Until then, tourism was going quite well: the money was good, and I enjoyed it. I was really happy. But then, tourists have such an odd mindset! I would explain to them on the phone that the situation in Syria was peaceful, and they'd say: 'But there's war in Palestine! There's war in Iraq!' – which would be like not going to Berlin because there is Basque terrorism in Spain, or not going to London because there are troubles in Ireland. Anyway, there's no point talking about how tourists think. We all know that by now. They do what they like and there's no arguing with them. Sadly, many of us here in Aleppo are having real problems because of that. Tourism is finished, the restaurants are empty and so are the hotels, but the saddest thing is that it doesn't make any sense. Yet you get a phone call from Canada, and they tell you they're going to India because: 'You'll agree that this is no time to visit Syria, not with everything that's going on there!' And I can't answer because otherwise they won't call me back again. Tourists are interesting people, and they can even be very friendly, but when they get something into their heads, there's no arguing with them: they shut the door and that's the end of it!

But I still have some savings, so now I'm piecing together the story of my father, who has been so important in my life and has now reached an age where all you can say is that he's still with us and his mind is still very sharp. But he's almost ninety years old and, well, he's no longer what he used to be. And my dad's story is interesting not only because of what he did but also because it's about a world that has now disappeared. We are really talking about a bygone era, and who knows whether it will ever come back or what the future will be like. It's not that everything was better or worse, it was just different.

I think the most dramatic thing for us who live in Aleppo was what happened in the late 1930s, when the French had the bizarre idea of giving Antioch to Turkey. That was our war, our tragedy. I don't have anything against the French, or the Turks for that matter. By the time I was born they had both left, and frankly, no one was sorry about that. After they had gone it was as if they had never been here. People were so happy that they didn't even want to talk about them. But, leaving that aside, I wonder what they were thinking about when they gave Antioch to Turkey. It's right here, just a few kilometres away from Aleppo, and it's practically our port. It's been our access to the sea for centuries. Aleppo was built here, inland, for a thousand reasons that I won't go into, but Antioch used to be its other half. What got into their heads when they decided to give it to another nation? What was the idea? There was a road that took less than an hour to get there, and then, in no time at all, you'd be by the sea. People went to the beach and merchants did their business deals in the various establishments near the port, loaded their goods onto the cargo ships and then came straight back to Aleppo. Antioch was so vital for Aleppo that the city of Antioch itself didn't grow because it was just an extension of Aleppo rather than an autonomous city. Wealthy people would come to live in Aleppo, and businesses had their offices in Aleppo and used Antioch as their seaport. It would be like taking Piraeus and giving it to Egypt. That would be pretty ridiculous, wouldn't it? Anything the Turks say means nothing at all to me. We know them very well; we had them in our homeland for almost five hundred years. There isn't a single person in Aleppo harbouring the illusion that they will give Antioch back to Syria one day. They belong to the great family of people who 'take the money and run' whether or not it's fair. Their attitude is: 'we are taking it and, as to returning it, that's never going to be on the table'. That's what happened with Cyprus as well, even though they were provoked into it. But the Colonels in Greece have been gone for at least thirty or forty years while they are still holding on to Northern Cyprus and will never let it go. That's what the Turks are like; they are only ever interested in Turkey and Turkish people. The rest of the world could die off tomorrow and the Turks wouldn't lift a finger, as long as Turkey is safe.

My father was born in the last days of the Ottoman Empire, though I don't remember when that happened exactly. I think Damascus had already been liberated by Feisal's troops and General Allenby had also arrived a few days earlier. My father was born into a family of grain merchants; they were very well off and had been in the grain trade for several generations. But my grandfather's properties and concerns went well beyond that. They included a large estate just outside Idlib, a number of houses, including their own house where they actually lived, plus a multitude of contracts signed with many farmers in the Aleppo area whose crops were purchased before they were even harvested. My grandfather's store was also a very large business. So, our family was already part of a small circle of families in Aleppo that had close relations with one another, had known each another for generations and were the masters in those days. I was recently told that back then the city was in the hands of a group of families which were responsible for its ups and downs and as a result weren't very popular among ordinary citizens. It's the same story you hear nowadays: that Aleppo is supposedly a closed city and that the middle classes would much rather mix with their own kind than with the rest of the population. Of course, it's difficult for me to judge these things as I was born much later, and we had already lost Antioch by that time. Also, Aleppo changed a lot as a result of the tragedy that took place in Turkey with the fall of the Ottoman Empire. The city had spread enormously and, in that situation, the fact that Aleppo's old citizens wanted to group together didn't seem such a negative thing to me. Although the thousands of Armenians first, and Kurds later, who fled from Turkey and came to live here in Aleppo integrated successfully and quite happily, they still had a different religion, a different language and were a different ethnicity. And while they were well received – they actually say so themselves – I don't think it was such a bad thing that the citizens of Aleppo protected themselves, so to speak, trying to preserve their community, their traditions and their customs.

Aleppo was a very important city at the time. I don't know if we can say that it was more important than Damascus, but I think if you had asked the citizens of Aleppo that, they would have been in no doubt about it, while if you had asked the people of Damascus, I'm not so sure. So, Dad was born in this wealthy middle class world of Aleppo: it was part of a trading and business community that didn't have many links inside Syria. The most important cities for Aleppo back then were Cairo, Aleppo and Istanbul. Aleppo considered itself superior to all the others, and although Damascus was incredibly beautiful in those days, it reflected ancient glories rather than recent ones like Aleppo's wealth. Damascus had been the ancient and glorious capital of Syria, but – and people still say this today – this closeness to the corridors of power had somewhat weakened its business community, creating a kind of clan. We've never had that sort of thing here in Aleppo. Here, if people have money it's because they've earned it through their work, not by asking favours from the government or from this or that minister.

With Dad, it was already clear from when he was a teenager that he wasn't going to be an ordinary person. He had blond hair, with big soft curls, and a white complexion that all the women wondered at and almost wanted to caress to feel how soft it was. We have some photos at home, and it's pretty obvious why Grandad didn't want to let him go around the clubs and parties in Aleppo to sing. People invited him, but Grandad probably thought it wasn't so much for his voice – which was certainly beautiful but had no kind of training – but for his charm as a 'blond angel'. Nothing was ever said about this at home, and Dad always brushed it aside and never talked about it. But I realize that, in certain circles, with a boy like that, it wasn't just the women who were crazy about him. So, when Grandad said he didn't want him to go and sing at the clubs, it wasn't just a question of age or family respectability, maybe he was more aware of things than other people. Besides, we all know the way of the world; certain things happen everywhere, and Aleppo is no exception.

But Dad always talked about the old houses of Aleppo. They were grand, opulent mansions with the first floor in stone and the second almost entirely in wood, with coloured glass at the top of the windows and, most of all, they were extremely luxurious. He told us about Persian and Turkish carpets, Chinese ceramics, Persian and Indian cloisonné, and magnificent and imposing Russian samovars. But however beautiful the objects, and the richer the family the more stunning they were, the most wonderful feature of the house was always the woodwork, not because of the richness of the materials but because of the craftsmanship. That was a different era: there were some incredibly skilled craftsmen back then who knew how to carve and decorate wood. Although they did things slightly differently than in Damascus, then as now, the approach was largely the same, and their crafts involved a range of decorations, intaglios and finishings, and sometimes also with inlays in other materials, including mother-of-pearl. Now there are very few of them left, and when you have a problem with a window, getting it repaired can drive you mad if you can't do it yourself.

We have a photo at home from those days which I think is very beautiful. It shows a group of farmers working in the fields and Dad standing bare-chested among them singing. My parents used to say that, despite the heat and the dust, he sang so beautifully that even the people from the nearby villages used to come and help out just to listen to his impromptu yet, in their own way, wonderful performances. In spite of my grandfather, the family and the strict code of behaviour of that period, my dad was a bit like that: I was as shy of a crowd as he loved being in the middle of it. His love of an audience — any audience, whether paying or not — made him a natural showman. He was really born to sing, to be admired, and to amaze. And I'm told that people absolutely loved him, even though he was still young, and his voice was still too spontaneous. As long as he was in their midst singing, people were always happy, including farm workers.

So, Dad wanted to sing, Grandad didn't allow him to, and things went on like that until he completed his education. Then my grandad died, and my dad began his adult life with a clear idea in his mind that he wanted to become a singer. But people were no longer as wealthy as they used to be, and my dad's Aleppo was no longer my grandad's Aleppo.

First there was the French mandate, whose only merit was to be a tiny bit better than Turkish domination. Then Antioch was ceded to Turkey, and that was followed by the Second World War, which for Aleppo meant French Vichy troops and de Gaulle's Free French forces fighting each other. The city had changed – I won't say whether for the better or for the worse – with the migration of thousands of families from Turkey, from the dramatic fall in trade and from the general decline of our society. In Syria this was perhaps felt more acutely than elsewhere, and its effects were also beginning to show in Aleppo. But that is what happens everywhere in the world when there's no money: in the first year you don't really feel it, and neither in the second year. But then, little by little, the parks and gardens are not so well looked after anymore, the streets begin to get dirty, and even the houses, which were once in good order, fall into disrepair, until one day you wake up, you look out the window and you realize they have become totally dilapidated.

During that period, Dad started studying the three forms of traditional singing in more depth. He usually chose to be accompanied by the oud,[18] the flute and the qanun.[19] The players were old and performed in concerts wearing the old red hat from the days of Turkish rule, the tarboosh.[20] But they were very experienced and had played in the leading orchestras at the beginning of the century and in the 1920s, when the city was still very rich. They played traditional genres: the muwashshah[21] and the qudud.[22] But when it came to the classical Arabic repertoire, which combines religious and love songs and transforms a large part of the religious literature into music, it was quite challenging for Dad. He said so himself many years later, when he was already elderly, in one of those endless monologues that went on for hours, in which he repeated the same old things that we all knew and had heard many times before. But sometimes he was also honest and would see things in a new light in view of what had happened. When he listened to Om Kolthom,[23] or to Mohammed Abdel Wakhab,[24] he realized that the skill of these great singers from Cairo was connected with a culture – the art of chanting the Quran – which he had never studied in depth. It was the foundation of every musical piece and every song, and he therefore couldn't put it off anymore. It is only by chanting the Quran, and by studying its various schools and interpretations of chanting, that you can learn the sophisticated technique of modulating your voice. A while this technique could be ignored if you were an amateur, it was vitally important for anyone aspiring to become an accomplished professional.

So, during the whole of the 1940s my dad looked after my grandad's shop and gave more and more performances, while also studying as he had never done in his youth and had now become essential. In this respect, he was very lucky to live in and to be from Aleppo, because all the great singers used to come here, and our theatre was a very difficult testing ground for anyone who wanted to become famous. There was a saying at the time that in order to become a great singer you had to have sung in Istanbul, Aleppo and Cairo, and you needed to pass that test first. But while Istanbul was the city of power, the cities that gave you access to the most important audiences, the cultivated ones, were actually Aleppo and Cairo. And singing here wasn't easy: Aleppo didn't give itself very generously. Once – Dad always told us this story – there was a great singer from Cairo who decided to see if he measured up to the traditions of Aleppo. He worked so hard to get an invitation to perform for a few evenings in Aleppo that he eventually succeeded. When he got to the theatre he was quite nervous and very excited, but when it was time to perform there were only five people in the audience! He was so dismayed that he went back to the dressing room, summoned the agent who had got him the contact and said he would leave there and then and go straight back home. Aleppo, he said, had insulted him, and he hadn't come all the way from Cairo to be insulted like that. So they called in the theatre director, who explained to him that the five people in the auditorium were the city's leading music critics. He told the singer that he had committed the unacceptable and thoughtless act of seeking an invitation before singing for them first, and this had not only seemed disrespectful but had probably also been interpreted as a sign of mediocrity. So, people hadn't gone to the performance but were waiting to see how the first concert went before deciding whether they would go or not. The singer was shocked at this and exclaimed: 'But even in Cairo people aren't so superior and snobbish!' 'Cairo,' retorted the theatre director, who was very familiar with that kind of world, 'didn't even exist when Aleppo was already a rich and famous city. We are not just over a thousand years old but go back two or three thousand years, and even more. Now go and sing. Get over your anger and go out and sing for those five people in the hall as if they were five thousand. If you're really as good as they say, people will flock to your performance tomorrow and also in the coming days. If you don't sing now, in front of those five people, you'll still be a famous singer, but only in Cairo.'

It was a terrible city: Aleppo could be terrible. Yet he could have handled it better, and not have challenged the city's traditions like that. Anyway, he was smart enough to understand and went back on stage, and sang all evening pretending that the five people in the audience were five thousand. They say the only liberty he took was to bow to the left and right of the empty house, as if there were beautifully dressed ladies leaning out of every balcony throwing flowers. But that wasn't such a big thing and, after the humiliation he had suffered, he was forgiven for it. Anyway, he went down well and the next day, and also the following days, the theatre was taken by storm. From then on he came back to Aleppo every year and his performances were the most important in the city's entire concert season.

That's why I don't think it's fair to say that Aleppo is a closed, snobbish and unwelcoming city. In any other Eastern city, this famous singer would have been listened to, acclaimed and then forgotten, whereas Aleppo welcomed him, turned him into one of its own citizens and gave him the kind of warmth and love that singers constantly seek but hardly ever get. Here, he could venture to sing pieces that were not necessarily popular, but which required the skills of a virtuoso to perform. And people didn't complain, as they would have done anywhere else, that they weren't getting the popular and catchy songs that everyone knows and people even sing in the street. How could anyone expect to gain so much affection and esteem without getting into the heart of the city, winning it over and earning its recognition?

At the time, there were many folk stories going around about stage performers. They are still told today and give you a clear idea of what Aleppo was like – and, I think it's fair to say, is still like. According to one of them, Om Kolthom was going through a crisis. It seems she couldn't get the right rendition not just of one song but of a whole section of her repertory. Suddenly, it was as if she realized that she had to mature, and that her voice and skills didn't allow her to go beyond what she had always performed. And while that may have been good enough for her audience – with Om Kolthom everything was always good enough for the audience – it was no longer good enough for her. I don't know if it's a true story, but I can understand this, I've seen it happening many times with my dad. I think it's what distinguishes great performing artists, the ones who not only do well what everyone else did before them, but also understand that they are being called upon to do something. They don't really know what that something is or where it will lead to, but they have to work towards it. And they plunge into uncharted waters, putting themselves to the test. Some might think it's ill-advised and dangerous. Dad was like that too: at some point he would feel irritated and bored by certain things and would explain to us – he always explained things to us at home, there was no danger of him keeping things to himself – that he had learned to respect this sensation. When he was tired of a song, whether a classical, a qudud or a muwashshah song, it was sign that he was tired not of the song itself but of his interpretation of it. The songwriter had clearly meant to say something more than he had understood up to that point, and that "something more" now demanded attention. He would then shut himself in his room and try singing the song again and again; he would listen to records with different renditions of it by other singers and would try yet again. Dad had an obstinate ability not to move from one step to the next until he was fully satisfied with it: he wouldn't settle for anything less. When he listened to others he was critical, but when he listened to himself he was ruthless. This, in our eyes, somewhat atoned for the way he would keep saying 'I did this,' and 'I did that.' We realized that there was something burning inside of him which we didn't have, and of which he was the first victim. And so, when people say to you, 'You're so lucky to have a dad like that,' I say – as my mum does – that there are a lot of folks who only speak for the sake of saying something...

... Ah, yes, I still have to finish the story about Om Kolthom. So, as she was going through this deep crisis in her singing career, Om came to Aleppo and wore a disguise so that people wouldn't recognize her (though, frankly, that sounds a bit far-fetched to me). She apparently spent days on end, and even weeks, in Aleppo listening to the muezzin chanting the call to prayer. It was only after she had gained a deep understanding of what the Aleppo tradition had preserved that she realized what she was trying to achieve. So, she went back to Cairo, introduced these new musical discoveries into her repertory, which she completely transformed and revolutionized through these new interpretations, with the result that the Om Kolthom legend, which was already huge, achieved the impossible.

Dad wasn't as famous as she was at the time, and perhaps not even in the Seventies, when he had the honour of being invited to sing in Paris. Yet, like her, he also understood that the secret of every music interpretation lies hidden in the call of the muezzin, that is, in the chanting tradition. That's because singing comes from the reciting of the Quran, or is measured against it at any rate, and that's how it's been for centuries.

He never told us who gave him lessons and we never found out. That was partly because he didn't want to tell us, but most of all, he said, it was because the sheikh, who was teaching him so many things, didn't want his life to be disrupted in any way by my father's fame. The sheikh had agreed to give him lessons because he could see that it didn't involve just the study of music but a deep inner search that my father would then be able to convey through his voice, which by then was almost universally popular in Aleppo.

So, in the evenings Dad would go to this sheikh, and we knew we shouldn't ask about it or it was best not to. Yet I think I understood something about it later on, from one of the many stories my dad told us when so many years had gone by that he had forgotten he had forbidden us to talk about it at the time. He had been fascinated by this sheikh and the way he spoke about things that people had always talked about in Aleppo but which maybe my dad had never heard or hadn't paid particular attention to. But I don't think it was a tradition restricted to Aleppo. This sheikh had travelled a lot, more towards Central Asia and Persia than towards Cairo. He knew the holy sites of Shia Islam and probably belonged to one of the many currents of Sufism.[25] My dad learned from him that reciting the Quran – as the muezzins do several times a day – has its own complexity and deep-seated rituality that goes back centuries. He taught him the different purposes of chanting: to explain, to glorify God, to remember His words and to celebrate feasts. But none of these forms, he said, has the power of the kind of chanting that forgets the words and the literal meaning of what is being read or recited. In this particular form of chanting – which only those who are fully familiar with it can understand in all its complexity – it is not the words that matter but the ability of the singer to attune himself to the emotion of creation and replication. And, after all, what is singing but the act of creation repeated freely and in a different way each time? The song cannot exist without the singer, and when the singer stops singing the song ends too. And so, in the mystery of this thing, which it would be blasphemous to call creation and yet is so much like it, men – this is what the sheikh told him – must learn to achieve inner emptiness, and silence. They must allow their body to attune itself to the Almighty through their singing, and when this happens, it's as if a new chord were being created, a new and very sweet music. Non one knows what it is or where it comes from because it is heavenly music, it is God Himself who has taken possession of the person singing and is using him to speak to his people, whether they are believers or non-believers.

I don't really want to focus too much on this as I wouldn't want to say anything blasphemous or inaccurate. Yet, as I talked with my dad I realized that the work that this sheikh did with him made him go beyond the text until the text itself had ceased to exist, as my father himself and the sheikh had ceased to exist, and everything became a sort of extraordinary and impossible reflection of the Divine, who understands everything and explains nothing. My father had pretty clear ideas about this: there was something more to singing than just words, and words are a very powerful yet only partial medium. He thought that singing pushes man into a sphere where the only Lord is God, a God that no longer needs to use words as the tool for communicating with human beings, but infuses them directly with His light, His warmth and His presence. It's something very similar to what the Dervishes felt through their dancing, in Aleppo as in other nearby cities. But while dance celebrates the body as the place where emptiness is created and the encounter with the mystical dimension occurs, my dad chose the path of singing. And although singing may have been less spectacular and less visually dramatic, it was nevertheless hugely powerful. That's because music goes straight to the heart as nothing else in the world does – and even I understand this, although I've never sung or played an instrument, and would never dream of doing so as I'd be hopeless at it. Music knows neither rich nor poor men: it is emotion pure and simple, it's an end in itself. And everyone can interpret it as they think best and as they like. All interpretations are okay because what matters is the emotion behind them, not what I or other people might think it means.

I don't actually think it's so hard to understand all this. I was told that some years ago there was a Pakistani singer – I suppose he was also a Sufi – who had this same exceptional gift.[26] I know that when he died – someone told me or maybe I read it in the papers – all the radio stations in Pakistan and India played his music all day long. It was the first time something like that had happened since the two countries were partitioned. And maybe it's not all that surprising: there are deep divisions between peoples in the West too, but however rigid and even dramatic those divisions may be, the various generations listen to the same music and are stirred by the same pieces. Whether it's the Beatles or Italian opera, there is something in music that doesn't belong to a given language but speaks directly to us all, the educated and the uneducated alike, Muslim and Christians alike.

I think these were more or less the kinds of things that the sheikh explained to my father and taught him during those lessons – although they are not really things you can teach. You need to experience them and develop a deep understanding of them, which is why my dad went to see him so often and for such a long period of time.

But now we've come to the Fifties and I realize as I speak that it's only by talking about these things that I can see how long my father's development path was. He was born in 1918, but it took him almost thirty-five years to acquire this complex set of experiences that ultimately became his voice, his way of singing. We may have been deceived by the photos of him as a young man sitting on the cart full of wheat sheaves. In actual fact, back then he didn't sing the way he did in the Fifties, so maybe my grandfather was right not to want him to waste his time on this just because he was tall and handsome and had a fabulous voice. Anyway, in the Fifties my dad was invited on a radio programme by a friend of his (who also had trouble being appreciated in Aleppo). The programme was called *Sheikh Ali Dervish*, and Dad went along under a false name, calling himself Sabri Ahmad. I'm not sure why he decided to do that but maybe he wanted to surprise the critics in Aleppo so that they wouldn't recognize him straightaway and would be forced to listen to him before expressing an opinion.

The rest is history and doesn't need my words anymore to be remembered. He became a celebrity overnight and his programme, the one in which he sang, became one of the most popular in the whole of Syria. A few years later, and this was possibly the greatest honour he received in his entire life, or the one he cared most about, he was invited to recite the Quran in the Al Abbara Mosque, the new one they built in the centre of Aleppo. Since then, his was no longer a family story but a national story, with radio programmes, records, concert tours in Europe and Egypt and then, in 1975, came the invitation to sing in Paris.

And my mum, left on her own in Aleppo, on receiving all her friends' congratulations would always say, jokingly but, deep down, very proudly: 'I must be such a blockhead; I really didn't realize he was so good.' And, for my brothers and me, it was the beginning of the refrain: 'You're so lucky to have a father like that! So lucky! I bet he sings lots of wonderful songs to you in the evenings at home!'

9 - The Chaldean Bishop

I don't know if I'll ever go there. But maybe it's actually the idea in itself that doesn't appeal to me. Although my family comes from there and so to some extent it's my region too, my brothers and I feel that we belong to Aleppo in every respect. Aleppo is our city, our memory. Our memories are all connected with Aleppo, and while certain stories belong to the past of many families, they are like somewhat distant chapters of our history, which we remember because it's right that we should, but they are not so important anymore.

We come from northern Iraq, from the mountainous region north of Mosul, where there is a high concentration of Chaldean Christians. My family comes from a village called Alqosh, on the border with Kurdistan. It's seen as a sort of legendary and personal cradle for every Chaldean in Iraq. My family had lived there for many generations. Both my grandfather and his parents were regarded as very important people in the village. They were landowners, with vast estates and livestock as well, but they also had knowledge of Arabic medicine, which meant they were the village doctors as well. They treated minor illnesses but also slightly more serious injuries, so they were landowners as well as *hakims*, which means doctors in Arabic. We were one of the many Chaldean communities in northern Iraq, north of Mosul, like many that are still in this region today, where I think there are over half a million Christians of our denomination.

There is a lot of confusion about our cultural identity and what it really means to be Chaldean. Maybe it's because there aren't so many of us and no one talks about us very much. As Chaldeans, we don't really like to refer to ourselves as Arabs. We prefer to say that we have an Arabic cultural background: we read and write in Arabic and Arabic is the language used in schools and universities, but

Chaldean culture is not exclusively Arabic. Our environment, the environment we have been living in for centuries, is Arabic, but it isn't exactly our own. We have our own language, Aramaic, which many of us still speak today. My mum and dad also spoke Aramaic at home rather than Arabic. But living in a city like Aleppo, where this language is not very well known and you never have a chance to practice it, obviously made things more complicated for us children. In my case, for example, I understand it, but I don't speak it very well, I only know the liturgical language, the one they call "Syriac with an eastern accent", which is actually just another way of saying Chaldean.

We would probably never have left Iraq, and maybe I would still be living in Alqosh, if my grandfather hadn't died when he was still quite young and if my father hadn't found himself virtually alone when he was just over ten years old. His relatives thought the right thing to do was to send him to Aleppo, where his uncle was living at the time. He was a sort of legendary figure in our family, a monsignor in charge of the Chaldean Church in Aleppo. So, my father came here, and his uncle placed him with the Franciscan friars where he received his education. When he finished his studies and got a job, he heard there was a girl from Diyarbakir here in Aleppo whose surname was the same as ours, A***, and obviously she was Chaldean like us. She came from a branch of our family that lived in Diyarbakir. They had lost all contact for many generations, so he knew hardly anything about them, but their name was certainly the same and the family had a Chaldean background.

And that too, you know, is one of the many stories that have never been told, or else have been simplified, because, you see, even without the bad faith that there often is in the region, the Near East is so complex and intricate that unless you know it very well and don't live there yourself it's sometimes difficult to understand what is happening or what happened there. Usually, when people talk about genocide in the early twentieth century, they tend to talk about the Armenians who were exterminated by the Turks and forced out of the Anatolian plateau. This is obviously true, but it's also true that the Chaldeans who were living in Anatolia in large numbers back then were also exterminated, just like the Armenians. In our community, over sixty thousand people were thought to have been killed. Of course, it's nowhere near the number of deaths in the Armenian community, but I think you'll agree that it's still a huge number, an awful lot, especially in those days. And so, sadly, it's the same old story you hear again and again: my mother came here as a child, fleeing with my grandmother who was widowed at just eighteen years old. They fled, leaving everything behind, losing all the men in the family, walking through the night and resting during the day, to escape their pursuers, the robbers, the looters, who are always around in that situation... You can imagine their plight and how much destitution was all around them. They reached Aleppo with a bit of wool and a few coins sewn into their dresses, having lost all they had and having to start everything from scratch. And once they got here, they had to adjust to working in the homes of the wealthiest families as cooks, housemaids and seamstresses, mending and darning clothes. I'm not suggesting it was hard, or any harder than what thousands of other people went through at that time.

But, of course, my mother's family was from Diyarbakir, it was a wealthy family from the city's middle class. Even now, people in Aleppo still remember that both the Armenian and the Chaldean families that came from Diyarbakir stood out for being highly educated and cultured, with important family traditions... high-level we might say. And even compared to my father's family, which also had quite a high social status, my mother's family had something that set it apart. I don't think it was a question of education or money, or anything like that. The middle class Chaldeans and Armenians who came here from Diyarbakir had been part of a city with an important urban culture and a longstanding tradition. My father's family had counted several illustrious personalities through its history. It had been a landed family for many generations, with many bishops among them, including one who had been quite eminent in the 19th century, as well as men of letters, interpreters, and so on. Yet they were still part of the rural nobility, while my mother came from the city – quite a rich and populous city, with distinguished middle class families. So the differences that existed between my mother and father were not related to religious doctrine or other such things but had to do with the social status associated with their different backgrounds.

This is perhaps something that ought to be stressed... In this land there are many religious faiths and many currents of thought, but not as many as people sometimes think. The differences are often social rather than religious, and are related to their social class, to the history of these classes, and also to their family's economic status. Syria – and I mean the Syria of the past, particularly when it was part of the Turkish Empire – had an extraordinary wealth of histories and cultures, probably even greater than its many different religions. In Aleppo it's normal to find families from all sorts of places. There is a social complexity that is often forgotten, especially in the West.

The events of the early 1900s and the genocide in Turkey added new factors into this already very lively and variegated situation, especially here in Aleppo. Why did all those who were fleeing come here? There were many reasons, all of them interrelated. Aleppo was one of the biggest cities in the region. It also had the reputation of being a tolerant and welcoming city. Aleppo didn't turn anyone away, whatever their race or religion. I'd say that thinking in terms of religion and race is totally alien to this city's outlook. And, of course, in the years after the First World War it was under French occupation, which gave protection to the refugees and promised them some kind of help and assistance. And I think many people saw Aleppo as the city from which it was easiest to emigrate to Europe, to America and generally as far as possible from the horrors they had suffered in Turkey.

And these wretched people, who were materially poor but spiritually rich from their strong religious faith, traditions and values, came here and organized themselves around what they felt represented them most strongly: the Church. The church steps were the place where families were rebuilt, where people exchanged information about those who had died or hadn't managed to escape. It was the place where you met people from your city and of your religion, and where people effectively rebuilt the fabric of their society and the relationships that had been torn apart by their escape, the slaughter and losing everything they had. So it was very natural for people in this situation to try and marry someone from within their own group, Armenians with Armenians, Chaldeans with Chaldeans –, and build homogenous families. It wasn't to comply with any rules, but to protect themselves, to group together and begin to build a new community.

The Church naturally played a major role during that period. The priest, or the bishop, was the first reference point for the refugees. He was the person they turned to if they needed a job, a house and all the usual things that refugees are in need of.

And so, when my father – who was studying at the Franciscan school at the time – found out that there was a girl who came from the same family as him, he did everything he could to marry her, until he eventually succeeded.

The custom of marrying within the same groups is still very strong today, perhaps not as strong as in those days but it still runs deep. In recent decades there's been a large migration flow, where many of us, many Armenians and many people from other social or religious groups have left for America, Australia, South America and elsewhere. But when the children grow up and it's time to marry, they prefer to come back and look for someone with their own traditions. And the custom continues to this day. For us Chaldeans it's perhaps not as strong as with the Druze Christians or other communities, but it's still strong. It's a way of staying within the family, of protecting ourselves and providing a degree of continuity which would otherwise be lost. I think it's a tradition that not everyone understands. For some people it may have to do with the survival of ancient tribal links, or possibly even with old fanaticisms. Nowadays the Chaldean community in Aleppo is more open-minded about this; they are also quite happy to marry someone from the Armenian or Greek Orthodox community. But if we think about what these families went through and the real danger they faced that their spiritual identity could be completely wiped out, then it's not so easy to criticize their wish to group together.

When my mother and father got married, Aleppo's Chaldean community was very diverse. Those who had come from Iraq or had fled from Turkey were suffering from great poverty. But alongside them there was also a lower and an upper middle class. Then there were also five or six families who had been living in Aleppo for many generations and had made a fortune, especially with the trade between Mosul and Aleppo.

In those days, the French mandate had a big impact on the life of our community, sometimes through mistakes that could have been avoided or weren't really necessary. I think the most unpopular one was the French effort to break up Syria into many small states: the state of the Druze, of Damascus, of the Alawites, and so on — not independent states but with a degree of autonomy. Each of these communities was encouraged by the French to become stronger, more cohesive and more organized. In some cases, things went that way of their own accord, as was the case with the Druze. But in other cases, many people thought that French policy seemed to do everything in its power to put up fences and create barriers of misunderstanding that didn't exist before. At home, but also throughout Aleppo, people said this was the classic divide and rule policy of foreign powers, in other words, creating as many divisions as possible so that they could rule or offer themselves as mediators between different and opposing forces. I don't know how much truth there actually is in all this. As a matter of fact, many divisions existed before then and, viewed from a historical perspective, the

French mandate didn't last very long at all, only thirty years or so. Yet people felt very strongly about the different attitude the French had towards the various groups within Aleppo society, and Syrian society more generally, and were quite aggrieved by it. It was as if the French were trying to do all they could to create divisions that may well have been real, but which should neither have been fuelled nor emphasized.

But, you know, these things I'm talking about are a bit general. They reflect the things I used to hear as a boy when the French mandate was over anyway, and Syria was already an independent country.

For us as Chaldeans, and for our family, the French years... if I may say so, were the good old days! No one yearns for them, because it's a good thing that they are over, but you can't help looking back on them with pleasure.

It has to do with French culture, the freedom, the fact of enjoying some sort of protection when those terrible things we all know about were happening across the border. And in this city of Aleppo dominated by a foreign power, with so many differences but also enormously rich in spiritual values, our family and the Chaldean community were living under this towering and almost legendary figure, Monsignor Jean A***. For my family he was a sort of patriarch, but for the Chaldeans and the whole of Aleppo he was also an institution. He had studied in Paris, at Saint-Sulpice, and also in Rome. He had taught French to the most prominent families in Aleppo and was in some way also a reference point for the French. At home, he was said to be very close to the French authorities and to be able to help people in financial straits, those from the poorest Christian families, to find a job. Thanks to him you could get a job in the railways, or with the customs office, as my father did.

My uncle, Monsignor A***, died before I was born, so all I know about him is from hearsay. But from what I was told at home or heard in town he was a very important figure for the Christian community and for Aleppo in general. During those sometimes very painful years, Monsignor A*** was the go-to person for many more or less desperate families, and even now his name is still surrounded by a kind of aura for both his legendary status and the deep gratitude that people feel towards him. So, for my family too, the fact that a person of such stature was my father's uncle contributed to fuelling this positive, almost nostalgic memory of the French period.

We were a simple family, with a respectable past you might say, and also with deep spiritual values, but we weren't rich, quite the contrary. We lived in this lovely neighbourhood of Aziziyeh, close to many Arab families that were much better off than we were and who had distinguished, and sometimes lucrative, professional lives. But although as kids we played with them in the street and they were our everyday friends, we weren't wealthy, and to be part of that set you needed a lot of money and a high-ranking profession, and we didn't have any of these things. But we lived there because the church was close by and it was natural for us to go and live near the church, which was so central to our community, not just in terms of religious practices but also as a meeting venue, a place of friendship and mutual support, or simply a place where you knew people.

Of course, the Aleppo where I lived as a boy was different from what it is today. Street life was more important. Everything happened outside the home and people were much more involved in their neighbourhood's social and community life.

In those days, when there was a funeral, it was an event for the whole community, and everyone shared in the sorrow. The blessing of the body was performed in the home of the deceased, but then the coffin would be carried on the shoulders to the church. And families sometimes hung black drapes outside their houses as a sign of mourning, while the relatives of the deceased would hire a band to play some funeral marches if they could afford it. Then there was the funeral service inside the church, after that people expressed their condolences the church steps, and finally the coffin would be taken to the cemetery. The whole neighbourhood experienced the event as a dramatic occasion. People leaned out of their balconies, looked on, commented and prayed. When the procession went through the street, the shops lowered their roller shutters half-way down, the men came out of the coffee houses, and for an instant everything stopped. It wasn't just the family that mourned but the whole neighbourhood. And while this may have been distressing for a child, it was an expression of sympathy and support for the whole family.

But then, to make up for a mournful event like a funeral there were many festive occasions, like the feast of the Corpus Christi. The procession would come out of the church carrying the Blessed Sacrament, and all the balconies – truly all of them – were decorated with drapes of white and gold brocade or tapestries for the feast. Then there was the incense and the singing, and as the procession made its way through the neighbourhood, people threw flowers or rose petals from the windows. And just as funerals were a time of mourning for the whole community, the Corpus Christi was a great feast, with a joyful and serene atmosphere. The men and women wore their best clothes, the church would be teeming with people, the streets were ablaze with flowers and the community would gather around the church to celebrate the holiest of ceremonies.

These things were not just peculiar to Aleppo. It was probably the same in other cities across Syria, and also in Italy and France. And now, I'm not saying it was a good or a bad thing – at the end of the day we have to live in our own times and not in the past – but from the mid-Sixties on people's sensibilities definitely changed, with cars and traffic and all that. But then, it wasn't even that so much. It was more a desire not to display ourselves so publicly, not out of fear or anything like that but so as not to hurt the sensibilities of those who didn't believe in these things or were of a different religion. Now everything takes place inside the church, and I suppose that's fine, it's more in keeping with the sensibilities of our times. Yet I sometimes wonder whether it was a good thing to stop going out into the street. I mean, looking at what the streets have become – with the traffic, the advertising and all these things –, I wonder if our city has really gained by it. I say this because, while it's always right to show respect for others and not to put ourselves on display, since we want to promote dialogue and not cause offence, these were actually moments of growth for our community, which all came together and felt engaged on these occasions. So, perhaps, faced as we are by so much loneliness these days, you do wonder whether it was a good thing to abandon a certain form of community life, which might have been important for many people. Having said that, ours is a small community. There are only around three thousand of us in Aleppo, and as to Damascus, once the Iraqis have been repatriated or have emigrated, there will hardly be more than a thousand or so left. So, our withdrawing inside the church and not occupying the city's public spaces is perhaps also a way of acknowledging that we are a small community. We've grown, our numbers have actually increased, but being a community of a few thousand in Aleppo before the war, when the city's population numbered just two or three hundred thousand, was one thing; now that it has reached almost two million it's quite another.

So, I grew up in this small Christian community, organized around the Church, surrounded and also protected in a way by the good name that my uncle enjoyed during his lifetime. I was a very conscientious student. I worked hard and tried to do well at school, and my teachers also thought quite highly of me. Then one day at school we were asked if any of us were interested in becoming a priest. And from our desks we all put our hands up while the teacher, pointing at each of us, said 'No, you can't!' or 'Yes, you can!' When he came to me, he said I could. So, I went home and told my parents that I wanted to become a priest, and it was obviously a very important moment for my family. My father was happy. The fact that one of his children would carry on the family tradition seemed a good thing to him. But my mother wasn't so happy. She thought I would end up being away from home and that we wouldn't be so closely in touch anymore. But she eventually accepted this decision as well, and I think she was happy. With nine children, my parents always envisaged the possibility that one of them would want to become a priest and saw that as part of the family tradition.

I was sent to a seminary run by the Jesuits, in Lebanon, south of Jounieh. It was a school for Maronites, but they also accepted Chaldeans, and now it's become the patriarchal Maronite seminary. The standard of education was very high, but they also charged fees. There were two annual rates to pay, and while they weren't very high, neither was my father's salary. So, I remember that sometimes, when I came back to Aleppo for the school holidays, I would go and see my grandmother and ask her if she could help me to continue my studies.

It was an important experience, but also a tough one, particularly at the beginning. I was only a thirteen at the time. I remember there were about ten of us in my group, some were Maronites and some Chaldeans. We would get the train to Jounieh and then continue the journey by car up to the seminary. It wasn't easy to leave my family and my city at such a young age. I used to get quite homesick, especially in the early days. I really missed my mum and my brothers and sisters and felt very lonely. On top of this, the impact of life in the seminary was very hard for me. At the time I spoke French and Arabic, but the French they spoke at the seminary wasn't like mine, it was like being in France. At the beginning, I found it really hard to do all the written work in French, including the maths, history and geography tests and the homework. Also, all of us in my group were from Aleppo, we came from Syria and had a different mentality, a different background. These kinds of issues were terrible for a teenager to cope with.

On top of that, the seminary didn't make my life any easier. I was a conscientious and hardworking student and was very proud of how well I did at school. As soon as I got there, they gave me an exam and placed me in the sixth year. That was a terrible humiliation for me. I was used to being top of the class and it's easy to imagine how I felt when they put me back a year. But eventually I got over this challenge too. My written French became acceptable and I started making progress towards achieving the standards expected by the school. And little by little, but with a huge effort, I managed to adjust.

We used to go back to Aleppo three times a year, for the Christmas and Easter holidays and for the three months' summer holidays. Here in Aleppo, the Christmas celebrations especially were a very strong tradition. This may have been partly to do with the years of French occupation, although those were over by then, but it was still seen as a major event. We had the Christmas Eve vigil, nativity plays, singing, scout groups, and so on. And then, just a few days later, there was New Year's Eve, which was a major celebration for the whole family. We had supper together, and then played cards and drank while waiting for dawn, always with our families. This tradition was very important and had been for many generations quite apart from the fact that it was also a French tradition.

I was at the Jesuit school in Lebanon until 1966, the year of my baccalaureate. When I got my certificate, I went back to Aleppo and spent a year there. I needed a break and to take some time for reflection. For a year I gave French and maths lessons, and I studied for the Syrian secondary school certificate, to safeguard my future, in a way. And I meditated. I pondered whether the calling I felt was truly a vocation and whether or not it was right to follow it. I considered what my role would be in the family, in society, and so on. That was a very important moment in my life. Maybe I also felt a little scared by the bishop we had in Aleppo at the time. He came from the Iraqi mountains and was quite old by then, but most of all he had an old-fashioned view of his role, of the Church and of society. Or, at least, that's how it seemed to me at the time. So, I asked myself if I felt like spending my life under the guidance of someone with that kind of mindset, and whether one day I would also find myself with such a traditional and, to me, somewhat unsatisfactory outlook. I had a spiritual father that I went to for advice. He took me through a process of reflection that made consider things very carefully. I was clear in my own mind that if I continued along that path I would do so as professionally as possible. I wanted to reach a final decision only once I had resolved all of my most serious doubts.

And in the end, as you can see, I decided to enter the Jesuit order. I was glad to have taken the decision calmly, after a great deal of reflection and without worrying about losing a few months over it. I pondered it and also discussed it in great depth with my spiritual father.

The Jesuits asked me to spend a few years studying at university before entering the novitiate. So, in 1968-69 I devoted myself to the study of Arabic literature. I was obviously interested in Islam, but it was also very clear to me that in order to understand this culture at all it is essential to have knowledge of the Quran. Islam and Arabic culture go hand in hand and there cannot be one without the other. And so, for two years, I developed my knowledge of the Arabic language, of the Quran and of Arabic culture – until it was time to enter the novitiate and make the decision. Back in those days there still wasn't a novitiate in the Near East, so the Provincial father said to me: 'You're young, you speak French... We'll send you to Toulouse.' I don't hold it against him: it was very hard, but it was a very important experience for me.

It was a great leap. Was I afraid? I was a bit, of course. It was one thing to go to a place just a few hours' train journey away from Aleppo and with other boys from my own city, but going to France, with everything that this involved, was another matter. But I remember that even when I spoke to my parents, I said things like: 'After all, I'm from Aleppo, not from some provincial town...' And that's something which everyone from Aleppo can really identify with. We see ourselves very much as belonging to a city with a long, complex and very ancient history – a city with countless ancient and modern aspects, and whose culture is used to constantly dealing with otherness, because we are all different here. After all, who is truly from Aleppo? Some came here yesterday, some two generations ago, some five... but if you dig into the history of each of these families, very few actually belong to the Aleppo of centuries past. So, I felt protected by this international dimension of my city. Toulouse was far away, it was France, and a great many other things as well, but I could face it with the confidence of someone who comes from a large metropolitan city and is used to seeing everything from different perspectives, to mediate a lot and to coexist with different languages, races and religions.

But I had miscalculated badly! Toulouse was so distressing! Not for the reasons you might suppose, or for the thousands of difficulties that I somewhat expected and had prepared myself for. I arrived in Toulouse in the thick of the 1968 protests, you see. Coming from Aleppo, and from Syria, I suddenly found myself thrown into a world that was changing at the speed of light, and into many things that I understood nothing about or couldn't accept. I was shocked. I had received a traditional, Catholic education, and I suddenly found myself confronted with the "global protest movement". I couldn't understand how some young people who wanted to become priests could spend all their time challenging the Church. What was the point of them coming here? What is it they wanted, if all they wanted to do was protest? I was alone, and all the French were with them. And I was the only Syrian there.

But once again I was lucky enough to be able to rely on the help of a teacher of great literary scholarship and spiritual depth, because what was happening there was not that young people were refusing to study or wanted the easiest or quickest solution. They felt passionately about things and were raising deep questions that shook the foundations of my religious identity. My very faith was being challenged by this need to understand all kinds of things, including sociology, the idea of seeing everything in relative terms, and translating concepts and values that suddenly seemed old fashioned into something modern, but without distorting them and without losing yourself. It was a great experience for me, but it was also tough and challenging. Then, when I was sent to Marseilles in 1971 to work with Algerian immigrants in the outskirts of the city, the universe opened even wider for me and became even more critical. Everything was new to me. Basically, for the first time in my life I found myself grappling with the question of man, with what freedom and justice are, and what the Church is in all this. It was a totally new approach for me, and it might have lost me completely. And except for my spiritual father, I had no one else to talk to. I wrote to my parents, but I didn't tell them about my inner thoughts and issues, they wouldn't have understood. All this might have proved too complicated for my father, so I only told him about the things I was doing. Dad had this image of France as a great country, but what he knew belonged to a different era and was really about the country that his uncle, the famous Monsignor A***, had known. But that France didn't exist anymore! It was like an old legend. What could I tell him, without making him worry unduly?

When I returned to Syria in 1971, at the end of my novitiate, it's not that I was a different person, but I was certainly very different from the somewhat overconfident young man that had left for Toulouse four years earlier. The two years I spent in Syria before setting off again helped me to digest a lot of things and to reflect on my past experience. Also, this was the first time I was living closer to my family after being away for some years. I completed my degree in Arabic then I took up magisterial teaching, which involved being part of a working group that taught catechesis in schools, although I still wasn't a priest.

Then, one day, I was sent for by the Provincial father and was assigned to the Collège de la Sainte Famille in Cairo. And that too was one of those transforming experiences that help nurture your modesty. In Cairo there was a very strong and very interesting religious community, with Dutch, American, French and Arab families. I taught students, but it was nothing like my experience in Syria. They came from the city's upper echelons and from the Egyptian middle class. I remember we had some of Nasser's and Sadat's grandchildren. They were brilliant and highly educated students, and I felt really small. I studied with them day and night to try to be up to their level as far as possible. Of course, there were also the usual things that I already knew but which weren't the less taxing because of that. There were differences in accent, cultural differences and national differences, and I was under constant pressure to learn, which on the one hand is enriching and makes you grow, but on the other hand it forces you to always strive to give your best and means you can never relax. I remember at the Collège de la Sainte Famille I taught translation from Arabic to French and from French to Arabic. And this too was something that aroused great surprise because I looked like – and I still look like – a European, and naturally no one thought or believed it was possible for a European's knowledge of Arabic culture to be good enough to be able to do that. Again and again, when I was teaching, I had to overcome an instinctive diffidence towards me and earn the confidence of the students and the people I worked with, also without having to explain, time after time, that I came from Aleppo.

There is no doubt that ever since I was young I had been used to seeing myself as a citizen of a city that had few equals in the Middle East. At home we always heard that Aleppo was second only to Cairo and Istanbul. And, of course, I thought so too. But now I was actually in Cairo and many of the things from my Aleppo became somewhat smaller or less remarkable compared to the cultured and international environment I found myself in. We studied, we read, and we worked, and all the people I lived with gradually accepted me as part of their community. I learned to speak with professors who were infinitely more cultured than I was, and sometimes I wonder what they must have thought of this young man who endeavoured to do his best yet was still so much their junior, not just in age but especially in learning. So, I can't but be grateful to this group of scholars who slowly took me in as one of their own, without making much of the great many differences that existed between us.

And finally, it was time to move on to philosophy and theology. I still remember how it all happened and how important it was for me. In Cairo I went to see the then director of studies and I remember that during our meeting I told him I didn't want to go back to France – not after all I had been through and after everything that had happened there. I wanted to go to Lebanon, I said, to a less stressful kind of world: all that tension you had to live with in France, which we were still reading about in the papers, was not for me. I think I told him I wasn't up to it and that perhaps I was more suited to a simpler, less ambitious life. My time in France and in Cairo had left me almost dazed. They had been good years; I had learned a great deal and had developed in terms of both my faith and my experience, but I didn't feel like starting again. I wanted... yes that's it... I wanted my own quiet and modest corner where I could be myself.

And when I got him to understand all this, he didn't speak very much. In fact, he only said these words: 'Then, stay true to yourself. And go!'

So, I had to face this experience yet again and didn't have the option of sitting back and going for an easier solution. So, I left and spent the next six years in Paris. I did four years of philosophy and two years of postgraduate work. I went through the whole course at the Sorbonne, got my degree in Arabic and did a doctorate on one of the founders of the Ba'ath Party, Zaki al-Arsourzi.

I chose to focus on him because I wanted to find out about the Arab world's response to modernity and what they understand about socialism, psychology and Marxism. My project was very general and maybe not even particularly clear. But it seemed to me that if we have to operate in this region then it's important for us to know what those around us think. Also, Zaki al-Arsourzi's works had just been published and I didn't know he was an Alawite. I got his books, studied his speeches and had a professor helping me. The cultural focus of the man I was studying revolved exclusively around Plotinus and Aristotle, and I couldn't grasp its deep meaning. It was an adventure into a mysticism whose contours were sometimes clear and sometimes blurred... the exterior and the interior, the image and the meaning, relationships and all these kinds of things.

One day I went to see my Iraqi professor with all my notes and ideas. And after a while he said to me: 'My dear boy, it's obvious. He's an Alawite!' And from then on everything became clear; the work was completed relatively quickly and was actually published in Beirut.

And so, finally, in 1979, I was ordained priest here in Aleppo, and the man who ordained me was the very bishop I had been afraid of when I was a young man and who I didn't feel particularly in tune with. I was sent to Damascus where I did basic catechesis work, so I prepared myself for another departure by studying Greek and Hebrew. But this time my destination was Rome, the Pontifical Biblical Institute.

And this too was an important but challenging experience, though in a different way from my previous ones. I didn't have much time. I had been given just two years and a task I found almost overwhelming at times because of its sheer scale. Looking back on that stage of my life, I wish I had had a little more time. The subjects of the examinations were important, and the professors and standard of teaching were outstanding, but I've always thought that two years were not really enough.

The environment in the International Houses in Rome was very stimulating and buzzing with ideas. It was bit like France, but the situation there was totally different. In France, especially after 1968, there was a lot of freedom and everyone did more or less what they liked. But in Rome I felt as if I was back in elementary school. The studying was very rigorous, and whether you accepted it or not, that's how it was. I spent my first month there asking myself whether or not I wanted to carry on with it, but then, you know how these things are – obedience is an important value for Jesuits. So, I tried to buckle down and do my best, and within the two years I was given I managed to complete a programme that at the beginning I had thought might be too big for me and too broad. And perhaps I still feel a lingering a desire to explore in more depth many things that I only got a sense of, deep concepts that I was only able to look into very briefly. But what I'll always remember is the community of scholars I came into contact with. In every subject – whether it was exegesis or Hebrew language – they were not just experts but absolute authorities. I was very fortunate to get to know them. With these heavyweights, and the concepts that nurtured me, I developed my potential to be... let's say, an original scholar, or at least that's my hope. But let me tell you, it was such hard work! Yet I had always known that: it's how things are with the Jesuits, you are expected to give your best, and, after all, it's only right that you should. If the people around you are confident that you are up to a task, even if the task seems greater than you can cope with, it's only right that you should find the drive and the concentration to accomplish it, so that you can become what you are expected to become.

So, in 1982, when I completed my studies, I was sent to Beirut, in the thick of the war. The residence was located exactly on the line of demarcation, where all the fighting was taking place. The Jesuits had started working on the translation of the Bible into Arabic at the time, and I was appointed to join a commission focusing on the Old Testament.

It was odd, though perhaps not really all that odd, to live through a war without being in it. The world around us seemed to have gone crazy. We could hear the bombs going off and all the fighting, but I can't say that our lives and our scholarly work were disturbed by all this. But then, you know very well what the battle of Beirut was like. In one street, people would be fighting to the death, while, in the next street, people went about as usual, doing their shopping. In one neighbourhood, people would be dying, while in another, the rich families of Beirut were sunbathing around the pool, as if nothing was happening at all.

In my working group there were two Jesuits, a Syrian and a French philologist. We did a huge job and the result was, in many respects, a remarkable work. We did something similar to what was done for the Jerusalem Bible, but in Arabic, and it was a very important work for Arabic-speaking Christians. I think I was appointed to the working group because of my knowledge of Arabic and maybe also for the two years I had spent studying at the Biblical Institute. But I have to say that without those two fathers, who were older than me and accepted, corrected and encouraged me, I would have struggled. I was much younger than them. Maybe the awareness that we were doing something which would be very useful to the Arab Christian world is what motivated us to respect and help one another, and to keep working in spite of what was going on outside our walls in Beirut at the time.

Then there was the teaching. I taught exegesis to the Maronites and the Greeks, and because I was so engrossed in the studies I had done and in the work I was doing on the Bible in Arabic, which was such a major undertaking, I think I made my lessons as academically rigorous as possible. Maybe I also felt glad that my lessons were difficult because the subject we were dealing with was so difficult. But the criticism I got from the religion students and seminarians who attended my classes, who complained that they were too rigorous, again made me realize that I had let all this go to my head a bit. I realized during those years in Beirut that studying also means being able to present what you've learned in a simple way, with a creative approach that is not pedantic, that is complex yet respectful of the need to understand of those who listen you.

While I was in Beirut I started going to Aleppo more often. I was able to get more involved in the life of my family and with the people I had left behind as a boy. And as I travelled on the road that took me back to Aleppo, my native city, I often asked myself what Aleppo had meant to me.

Before leaving for France I believed that Aleppo was the centre of the world. And when people told me it would be tough, in my own mind I said to myself: 'But I am from Aleppo!' But then I realized that things are not like that and actually turn out a different way. Discovering France and the extraordinary rationality of French people made me grow. They had the art of exchanging ideas through discussion, reading and addressing issues. And the idea that rationality can also certainly be a path of freedom is something I am glad to have understood and which I never want to forget. Aleppo, by contrast, was the place of my early certainties, a place with the attitude of a city that is the top in everything: we have the best cuisine, the best clothes, the best city life... Aleppo, the citizens of Aleppo... Aleppo's culture, its morality, its tradition, and so on and so forth. Then you leave. You go away and you learn to put a lot of things into perspective... You are confronted with other cultures and things that are foreign to you. On the one hand, I wanted to open my mind and discover the worlds I found myself in, or had been sent to, but, on the other, I didn't want to change: I wanted to stay true to myself. And it was the same during my experience as a novitiate, with everything that happened then. For a while, I wanted to imitate the French in absolutely everything. I wanted to speak like them, think like them... But over time I realized that, ultimately, I had to stay true to myself. I had to grow and become enriched with values and learning, but without losing my identity, my history and the history of my family and my city. It was, in fact, just as the present Jesuit Father General said to me all those years ago in Cairo: 'Stay true to yourself. And go!'

And it wasn't easy. It really wasn't easy at all to open myself to the world while staying true to myself at the same time. It meant learning to respect differences and accepting them in your own mind without being afraid of them. It meant learning to see our limitations as individuals and the limitations of our own background or the environment in which we were brought up as something natural to the human being, but not absolute.

And then came 1990. The old Iraqi Bishop of Aleppo died and people in Aleppo started saying that the dioceses was going through a difficult time and that Antoine A*** had to come back. I was Superior at the House in Lebanon at the time, and a few days before Christmas I received a fax from the Patriarch telling me that I had been appointed "Patriarchal administrator" of the Chaldean diocese of Syria. I remember going to an elder father, a great authority, and asking him what that meant. And he said to me: 'You have all the powers of a bishop, all except to ordain new priests.'

So, I gradually gave up my commitments at the House in Lebanon and came here, and in 1992 I was appointed bishop by the Chaldean synod. I've been here for fourteen years now and it isn't going too badly. I'm happy to be back, but I'm also happy to have learned that responsibility is something that can't be refused, and also that perfection doesn't belong those who operate in this world. Solutions are never perfect, but they must the best ones possible.

Sometimes I miss my academic studies a bit, although I still manage to make time to read and study. Every week there is an article to write for an Arabic-language patriarchal magazine, and every two years I collect these articles in a book. It's a way to carry on studying, publishing and keeping in touch with the scholarly community.

But except for all this, I devote all my time to the community – which now counts almost six hundred families – with catechesis, scout groups, community centres, young people, marriage preparation, and so on. Then there are church celebrations, weddings and funerals to perform and take care of, and the old and the sick to visit. In Syria there are ten parishes like this one, around twelve thousand Chaldeans and five priests that I have ordained myself, and soon I'll be ordaining the sixth. It's a growing community, not as fast as the one in Iraq, but it's still getting bigger by the day – despite all the things that happen daily in this part of the world and the ongoing emigration.

What has happened to my Aleppo? To my centre of the world? It's still pleasant. It's still my city, my childhood, my recollections, my places and my memory. There is a vital connection with the places, the climate... It's just Aleppo. It's easy to love it, even now that the population has grown from three hundred thousand to two million.

But the old Aleppo is still there, with its customs and traditions. And maybe it's not so inclined to see that there is a neighbourhood in the suburbs with a large concentration of Kurdish migrants and, after what happened in Turkey, there are now almost six hundred thousand of them. Of course, I fully realize that they are now a bigger community than all the Christians in Syria put together... Some people say that Aleppo is an aristocratic and somewhat closed city... No, I don't see it like that. Aleppo knows how to cope with the new, it knows how to accept it and embrace it, as it did with my father who came from Iraq, and as it did with the Armenians... It's just lazy, and concerned that the new, which is advancing and will keep advancing, should not disrupt too many customs.

Aleppo? It isn't closed. Maybe, through the centuries, it has simply learned at its own expense how important its identity is and how to go about protecting it.

10 - The Druze Officer

He's never said a word about it. When he comes home, he sits in the yard, takes his off shoes and starts smoking. He can sit there for hours, sometimes until nightfall. At home, we all know what he's like by now, that's just the way he is. He doesn't talk; he doesn't say anything. When he does speak, he measures out his words carefully, in the way a spice merchant might do. And it's best to listen to him as you never know when he's going to speak next. Sometimes I wonder if he also speaks so little with the farm workers or with the shepherds when they come and report to him how the grazing is going. Surely he must say something. He can't just keep quiet like this, like he does at home. Last week we spent a whole evening together. My wife and his daughter were also here, we had come over together from Damascus. He could have said something to me then... Instead, he listened to the usual women's conversations and the two of us just sat there, like two old brothers who have nothing to say to each other anymore, or perhaps have too much to say.

The women wouldn't even have heard us, so he could have told me then that there was blood in his urine, and that he was concerned and was waiting for some test results. Instead he didn't say a word, as if there was nothing to tell, or it was such a trifle that it didn't deserve the slightest notice. And she called me yesterday and said: 'What do you mean? Didn't he say anything to you?' 'No, nothing at all.' 'Didn't he even tell you about the test results?' 'I didn't even know anything about the tests.' She just kept silent. 'How did they go?' I asked, 'What were the tests for?' At that point I heard her cry. It was a heavy cry, like a stone. I was silent too, until she told me about his prostate cancer, and that it has spread so far that it's not even prostate cancer anymore, it's everywhere. And the doctor didn't even tell him to stop smoking. It's too late for anything... a few weeks, a couple of months perhaps, maybe three.

Like my brother, I am also a man of few words. Only people who don't want to see or to understand have any use for words. But those who don't want to see also manage not to hear. What's the use of words? But, really, in this case, Ma'an, wouldn't it have been better to tell me what was happening? At least to prepare me, or to see if there's anything I can do.

So, here I am now, in the car, behind this truck, heading south towards the border with Jordan. And I don't even know if I'll be happy, as I always am, when I see the sign for As Suwayda and the al-Arab Mountain. And I feel ashamed that I can't even cry inside me. I feel ashamed to be thinking about the property we inherited from our grandfather and then our father, and to be wondering who is going take care of it from now on. How long have I got before I retire? How much time will my brother give me? My sister-in-law is alone; if I take her to Damascus to live with my family she'll also be closer to her daughter Asma. But who is going to stay on here? And how can I carry on in my current job while going back and forth from Damascus? Also, we are talking about a six-hundred acre plot, and even if it's not very profitable, you can't manage it from Damascus. You need to be here and spend the whole day here. And this is a possibility I've never even considered. When I was born he was already in this world, and at home everyone took it for granted that he would inherit it while I would go away and study. I've never been a farmer or the owner of the family holding for a single day. I used to go over to the fields with my grandfather – my wonderful grandad – and my father, and even back then everyone looked at me and called me "the student". So I grew up knowing that I would be going away, I would study first in our village of Zibien, then in As Suwayda and eventually in Damascus. My mum wanted me to become a doctor. Sometimes she tried to tell me this and said: 'If you study medicine we'll have a happy old age, with you and your brother we won't want for anything.' And maybe I'd be a little more useful now than I am as someone with a degree in Arabic literature from the University of Damascus who has spent most of his life serving as an officer in the Syrian army.

I could take care of it. I could live in Damascus in winter, when almost everything in the countryside stops, and I could come here in the summer through to September. But is seventy the right age to start? When we came here, the mountain was more arid and poorer. It has taken the Druze generations, generations of solid Druze wisdom, to transform this place. It isn't fertile, and probably never will be, but at least our land has started to make a return. It isn't a cost, and sometimes you can even make a profit from it. But there is a whole history here that I know nothing about; there are skills and knowledge that are totally foreign to me! I know nothing about this farm, nothing at all. I used to come here to visit my brother and sister-in-law, to tell them about their daughter Asma who lives with us in Damascus, never really thinking about what was happening here. I've never asked myself which well they get their water from, where the water tanks are, where they store the water in winter… and not even where they keep the ladders to go up the cherry trees! And everything has changed so much since we all lived here together, with our parents and grandfather. It's all different now. I wouldn't even know where to go and look for farm labourers to hire for the grape picking season… Of course, I could ask the people who know my family. If I'm no good at it, I can rely on my family's name to get good helpers. Maybe that won't be too difficult, there's still so much poverty on the mountain that you're spoilt for choice… They've done nothing to help this region, nothing since I went away. They couldn't have cared less about it, even though they always knew it was one of the poorest areas in Syria. There is a company that produces arak,[27] a small carpet manufacturer and nothing else. And the families here live on very little, on hardly anything in fact. People work the land, but nothing grows in this volcanic soil. They keep flocks of sheep, but the grazing is poor, and the sheep are so thin that you wonder how they manage to stand on their legs at all.

But then, that's what always happens when you never complain, when you have the utmost dignity and self-respect – when you don't go around offices begging for things from this or that person. Like that idiot I had in my office for years, who used to say: 'But you Druze people are rich!' I eventually asked him one day what made him believe such a thing, and he said that our houses always have huge, comfortable sitting rooms, and that during the many years he had been working at the ministry of agriculture he had never – not once – seen a Druze coming to plead for a recommendation or any kind of help. That's how it's always been: dignity and generosity are mistaken for wealth and pride, for arrogance almost. If you don't act like a beggar then it means that you are rich.

Or maybe it's Syria that has changed. It wasn't like that in the old days, not in the days of Sultan Pasha, in my grandfather's time. This idea of not working but being entitled to this, that and the other, always demanding things as if one had a right to them, this inability to live with dignity, it's all new. My wife won't say it, but I can tell she disagrees. But I believe, and will always believe, that this change that has disrupted our ways can partly be blamed on Zionism, on this cancer that has attacked us and which we haven't been able to free ourselves from. We belong to a sad generation, my brother and me. We grew up with outstanding examples around us, and cherishing hopes and ideals that we thought were universally shared and attainable. Or perhaps we just weren't up to the challenge of the times. We failed and the world has turned another way. But the things we believed in, and which we still believe in, weren't crazy. They were right...

Still, my father and my brother did a sensible thing. They had heard from somewhere that in certain volcanic regions of Europe people produce good wine, so they planted the vineyard. Also, you can see from the Christian churches on the mountain that grapes had been grown here before. So they said to themselves that if winegrowing had been done in the past, they could try it again now. What a business that was! For a while it seemed to be going well, but eventually it turned out to be a never-ending disaster. Grapes are not wheat. Grapevines need ongoing care and attention, doing this, that and the other all the time. And when things have to be done it's already too late and it's always a rush. Also, there isn't enough water, and the grapevines have to be kept low. But they don't "stay" low! You have to work to keep them low, so you're always cutting and pruning and all the rest of it. But my brother's grapes were se delicious! And for a few years he got a good price for them and made a profit. That was before everyone else started doing the same thing.

And I have my job in Damascus. What will I tell the director? That I'm going off to be a farmer? If I don't tell him, how will I be able to be away for months? Thank goodness my brother planted some cherry and apricot orchards on the eastern ridge of the plot. You earn hardly anything, or very little, from them, but at least looking after them doesn't drive you crazy.

And then there is Asma, my brother's beautiful daughter Asma. What will she do? Will she be left on her own in Damascus? She is grown up by now, very grown up. She won't see it as a problem, but I will. Poor Asma, so beautiful, so proud… And we are her family: we are as a husband, mother and nephews and nieces to her. She, who was the most beautiful woman in the house, and at school even her teachers were in awe of her beauty. She looked at them with her steady gaze and my brother used to say they were hypnotized by her. With her pure white skin, black hair and green eyes… One of her teachers used to call her "the cat", because he said she had a feline gaze: if you looked into her eyes you'd see a sudden flash and you didn't know where it came from or where it would lead. Of course, he too fell in love with her, as did her father, her uncle and everyone else. Who hasn't been in love with Asma at home? How many times have we said jokingly that we would never give her to anyone because nobody was worthy of her! When she grew into a teenager and then into a woman she would come in from the courtyard, perspiring and unaware of the charm she emanated. She would sit on her father's lap or mine, and as you sought her eyes you'd see her heaving chest, a woman's chest by then, and beads of perspiration, like pearls, on her lips. My brother always said that picking her up in your arms was like opening a pomegranate, it sparkled all over, so brightly and so completely that you didn't know which way to look anymore.

When did she become aware of her beauty? When she was six years old? Maybe seven? None of us know. The kids would wait for her in the street and run after her. Whenever she made a suggestion, they were proud to do just as she said. If she had a project, it became the project of all the kids in Zibien. She was like her grandfather, and her great-grandfather. She didn't like to lead, but she *was* the leader. Like her great-grandfather and her grandfather, she didn't need to fight for things, raise her voice or prove that she was better than the other girls in climbing up a tree and coming down with a daring leap. Ever since she was a little girl, when she walked in the street, you'd look at her and think: 'It's her great-grandfather who's back among us, with the same incredible eyes, with the same ability to make others obey her and to lead.'

I've never understood why she hasn't got married. They say that more girls than boys are born in our community, so for many women there isn't a husband. And obviously you can't look for a husband outside of our Druze community. But none of this has anything to do with Asma. Asma has had more offers than anyone else. In the evening she would come home and tell my sister-in-law what she had heard in the street and what the boys had said to her, looking almost embarrassed about it. At the beginning my sister-in-law was amused, but as Asma grew up she became a little concerned. But then she stopped taking any notice of it. Asma has never been a sensual beauty, the sort of girl for summer evenings, full of tension-charged silences. I'm not saying this just because I'm her uncle. Even if I were the thirstiest man on earth, I couldn't think of Asma in that way. There has always been an intangible aura around her, the same aura that made everyone obey her, that protected her and kept her at a distance from ordinary mortals. Asma didn't receive cakes as presents, or invitations to parties with people her own age, or offers from regular young men who in their own way were right for her. Asma was not someone's girlfriend-to-be but everyone's leader. And she walked, she studied, and she spoke as if she knew it. After getting over certain stages of her adolescence – when she too asked herself questions about her body, and had an almost tender expression in her eyes, as dangerous as an embrace –, her face regained this kind of... sunny purity, like a goddess, like an ideal. It was as if what made her beautiful was not for ordinary men but was waiting to meet an exceptional person – the only one who would be able to resist her and not be burned by her in a flash.

Once, not so many years ago, a young man she was working with came to our house. He was a handsome fellow, a Druze, who came from the Druze area of Beit ed-Dine, in Lebanon. His family had moved to Damascus three or four generations before, but although they lived in the city, they kept their traditions alive. I don't remember what he did for a living, but he followed Asma with a tender and worshipping look that was almost disconcerting. Asma would go to the kitchen and he would follow her. If she wasn't there he almost seemed lost. When he spoke, he looked at no one but her. He seemed like the right person. He was a few years older than her and had a good job. Over time, he would learn to be with her and to have the right approach with her.

My wife wasn't so convinced. We talked about it and although she did her best not to dishearten me, she never encouraged me to believe that Asma had found a husband. She tried to console me when Asma eventually spent a whole weekend at home, and then another one, without him calling or coming by. I remember saying something like: 'That's no way to behave.' And she looked at me with a forbearing expression I knew very well and said: 'It wasn't him; it was her.'

I was desperately upset. When she told me that, I got out of bed and wandered about the house all night. Even though I wasn't her father, I felt responsible for her. At twenty-seven years old, did she feel she could discard a young man just like that? What did she expect in life? In the morning I stopped myself from reproaching her and kept silent throughout breakfast. Asma kept running her fingers through her hair; she knew she had to say something. When she turned towards me and said, 'Uncle, I have something to say to you,' I realized she had been crying all night.

She told me she knew that time was getting on, and that she could see for herself that her girl friends were already married and some already had two or three children. She said she realized what a great joy it would be for her family and for us if she got married. Yet she couldn't give up hope, she could accept anything, but not give up hope.

'But, my dear girl, what hope?'

'I want to be loved, uncle, not worshipped. I want to be a woman for someone, not a boss. I want someone who won't wait for me to speak but will tell me what to do. I want a man, uncle, a man like you, like my father, like my grandfather. I don't want an admirer; an admirer is no good to me! Can you understand that?'

Of course, I understood her, and I suddenly thought back to the empty, almost insignificant gaze of the young man who had raised my hopes. And I realized that she was right. But I also realized that it was us who we to blame for that. We had encouraged her to study like a man, we had given her the freedom she deserved and had treated her no differently than if she had been a son, in every way. Of course it was right to treat her like that; of course it was right to nurture her abilities and her gifts. But, as a result, the woman we had helped to grow and to mature was not an ordinary woman but an exceptional one. She would never be satisfied with what other women thought would bring them happiness. Her beauty, her independence, her French, her English and her degree had only strengthened the aura she had always had since she was a child.

Maybe… was there any other way we could help her? Should we be less proud of her? No, we did the right thing. We had brought her up as her character deserved and as her intelligence demanded. But now she was almost a victim of what she had become. It might be difficult to find a young man that was right for her, not just in Damascus but in the whole of Syria.

We would have been in trouble and wouldn't have known what to do if the memory of Grandad hadn't still been with us – if when looking at Asma we didn't see him standing before us: a big, awe-inspiring man, with fiery eyes that only my grandmother knew how to handle, with her long and patient silences. She was a tiny woman who looked as if she would break at the slightest touch, but she was totally undaunted by Grandad's huge frame and his wild physical strength. And, like Asma, he had leadership in his blood. People followed him as you would follow a prince. Maybe that's why Asma hasn't married. In her eyes and in her body there is too much… too much for an ordinary man like me, or like many other men. Is Asma still waiting for her prince? I wonder whether she's found him in the place where she's working now, where they deal with the plight of the Palestinians and war refugees, day in day out. But even if she has found him, Asma will never take him unless he's a Druze like us. Asma won't do what so many have done here in Damascus or in Lebanon. Too many – unable to endure the persecutions and intolerance regularly unleashed against minorities throughout history – have betrayed their faith. They have become Maronites, Sunnis, anything, as long as they were left in peace and could blend in with the crowd.

But now that I think about this, I wonder if it wouldn't have been better to… I mean, she would have children and a family now… No, no, her light would have broken. My niece Asma is like her great-grandfather. We are a people that never surrenders, we don't bow our heads. All our strength lies in our religion. If we lose that, the very light in our eyes will die out, isn't that right Asma? What's the point of a life that isn't worth living? You would never live with shame, the shame that I have to live with. I, who once had hope, who cherished the dream of an anti-colonial and anti-Zionist Arab brotherhood... And today I have to face this world where compromise and corruption are the rule, where there are no values anymore, where men seem to be dominated by an evil disease that everyone pretends isn't there, yet we all know very well what it is. This sweeping plague came with Zionism. It's this cancer that they have transplanted into Palestine and which spreads evil, kills people, annihilates our consciences, humiliates men and makes them used to the idea of living in humiliation.

But as to us... We will never be humiliated. And Asma knows that. We moved here from Lebanon, I don't even know how many years ago, in order to escape persecution but not to hide and be humiliated. And it is here, on this mountain, that my family has written the most beautiful chapters in its history, which we are all proud of.

It was the time when my grandfather, who today would be called the "mayor" of the village, along with my dad, led our whole community in the war against the Turks, when, alongside Feisal, he entered Damascus, freed at last from the foreign oppressors, the Turks. What a September that must have been! The Arab flag was fluttering on all the landmark buildings of Damascus, liberated by the Arabs themselves. Sometimes I understand what they must have been hoping for — what my grandfather thought he had achieved when, after months of guerrilla war, he was finally parading through the streets of Damascus cheered by a rapturous crowd. But it was all an illusion, followed by tragic disappointment when the colonial powers carved up the Middle East and divided it among themselves, deciding this, that and the other as if we were nothing, "nothingness".

It all happened before I was born, but my dad used to tell me that Grandad never wanted to say a word about it – do you identify with that, Asma? I think you do. He didn't oppose it; he didn't fight it: but a fleeting glance at him was enough to make anyone realize what a huge storm would be unleashed if he had. It took a man to lead all this, a pure man, Asma, like all of us. So when Sultan Pasha al-Atrash led the Druze revolt against France, my grandfather and my father joined him as they had done before with Feisal. They were never defeated. In the only battle the rebels lost, they weren't fighting because they had been wounded.

What a time that was! And Europeans wonder where certain feelings of resentment, of deep hatred, come from. They don't understand our intransigence, they don't understand how we can be so unyielding... They don't understand because they don't want to understand. They don't want to remember. They turn the page and that's it! It's all new, all different, all clean.

And they come and give us lessons in democracy, in economics, they of all people! They who stole from us the country we had liberated and gave it to France under the "mandate". The very word – mandate – says it all. But here they acted like conquerors, dictating matters left, right and centre. So much for the mandate! They couldn't have cared less about who we were, what we wanted and what we were doing. France, which invented an independent Lebanon (1926)! When did Beirut and Damascus ever belong to two different nations? France, which also gave away our port of Antioch, Aleppo's seaport, to Turkey! And so the citizens of Aleppo, who were used to being just an hour away from the sea and the docks where they loaded their goods for shipment all around the world, suddenly found themselves without their access to the sea. So they were forced to look for another outlet, the port of Latakia, beyond mountains always covered with snow and difficult to cross. A great lesson in democracy, no doubt! I'd like to know what the French would say if someone gave independence to Brittany and gave away the ports of Normandy to Belgium! I'd like to know what they would say if they were forced to reroute all their commercial traffic to Marseille. Would they be happy? Would they like that kind of democracy?

And then they come and tell us that everything is different now. What's different? Who is it different for? Antioch is still Turkish, and Lebanon is still independent. Where are the new things that were supposed to happen over these years? Where is this new path supposed to be? There's nothing new at all, everything is old, as decided by European colonialism. It's just the same for Palestine, and goodness knows for how many other places around the world.

Then, during the French mandate, there was that fellow, that Captain Cabrillet. He came here, to our lands, the very ones I am travelling through right now, and presumed to administer all that belonged to us. He, a Frenchman, here among the Druze and in our lands, telling us how we should do things, who we should be governed by, whose backing we should seek… until he made the mistake of arresting some of our key leaders.

It was like setting a powder keg on fire. All the distinctions between Druze, Bedouin, Christians and Shiites disappeared: we were all Arabs fighting against the foreign occupiers. It was we who had liberated Syria, not the French. And just as we had driven out the Turks, we would drive them out.

Those were different days, with different men. At home we were often told the story of a battle in which my grandfather was wounded by a gunshot to the chest. Luckily, the bullet was diverted by a bone and became lodged inside his flesh. He tore off his jacket, plunged his knife into the wound and dug out the bullet. Then he put his jacket back on and carried on fighting for the rest of the day. I still remember Asma's eyes when she was only a child and my brother used to tell her about her great-grandfather! She looked as if she was seeing the battle with her own eyes and was simply reliving it, hour by hour. Tough times, for real men, free men. When you were wounded they treated you by cauterizing the wound with hot sheep fat. There were no medicines and there weren't any doctors. You either survived or you died, there was nothing in-between. Yet the French were defeated and driven out. We entered Damascus once again, and Sultan Pasha al-Atrash restored our city to us, our "eye of the East". The revolt was no longer a Druze revolt, my family's revolt or the Jabal al-Druze revolt: it was a revolt by the whole of Syria. And when revolts put up such a united front, no imperialism in this world can do anything. A people with unshakeable beliefs and guided by good leaders, is invincible... This thought always goes through my mind when I go by the souk in Damascus and look up at the thousands of bullet holes from those battles in the 1920s. No one has ever repaired them, and they are still there for everyone to see. My grandson once asked me what they were. I don't know, maybe it was wrong of me, but I couldn't bring myself to tell him. I asked myself whether it was right that young people too should see how badly my generation has failed. Everything seems so distant, also painful in a way, but wonderful, nevertheless.

That was when "civilized" France delivered to us the first aerial bombardment in our history, perhaps the very first in human history. I don't know why they say that the first aerial bombing of civilians was in Spain.[28] If that's the case, then what should we call the bombing of Damascus in 1925? When an aircraft fires machine guns against the crowd and drops bombs, if that isn't a bombardment, what is that supposed to be?

The French came back and Sultan Pasha al-Atrash went into exile, first to Jordan and then to Arabia. He went into exile in order to survive, but many died – many were killed. Pasha saved himself, but how many people died? They say ten thousand or five thousand, in any case not that many more than on the French side. They reoccupied Damascus but from then on they carefully avoided interfering in the life of our Druze community. But the French had other skills... They told us that we were the best, and shouldn't mix with the other communities; they told the Maronites that they were Christians like themselves, and this made them a privileged group; they told the Armenians that they were virtually European, and the French therefore felt closer to them than to any of the other groups... What mattered to France was that there should be no such thing as Syria, and that each group should believe that the only way to survive or find protection was through a close alliance with them. It's the old story of "divide and rule".

They didn't defeat us, but they won all the same. This all happened before I was born, but when I saw Damascus for the first time I understood everything, or quite a lot of things, at any rate. I still remember very well the look on my grandfather and my father's faces. We were driving south from the Jabal al-Druze to see some relatives who lived on the way to Beirut, where the Beqaa Valley begins. They were distant relatives who had stayed on in the Lebanon Mountains when our branch of the family moved to the Jabal al-Druze. It was one of the many Druze families scattered across the mountains in Lebanon, Palestine and Syria who don't have a nation or a homeland, but know very well what they belong to and who they are... Although the situation is no longer what it was in the old days, choosing to stay in the mountains and not to live in the city is still in our blood. Or maybe it's the city that isn't made for us. There's something in the city that isn't right, that doesn't work for us. That may be why so many Druze who have gone to live in the city end up becoming Sunnis or Christians... Or maybe they would have done that anyway. My family has been living in Damascus for years, but none of us has even remotely considered the possibility of changing religion.

So, my brother, my dad, my grandfather and I were in the car. For almost an hour, after Bosra, the road was dusty and dry. There were dromedaries, some army trucks and a few people walking along the roadside amid clouds of dust and the scorching heat. Dad and Grandad seemed cheerful and were chatting away. Every so often they would greet someone along the road, an acquaintance or someone from our village. Inside the car there was a happy, festive sort of atmosphere. My brother and I were fooling around, but then, quite abruptly, we became aware that there was tension in the car. There was a different mood.

Everything around us began to change. First some plants began to appear, followed by cultivations, more and more of them and packed closer and closer together. After a few kilometres the temperature had become delightful, the dust had disappeared and the air coming in from the open car windows brought us the scent of moist earth and flowers. Jasmine, lemon blossom, orange blossoms, I'm not sure what, but it was a sweet, fresh fragrance, like the one you sometimes smell on summer evenings when the vegetation seems to come back to life after the sweltering heat of the day. Then Damascus appeared at the end of a straight stretch of road. I remember very well the excitement my brother and I felt, and the deathly silence that fell inside the car. Neither Dad nor Grandad was smiling anymore. It seemed as if there was something terrible hanging in the air, something that clashed with the sweet scents, the bustle in the streets and the fruit displayed on the street stalls. Then my dad turned off to the left, the city suddenly disappeared, and we were on a mountain road. I had caught a glimpse of a dream made of pink and white stone, nestling in such thick vegetation that it seemed like a fairy tale… and it had disappeared. We were on the road climbing up the Anti-Lebanon Mountains and all was dry and dusty again. But the people around us were no longer sharing our journey; they were travelling in the opposite direction, where my brother and I also wanted to go.

That's how we found out about the revolt led by Sultan Pasha al-Atrash, and about the French bombing of the city – and of my father and grandfather's promise never to return to Damascus for as long as the city was in foreign hands. To them, Damascus had become an open wound, so painful that they couldn't even talk about it. It was a zone of silence and anguish, to drive through as quickly as possible, pretending not to see the French troops and the French road patrols.

I remember a university professor I met many years later. He talked about the French Revolution and how it had betrayed many hopes and expectations. His French was very good, and he often amused himself with wordplay, though most of the time it seemed to be an attempt to show off rather than a mark of intelligence. He had a high opinion of himself that I didn't feel was particularly justified. But once, out of all his stupid little puns, he came up with a play on words that was very sharp and effective.

He was talking about the motto that the French Revolution has exported throughout the world: "Liberté, Fraternité, Egalité". 'These are wonderful words,' he said, 'but they are words, and, as always with words, you have to be very careful about punctuation!' We listened to him, a little bored as it didn't seem to be anything new compared to the silly things we heard every day. 'If you look at the French constitution and study the texts of the great French revolutionaries or of the Enlightenment, do you know how you'll see it written?' He was already chuckling to himself, with his usual, slightly hysterical and slightly stupid, grin that we had learned to scorn. He went to the blackboard. 'This is how you'll see it written: *Liberté* comma *Fraternité* comma *Egalité*. But if we look at the way it's written on the buildings in Damascus where the French governed our nation from during the mandate, what do we see? *Liberté point Fraternité point Egalité point*. Do you get it?' And he laughed, greatly amused. But, this time at least, we appreciated his play on words.[29] He had probably learned it in France when he was studying there, and maybe he had been taught it by some old anarchist or whoever. But it perfectly summed up what France meant to Syria. It meant privation of liberty, no fraternity, and, as to equality, that was unthinkable.

At the time I didn't know that I too would keep my grandfather's promise. I went back to Damascus many years later, in the mid-1950s, for my course in Arabic language and literature. I remember very well how proud I was when I talked to my fellow students about my family's past, and how emotional I felt the first time I saw the old French colonial buildings now housing the Syrian government. To me, they seemed to be living proof of our victory, of the Arab people's determination and also of their strength, if they were willing to stay united.

But no one was thinking about France or Britain anymore. Suddenly they no longer mattered: our enemy was within our own country by then and had already won a war. So my grandfather and my father's feats, the Druze resistance and the Jabal al-Druze revolt were things that no one felt like talking about anymore. They had slipped away into a very distant past, almost like Saladin or the Arab revolt against the Turks.

And so, my brother devoted himself to apricot and cherry trees. And I, who couldn't bring myself to believe that my family's and our nation's entire heritage had died out, turned to teaching. When you no longer have a present, it becomes easy to think about the future, and teaching then becomes a kind of gamble against history. What history has denied us, it will not be able to deny to our children.

I sometimes think he made a better choice retreating into silence, the same silence as our grandfather's and our father's, and not wanting to talk about it anymore. Or maybe not, perhaps it wasn't a good thing to do, you had to carry on believing in it right to the end, and fight. But when I was called up to the front for the so-called Suez Crisis, I realized there was no longer a will to fight. At the time, the idea of waging war against the French and the British seemed to me to be the ideal way to continue the battle we had lost in 1925. But times had changed: the era when men plunged a knife into their flesh to dig out a bullet and carried on fighting was over. But the enemy was still the same as it always had been, hateful and unacceptable, like any foreigner in one's homeland. It was we who were no longer the same. We had weak, divided and sometimes corrupt governments. And we were incapable of recreating the unity that had made us great. Instead, we were living under the foolish illusion that we would be able to survive this cancer that Zionism has planted into our very flesh, each fighting on their own. It's as if a body was being attacked by a virus and each organ decided to fight by itself: the spleen ignoring the liver, the blood and the lungs. Our cities were rapidly growing. And this flood of desperate people flowing into Syria from Palestine, although it was impossible not to take them in and treat them with respect, has changed our cities, our nation and even our people. It has become living proof of our failure, of the end of all our hopes.

Maybe that's why I am happy to go back to my brother's house. I have something like a suspicion that it was all too sudden and it happened too fast, but that there may be a message in it for me as well. Maybe it's time I should retire to the countryside, just as I retired from the army and from teaching. It means going back to the mountain where we are still respected as my grandfather's descendants. And maybe without me, and now without her father, Asma too will find a path that may be less epic but happier. Maybe I could start beekeeping. In the hotel where I used to work, the tourists always said that the flavour of our honey simply doesn't exist in Europe anymore. Maybe initially I'll get some help from that young man, that friend of Asma's, who opened a honey store in the al-Hamidiya souk and isn't doing too badly. After all, I don't need to earn so much money. And the work shouldn't be too demanding, or at least not as demanding as the vineyard and growing grapes. Maybe my wife will also be glad to come and live in my parents' old house, the only traditional house left there.

Jabal al-Druze is now completely transformed thanks to the money sent home by those who have emigrated. Many families have really lovely houses, even though I can't understand why they had to build new ones. Why didn't they just restore the old mud-brick houses? They are so cool in the summer and warm in the winter. Instead, with those awful windows, they have to have air conditioning in summer and central heating in winter. And since many people can't afford them, the houses end up being unbearably warm or unbearably cold.

Then, maybe, if beekeeping turns out to be a good business, we could set up a cooperative with all the honey producers in Jabal al-Druze. It could provide employment for some young people and bring some hope to this land, which is so poor. As a matter of fact, we don't need anything... There would be everything we need. Flowers in springtime, in autumn... but if we managed to get some Bedouin families involved, the ones living in the Hauran plains to the south, we might also be able to take advantage of the short-lived desert bloom. The young man at the al-Hamidiya souk was telling us that the honey made from the desert blossoms is superb. Maybe the tourists would like it too. Actually, I could speak directly with the hotel manager and maybe he'll let us open a little shop. I think the customers would be very impressed to see adverts for desert blossom honey. After all, they believe that that nothing grows in the desert. That day we'll take a picture of Asma and put it on all the adverts. And maybe the tourists will begin to travel north from Bosra up to As Suwayda, and there they could visit the Roman and Byzantine ruins.

I am not actually interested in those ruins at all, the tourists already know about them and realize how important they are. We'll open a museum, maybe in that house next to ours; it may be a bit run down but it's structurally sound. We could put together the photos of the revolt led by Sultan Pasha al-Atrash, the ones of Damascus and the Jabal al-Druze in the 1920s, those of the Arab revolt that took us into Damascus or the ones of the 1920s' repression. No, no. We won't have any pointless violence, there's no need for it. Also, tourists don't like to feel guilty, why should they pay to get into a place like that? Maybe we could display some period costumes, in a sort of journey into the Jabal al-Druze of the past. The museum should have a big sign, placed right next to the photo of Sultan Pasha and of my grandfather. It should say something like: "History of a people that never surrenders" ... No, actually, what we'll do is put up a sign by the museum entrance with such a big inscription that no one will be able to ignore it. Yes, that's right.

Maybe Asma knows someone in Damascus who could turn it into something bold and modern. But no one must touch the text, it will read:

   "Liberté virgule Fraternité virgule Egalité".

11 - The Lorry Driver

I don't think my life story is a very interesting one. I've done some very ordinary things and I've lived like many other people. And I'm not even old. It's not as if my working life is over, I'm still actually working. And I think I'll be working for many years yet, even though it's tiring, and I'd like to retire. No, I actually like my job, I like driving, especially at night, when the roads are empty, and you can go faster. I've always had this ability not to fall asleep at the wheel. The road keeps me awake, even when it's a long and apparently boring straight stretch of road. But the engine works better at night, it's under less strain and there are fewer people on the road. Only when I go to Turkey and have to cross the Taurus Mountains... there I actually stop and wait for daybreak. The road is narrow and full of bends, some of them dangerous, and the Turks are crazy drivers... no, I'm saying anything specific about the Turks, it's just that on the Taurus Mountains they drive dangerously. It's best to drive by daylight, when you can see them, they can see you, and you can see everything more clearly. Once, a friend of mine was second driver on a Turkish lorry and, as they were driving along, they came across a lorry with more or less the same engine power as theirs and carrying a similar load. And his co-driver started racing the other lorry, so my friend said: 'What are you doing? Are you crazy?' He didn't even answer but instead started tooting his horn and trying to overtake it, once, twice, three times... And the other lorry, which had seemed to be going slower, started speeding up just as they were overtaking it... I mean, they're not cars! It's really frightening to see two trucks speeding at ninety kilometres an hour side by side on a straight stretch of road. So, after a few attempts, they eventually managed to overtake it. But now the other lorry wasn't so slow anymore and started going at the same speed as them. So, when they got to the next straight stretch of road, my friend's co-driver drew closer to his nearside as if to let the other lorry overtake him, and – how crazy can you get? – just as it was overtaking him, he suddenly veered into its lane and cut it off. The other driver started tooting like mad but just kept going until the wheels on the left of his truck went over the edge of the tarmac and sent the lorry off the road. And I suppose, I' not sure of the exact details as I wasn't there, but a lorry of that size, unless it's fully loaded or if the load isn't perfectly balanced, tends to lean over to one side, and that's probably what happened, it almost rolled over. So my friend started shouting like a madman: 'You've killed him! You've killed him, stop!' But his co-driver kept going at full speed, and when my friends asked him if he had gone mad, he replied that he had seen the other driver get out of his overturned lorry and was fine. If he stopped, he said, the fellow would stab him to death, and he didn't want to get involved in a knife fight with anyone. 'And where are you going now?' my friend asked. 'To the nearest police station. We'll stop at the first one we come across and sort out this business somehow.'

That's what Turkish drivers do, or at least that's what they did when I used to go to Turkey. I haven't been going there for many years now. No, for no particular reason... I'd just rather not go there. I've never liked them, partly because they are different, partly because they behave differently, but on the whole, if I can avoid going there I will.

But let me go through things in the right order. I've lived an ordinary life. I've tried to do my best in whatever I've had to do, but I've also had fun compared to many people. I like my job and I'm quite good at it – at least I think I am – and when I'm driving a lorry, I feel free. I've got a bit of money, I've got my lorry... It's not as if I can go anywhere I like, but when I'm tired I stop, I keep going when I know I'm up to it, and I don't have anyone telling me what to do and how to do it. When I worked at the factory it was a completely different story. That was terrible! There were hundreds of us working in a state-owned textile factory. And there really wasn't anything you could do there except work, do what you were told and keep quiet. And in the evenings, a bit numbed by the noise of the machinery, I would go around Damascus with my friends... And although you feel like fooling around and having fun, you're so tired that you can't keep your eyes open. But I think tiredness has nothing to do with it, it's the boredom that kills you. Every single day is the same, it's always the same, day in day out. No, it really wasn't for me. I was born to be free and, even though it often isn't an advantage, I prefer to be free.

My parents came from Maaloula, not far from Damascus, they were *fellah*.[30] They were also self-employed, they owned the property, a plot of around three hundred acres.[31] That may sound quite big, but you couldn't make a living out of it at all. There was no water, the land was almost entirely rocky, and it was dry all year round. Even the goats didn't produce enough milk. Although there weren't many of us in the family compared to the standards of those days – there were still nine of us, my parents plus seven children, four boys and three girls –, we couldn't survive on it. So, my dad decided to move to Damascus before I was eight years old. He kept the plot – who would ever want that kind of land? – and took us to live in the old city, in one those big old Damascus houses. I remember there were other families, who had also moved from the countryside... all living all around this courtyard, which may well have been beautiful once, but when I lived there it was just filthy and foul smelling. There were no toilets then, so everyone just used the courtyard, but all the windows looked onto it and it really wasn't so nice, everything was much cleaner in the country. But then, my father had no money, he was looking for work, sometimes as a builder, sometimes as a porter. It couldn't have been very nice for him to leave the countryside, knowing he had to provide for so many children, and working as a porter at the age of fifty. But these are the sorts of things you get to understand later, when your parents have already gone and you'd like to say things to them but they aren't around anymore, and so you wonder if you could have been kinder to them and less bad-tempered. When they've gone, who is there left for you to thank? And yet, without my father's act of courage, my situation wouldn't be what it is now. I wouldn't have this cigarette lighter, this watch, and I wouldn't be able to afford to smoke American cigarettes, even though our Latakia tobacco is far better... I've only ever tasted one similar to it once, in France. Latakia tobacco isn't sweet like American tobacco, it's almost bitter but it's much nicer.

Anyway, I came to Damascus with my family, and when I left school at the age of twelve my family said it was time for me to help, although by then my dad had actually found a job in a big textile company and we weren't as poor as we had been when we first came to Damascus... I remember once, I was standing outside the door of the bakery without saying anything, just to enjoy the smell of the bread that almost seemed to take my hunger away, and a few hours later one of the people working in the bakery came out and asked me if I had eaten that day. And I said: 'Yes, thanks, I've had enough to eat.' The man started laughing and said: 'Have you been eating "enough" for a long time?' And without waiting for an answer he threw me a loaf of bread that smelled better than all the flowers in Syria. So I sauntered happily home to my mum and my brothers and sisters. My eldest brother wasn't at home, he had been working at my dad's company for several years by then. When I told my mum I had been given a loaf of bread she started scolding me and accusing me of stealing it. 'Oh, what a disgrace in the family!' she shouted out the window, 'my son has started to steal bread!' And all the while I tried to tell her it wasn't true. But by then, the other women had appeared at the window opposite us and were all chattering and commenting. So, I just kept quiet and waited for my father to come home, but he was even angrier with me than Mum. 'Have you been begging? Go on, admit it, you've gone around begging!' he shouted, and went on to beat me – it didn't hurt but I felt very humiliated. Then Dad said we would take the bread back to the baker's because some things just wouldn't do. We may have been poor, he said, but we didn't beg, and we didn't steal. So, with a dark look on our faces we went back to the bakery and I watched my dad as he spoke to the bakers. They explained to him exactly what had happened and he came out looking very cheerful (they had given him a fresh loaf to replace the other one, which had gone cold by then) and said to me: 'This time you didn't do anything wrong, but let's say that the beating you got was for something else you've certainly done but have never told us about.' And he smacked me on the head, but playfully this time, and I realized that Dad was proud of me, and I felt happy too.

But the next day, when I walked past the bakery again – this time I didn't stop and never said a word –the baker came out and told me he had some bread he needed to deliver to a place where lorry drivers stop to eat. So he gave me a few coins and I carried the bread, still warm and covered in flour, up to the gate of the old city on my back. There was a café there – it's closed down now and I don't even know what happened to the owner, although it was nice and very popular among the customers –, and when I delivered it, the owner asked me if I was looking for a job.

So, I ended up working as a waiter in this café that had a big car park. The lorry drivers would come, park their trucks, and sit there drinking tea, smoking and eating the bread from the bakery with some garlic and cucumbers. They were all huge men with arms like tree trunks, and I remember there was one of them with a moustache that made him look like Sultan Pasha, and another with dragon tattooed on his arm. I don't know where he had it done, because tattoos weren't as popular at the time as they are these days. For some reason, I was sure it had been done in Germany, although I have no idea what Germany has to do with tattoos.

Anyway, I spent several years working in that café, and everyone knew me there. Some of the drivers asked me if I wanted to go with them as the third man, who is basically the boy that gets out of the truck when it has to reverse and guides the driver. But my father had met one of these boys and didn't want me to do it. The boy he knew had been on a lorry struggling to go uphill and was told to jump off and put a rock under the wheels before the lorry stopped because it wouldn't be able to go any further. But the wheel had slipped back and sadly he lost his hand as a result. My mum also didn't want me to go because she said that lorry drivers are often not very reputable, and it wasn't good for such a young boy to go off with them. So, I started back at school and in the afternoons and evenings I worked at the lorry drivers' café. Everything seemed to be going very well when, one winter morning, my brother, who never came to the café because he was too busy working, turned up and said that Dad had died of a heart attack. He also told me that, from then on, all the responsibility for taking care of the family fell on the two of us, so I had to look for a better paid job because his earnings alone weren't enough to make ends meet. I also knew he wanted to get married and that dad's death was a great sorrow to him, but it was also a problem for us all, including for his new family.

So, I went to the textile company where my dad worked and they said they needed people, so they gave me a job as a factory worker, and I did that until I was seventeen. That was very grim, because the people I spoke to were always the same and everything was so precise and so neat that I felt as if I was turning into a machine myself. But the wages were good, so my family had some respite and it was easier for them to endure the loss of my father. And my brother could also look forward to his future and not feel too worried about us.

But it was very dreary. I would try to stay up in the evenings and used to hang out with four friends. One of them is now a doctor, one is a cobbler and one is an architect, though I've never understood what sort of an architect he is because I've never actually seen any houses built by him. The doctor now has a very successful practice and earns a lot of money – he's become the richest of us all. Not that I'm complaining about my situation, but he's much wealthier than I am. But even in those days he was the one that went out the least and knew exactly what he wanted in life, and he was clearly in a different league from us where work is concerned.

There was very little to do in the evenings. We would go for a walk, talked about work, and maybe if a girl we knew went by we'd pass a few comments about her, but everything was very different then from what it is now. We were sixteen or seventeen, but we were like grownups, so it wasn't proper for grownups to say things about girls, which were all lies anyway, and no one believed them. But still, it's fun to tell them, so you keep doing it even though it isn't a nice thing to do. The only form of entertainment we really enjoyed was going to the movies. But even then, to be honest, I used to fall asleep quite regularly. The shows started late, and halfway through the film I'd nod off in my seat because I had been up since five in the morning and at eleven in the evening I was ready to go to bed. But there was one film that I watched all the way through, and went to see again the next evening, and again the next. It was an Italian film, I remember it starred the actor Franco Nero, and it told the story of the Israeli athletes taken hostage at the Olympic village in Munich during the Olympics.[32] We sat there watching the film, thinking it was wonderful, and when the Palestinians took the Israelis hostage the whole theatre was excited. I remember that during some of the scenes a few people even clapped... but these are the sorts of things that happen, it wasn't as if the whole theatre clapping. We just wanted to watch the film, but of course we were all on the side of the Palestinians and were very happy to see the Israelis in trouble for the first time in their lives.

I don't remember if this happened before or after I did my national service. I was lucky enough to avoid the war, but that wasn't my only lucky break. When I was in the army I asked to be assigned to a unit where they needed people who knew how to drive trucks. I already had my driver's licence, but it was only for driving a car. During my military service I was able to get it upgraded to a lorry driver's licence, so when my draft was over, I actually held a licence that would enable me to do the job I had always wanted.

But during my time in the army I also got the opportunity to see more of my country, because until then I had never been outside Damascus except to take my dad to Maaloula to see some relatives who had decided to stay on there. They were farmers and were much worse off than we were. I saw a lot of Syria during my national service, although our commanding officers always told us that when we went back to civilian life we were never to say where we had been sent to, as that was a military secret and if it got out it could be damaging for the whole nation. So, I'd rather not go into the details now because I've been asked not to. Let's just say that I saw a bit more of the country than I had seen up to then. I can also say that Damascus seemed to me the best that Syria had to offer, and I felt lucky to live in the biggest and probably the wealthiest city in the country. Maybe I wouldn't say that now, as I've realized through my job that Aleppo is much wealthier than it seems, it's just that it doesn't want to show it. But anyhow that was my impression at the time.

So, after doing my national service, I went back to my factory and in the evenings I'd go to the café where I had worked as a boy and I spread the word that there was a young lorry driver willing to travel and who had a military driver's licence, something that was highly rated because people said that if someone wanted to learn to drive a truck, there was no better place than the army for that. After a while, I was offered some work for a few days, but I turned it down. If I left my job it would be for another proper job, not for something lasting two or three days. But then a lorry driver told me that that's how it always is in their world. No one hires you permanently and it seems as if you are never offered more than one trip, but in actual fact it's hard to have even one week off in any two-month period. So I said yes and started going back and forth between Damascus and Aleppo, and that was very rewarding. When you're on the lorry you feel as if you own the world and it's very exciting. I was young, I was driving a lorry, and I was also beginning to make a bit of money, so I felt really satisfied.

Then, one day, three lorry drivers came up to me and said they were looking for a fourth driver for a delivery they had to make to Germany. It involved driving a lorry to Munich to deliver some goods; then from there, one driver had to bring back the lorry loaded with other goods, and the three other drivers each had to pick up a brand new Mercedes and drive it to Syria. It was only one trip, but they said it was a great opportunity because we would need to make at least four of these trips every month. The road wasn't bad. The worst bit was going across the Taurus Mountains, where you met the sorts of Turkish drivers I was telling you about, and you also had to be really careful when driving uphill as the lorry was so slow that there were boys waiting around to take advantage of that to get into the back and empty it out. And people said that, especially at night, a few Syrian drivers had found themselves with a gun stuck to the back of their neck and being told to get out and walk back to the first town, or else... And when someone finds himself in that situation you can understand why he doesn't like the Turks. Anyway, forget I ever said that. After crossing the Taurus Mountains, you headed for Konya and then it was a fairly quick drive to Istanbul. The journey from there to Munich was really short. You drove past Edirne, then Sofia in Bulgaria, then Nis, Belgrade, Zagreb and Ljubljana, and finally to Munich.

The first time I made that trip I was really impressed with the beauty of the scenery in Bulgaria and Yugoslavia, it was so green. But then, past Sofia it started to rain, and it rained for three whole days. It was a heavy, miserable drizzle, and the wheels of the lorry skidded on the road surface, so you had to drive extremely carefully because if you so much as touched the brakes you would skid off the road like a bar of wet soap. I don't know what kind of tyres we had or how Yugoslavia's motorways were built, but they didn't seem all that great to us. Also, the journey between Belgrade and Zagreb was so dull that if you didn't enjoy driving, it sent you to sleep. And I thought the trip between Aleppo and Damascus was boring! So, partly out of boredom and partly to kill time, we started thinking about the movie we had seen and decided that when we got to Munich we would go and see the stadium where the Palestinians had captured the Israelis… No, it didn't end badly, quite the opposite in fact. The Palestinians all managed to get back home and it was a very successful operation. We were all very proud of that. Nobody likes death, of course, and those poor athletes had probably done nothing wrong… But I guess that's not how we saw it. To us, that was a place where the Palestinians had acted like heroes and, even though none of us were Palestinians, we decided we'd go there in the few spare hours we had between jobs. We just wanted to have a look at it to get an idea of what happened.

But when we got to Munich to deliver the truck, the owner of the company, who was also a Syrian, was waiting for us and asked us if we wanted a bite to eat before heading back. So we told him we wanted to have a look at the Olympic Village, but he said that this sort of escapade was a bad idea and that in Munich it was the wrong time to be doing something as foolish at that. In any case, we weren't there as tourists, he said, but to do a job and if we felt so refreshed then we might as well pick up the Mercedes cars and drive straight back to Syria. So, our excursion to the Olympic Village remained stuck in our imagination, although I didn't say anything about it. But a few years later, when I went back to Munich for another delivery, I said I was dead tired and wanted to go and have a shower and get some sleep. Instead, I took a taxi and went where I wanted to go, although I never actually got to see what I was looking for. But I must say, the football stadium is great, I remember how amazing it was, even though it all happened such a long time ago.

Anyway, after that trip things started getting better and better. I was young, I didn't have a family and I really wanted to travel, and there was great need for that. I didn't go to Europe very often, and I didn't like the road between Belgrade and Zagreb at all. When you had to stop off, there really wasn't a good atmosphere. People gave us unfriendly looks, or odd looks, but, after all, I was only doing my job. I was tired and they were tired, couldn't we all just let it go? Why should they treat me like that? No, I'm not saying that the Serbs and the Croats treated me badly because I am Syrian, it wouldn't be fair to say that... Maybe they just treat everyone badly in that country. And then in 1990 they started killing each other, so now it's their problem and that's put an end to driving the lorry to Europe.

Before 1990 we also very often went to Baghdad, and to other cities in Iraq. But when the war broke out the transport company didn't need us to go anymore and we started to travel south.

I've been going south for almost ten years now, driving through Jordan and then Kuwait, then crossing the whole of Arabia up to Qatar then Dubai and the Emirates. I think I've been to Mecca at least forty times. From there, we would go on to Yemen, sometimes doing some short deliveries, from Mecca to Sana'a and from Sana'a to Mecca. It sometimes happened that we'd get in from Damascus and, after unloading, the boss would come over and ask us if we wanted to go to Yemen to pick up some goods for him, and said he'd pay us very well for it. So, I'd call Damascus and they would tell me to go ahead... But occasionally some of us tried to get clever and didn't say anything about it, but when we got back to Damascus the boss could tell from the tyre tread wear how many kilometres we had driven, and so if we hadn't told the truth we were in big trouble.

Yes, I say "we" because we organized ourselves into small convoys, and we still do that now, even though the situation has improved a lot since then. For a start, we would try to set off from Damascus in groups of two or three, and then, before going into Arabia, we would stop in places where we knew that lorry drivers usually stopped and we tried to join a convoy, making up a sort of caravan. Of course, this meant eating dust, but those are not areas that you can travel through on your own. There are some dirt tracks, and sometimes even paved roads, that can get completely covered over with sand, and all it takes is for a lorry driver to lose concentration even for a second to end up stuck in the sand. When that happens, we give a signal and the whole caravan stops. Every driver knows he must help because next time it could be his turn. So, we take down some long wooden planks that we always keep strapped to the body of the lorry and place them as close as possible to the wheels that are stuck in the sand. You then drop the pressure of the tyre, even just a little, so that it sags over the plank surface. Once you've done that, you slowly drive the lorry forward so that the tyre starts to drag the plank underneath it and eventually becomes unstuck. You then re-inflate the tyre, strap the planks back on the lorry and drive on. The fact is that all this takes place in the scorching heat, or sometimes in the middle of the night, so, it's not that it's dangerous to be on your own – although every now and then you do come across someone who was robbed by lorry thieves – but managing on your own is unthinkable.

Then, when you stop, you take the opportunity to have something to drink, maybe make some tea, and it's also a way to tell each other what the roads are like, what the border posts are like, which customs are harder to get through and which are easier. Once, there was a customs officer at the *** border who said there was a problem with the visa we got from Syria and that we had to apply for another one in ***. I don't know if you get the idea. It meant driving all the way back for hundreds of kilometres. So, when this sort of thing happened we'd drive to the nearest city, go to the police authorities, hang around there for a while and let them see us, without raising our voice as that doesn't get you anywhere. The point is, they don't actually want a convoy of twenty-five lorries parked in town with their engines running, so you just have to keep calm and wait as they'll be the first to do everything they can to sort out the problem.

Then, sometimes you're forced by circumstances to join a caravan, whether you like it or not. For example, none of us would ever willingly to go to Mecca during the Hajj. Going there once in your lifetime is a good thing, you get to see the holy places and also to fulfil one of the duties of our religion. But the problem is that Mecca is almost impossible to get to during the pilgrimage season. Sometimes, after hours of driving in the desert in the sweltering heat, you reach the outskirts of the city and you come across a procession of worshippers. In that case there is nothing you can do. The authorities tell you to park on the roadside and make you wait until there are enough lorries to form a convoy that is as long as possible, and then they wave us all on in one go. But at that point, you're locked into the convoy and you can't leave it. Once I had to wait for over a day...

That's the upside and the downside of those regions. I enjoy going to Arabia, I like it there. Some people might think there are also other reasons why I like it, but even without that we Syrians are treated well and with a lot of respect. When we say we are from Syria, and from Damascus in particular, it's like city boys coming to the countryside, you can tell from the way people look at us. They have more respect for us than they have for Jordanians or Yemenis. It's partly because we are ahead of them in a lot of things, and partly because we come from so far away. And people in Arabia are curious, they are immediately interested in anything new. But after a while, you realize that what gives us a special glow in their eyes is the city of Damascus itself, maybe because it's beautiful, maybe because it's a city of great culture... I don't know, I can't really say why that is. It's true that in the past you used to be able to get things in Damascus that weren't available in Arabia, so that might explain a lot of things. But Qatar and the Emirates, and even Arabia itself, have made huge strides since then and, if anything, the opposite is now true. These days we feel as if we've come to New York. Yet, despite their giant leaps forward, they still look on us with the kind of respect you feel for people of a higher status or who are part of a higher world.

Actually, there is still something different. When we used to go all the way to the Emirates twenty years ago, and that meant many days of really tough driving, there was a river – in fact, it isn't even a river but a deep sea inlet – and such a small, modest city that it felt as if we had reached the edge of the world. And the whole of Arabia was like that. It was so poor, with very few houses and even fewer people around, and the people who came up to you were very simple, almost simpletons. They would ask us what the road was like, what Damascus was like, what was happening in the Middle East, and so on. I felt as if I had arrived in my Mercedes in a mountain village, like the ones that are so cut off from the world that you almost wonder if they even have a television or receive a radio signal. Of course, everything has changed now... or, at least, it's changed quite a bit in many places except for Yemen. We have a saying in Syria that's very popular among us lorry drivers, it goes: 'If Adam came back to earth, he would say that his people are the Yemenis.' So, when we leave Damascus for Yemen, we always say we are going to Adam's land, and everyone knows exactly what we mean.

Only the people of Kuwait are different, very different. But they had that nasty business of Saddam Hussein's occupation, and they felt betrayed by the whole Arab world so now they only believe in the Americans. I think if they could, they would make English the country's official language and if America was willing, they would apply straightaway to become a republic of the United States. And since they felt betrayed by us and only saw the Americans coming to their aid, they treat you like a beggar. When you deliver goods to them, they treat you as if you wanted to sell them coloured mirrors, even though they ordered the goods themselves and you're just delivering them. On the road, you can't stop here, you can't stop there, you can't do this, you can't do that and... always with that look on their face that says: 'We're much better than you.' That doesn't bother me at all, but if they've ordered some goods and want me to deliver them, they had better change their attitude or else I'll take my truck and go back home, and they can have their goods delivered directly from Washington, including their fruit and vegetables. As a matter of fact, none of us want to go to Kuwait anymore. They may even be right, but it wasn't us who destroyed their country. I don't see what I or my lorry have to do with all these things.

In Yemen things are still different. Years ago, the country was divided and there was also a war, but I've only ever gone to North Yemen, never to the south of the country. And the situation there is really different, it's like going back in time. There is a road there, but sometimes you can drive through it, other times you can't. Sometimes you come face to face with children carrying Kalashnikovs who tell you to get out of the truck, and there you have to be careful. You can't be complacent because you never know if the machine-gun has bullets in it or is unloaded. But then, someone from a nearby village comes over and sees that you speak Arabic like them. After a while they ask you for something and might offer you some tea. It's not that they want to rob you, but I think the way they see it is that the area that the road runs through has been theirs for centuries so... They know as well as anyone that they can't just kill a Syrian lorry driver and steal the load because the consequences for the country would be disastrous, and maybe they don't even want to. All they want is a small payment from you, to show them that you are aware you've crossed a territory that isn't yours and you don't want to offend anyone but are looking for a solution that everyone can be happy with.

But, except for Mecca and Medina, which are holy cities and there is too much to say about them and maybe I wouldn't even be able to do that, the places I especially like are Arabia and the Emirates, and Qatar as well. There too people have the reputation of not being very nice, but I think it has to do with the way they treat the Pakistanis and Indians that work for them. And it's true, these people don't seem very well integrated to me, in fact sometimes you get the feeling that they are nothing but underpaid menial labourers that the locals just use to do their dirty work. But the people of these places are sweet, naive and simple, just as they were in the old days. They have a hospitable manner and speak with a soft inflection; it's as if they had all the time in the world and won't be rushed by anything or anyone. Yet these places seem to me to be much more modern than many others that act so superior. And when it comes to certain things... they are also a lot of fun. I'm not saying it only happens there, it actually happens everywhere... But then, everyone knows it, we are men, and maybe we've been driving in the middle of the desert for days, and if a woman doesn't ill-treat us, we may even make a pass at her. All this business of covering themselves in black and hiding their faces is something you rarely saw our women doing in the past, but these days even in the Damascus souk you can sometimes come across a woman with her face all covered up... as I was saying, all this hiding of their faces doesn't really mean that are so different from us.

Well, there was one occasion that was a bit unusual. I was waiting at a red traffic light with my window down and a woman in a great big car that must have cost at least eighty thousand dollars said to me: 'Are you from Syria' 'Yes,' I said, 'I'm from Damascus' 'Really?' she said, then she shouted that she had some goods to deliver to Damascus and told me to follow her to the warehouse... or maybe she threw me a card with her address on it, I can't remember exactly. Anyway, after I had sorted out my things I went there and was met by a boy who said to me: 'Go into the house, sir, madam will be with you right away.' Talk about a warehouse! I found myself in a flat ten times the size of my house and it was all mirrors, bright lights, little water fountains in the middle of the sitting room... and things hanging on the walls that I didn't look at very closely, but if I had I would have understood it all. And she soon arrived, an attractive lady, still beautiful even though she wasn't twenty anymore – but then nor am I – and she asked me how things were going in Damascus, if I knew so-and-so, or so-and-so... I didn't know anyone and got the impression that she didn't know anyone either but was just filling in time. But by then I knew exactly where things were going. So, after telling me that she liked doing good business deals, buying and selling goods, because her husband was the boss of all sorts of companies and basically owned half the city, I asked her where the goods that she wanted to send to Damascus were. She looked at me, took off her veil and said: 'Are you always in such a hurry? Have a look at this and tell me if you like it. Would they like it in Damascus?' And in the blink of an eye she stood stark naked before me. She started caressing me and telling me she wanted to give me a bath... Well, I'll leave the rest to your imagination, don't think I need to go any further.

That situation was actually a bit unusual because we saw each other for a few years, and every time I went to her city I'd go "and pick up some goods to take to Damascus" and, by then, when I said goodbye to my friends, they would make fun of me and say: 'we've got room in the lorry as well, if the lady would like to...' Once, just as I was leaving and she was saying the usual things – like, 'Darling, don't be away too long, it kills me to be apart from you', or 'My love, I'll be tossing and turning in my bed like a restless teenager without you! The night will feel endless!' ... as if I didn't know that once I was gone someone else would turn up –, I asked her right out: 'You're beautiful, you're incredibly rich, how come... what's going on?' And she told me some weird story, of which all I could make out was that she had an agreement with her husband. That scared the wits out of me, and I was ready to run home with my pants in my hands. I thought her husband might be at home and was perhaps one of those men who like peeping and maybe even recording everything on video, but she told me not to worry. He had bought the flat for her, she said, so that she could have her little romantic affairs. Then she told me that many years before, when she was still young, one evening she was crying and said to her husband: 'Why is it dangling like that between your legs? Am I not beautiful? Didn't I do what you want me to?' And he had told her that it wasn't her fault, that she was very beautiful, but he had always had a passion for boys and had no interest whatsoever in women. So to avoid any scandal, her husband had bought that house for her, and she pretends not to know what's going on when he calls over some new Indian boy to the house to take care of him when 'he's tired and it's terribly hot.'

This is a bit of an odd story, because there aren't so many husbands with those kinds of tastes, at least as far as I know, but in Yemen everything is very free. You see a beautiful girl walking along the road on her own and maybe you make a pass at her. Most of the time you get a stone thrown at you, sometimes you exchange a few words that don't lead to anything, and... sometimes they get in... it makes no difference whether they are married or not. And if a girl has never done it before, you can always do things in a different way, I don't want to cause the family any trouble.

And anyway, these little escapades are often fun, I mean, they're not done in order to upset the husband or to fool around. They are genuine, just as the whole country is genuine, and they are also good in bed, they don't like to pretend that they're not interested and all the rest of it. They are graceful about it, that's true, but they don't wait around!

So, it always makes me laugh when I hear people talking about the women in Arabia who are apparently like this and like that, and apparently can't do this and can't do that. Maybe it has to do with my job, or maybe it's because I'm someone who always comes and goes, so I don't cause any problems except for the occasional night. But, to me, they are just like Syrian or European women. If they feel like it, they let you know, and they don't worry too much about it. There again, there is a proverb – I'm not sure where it comes from – that says: 'Court a woman but never declare yourself. If she wants it too, she'll be sure to let you know. Has anyone ever heard of a woman who doesn't get what she wants?'

12 - The Sunni Sheikh

I can't work out if they are looking at me and greeting me as usual, or if they already know. Ahmad the ironmonger was too cheerful, he would have been concerned about it. But the people at the soap shop and the bakery… I' don't know. Today I feel as if I've grown old, or maybe it's this frosty wind and cloudy sky. Autumn is definitely over. The fact that they didn't say a word at the café doesn't mean a thing; people never talk about anything there. Whenever someone starts talking about something even vaguely serious, people get up and move away. And then, there's a chill in the air that gets into your bones, and the daylight disappears so quickly, it's already dark by mid-afternoon. People are looking at me, and I don't know if they know yet. In any case, they'll find out by this evening and they'll say: 'That's why the old sheikh was looking so worried this afternoon! Now I understand!' And some may even add: 'The decision was long overdue; he lacked a sense of proportion. He had no respect for ordinary people.'

Maybe they are right, or they might have been right, but I know the kind of people who will say that: simple folk who think they know it all and are always finding fault with others. They are the ones who congratulated you on your speech even though it was terrible. The ones who really thought highly of you would shake your hand and say 'Good, good, but last week's was also very good!' And that was the politest way of telling me that they really didn't like my speech. But then, everything is normal. What really happened, after all? Is there anything I might define as serious, or that I didn't expect sooner or later? Everything looks bad to me because it's so cold out here, and it's almost dark. I've long realized that with old age I've also become dependent on the weather. I'm more bent-over when I walk, and I keep my hands crossed behind my back to try and straighten myself up, but then I realize that I'm even more hunched-over, and I'm beginning to look at people from the bottom up, despite my height.

There it is. I really don't want to walk past the front. Now I'll turn right, and in a hundred metres the columns of the Roman temple will appear before me, and then the entrance of the Great Mosque, with the illuminated minarets. Dad was so happy the first time he saw the minarets lit up at night! My wife and I took him there, walking through the dark streets of the old city. My wife kept saying: 'You're in for a surprise Dad!' And she said it louder and louder because he had gone deaf by then, and I was the only one who refused to accept it.

And this old man – unlike me, he was a really tiny man even before he became wizened – with the sort of dreamy but happy look of someone who knows that something is about to happen, pretended to grumble about a book he had left open at home. My wife said: 'You'll find it just where you left it. Don't worry, no one is going to steal it!' Masha was good with my dad, although I was little disturbed by that daughter-in-law's worship which, as time went by, turned into familiarity first and then into overconfidence. But there was so much fondness in Dad's eyes that there was no point saying anything. It's just that it bothered me, it seemed not to show enough respect for his learning, for what he had been.

And so we walked through the old city, I a little ahead of them, just to make sure that my wife could say to me 'Don't run! Your dad is with us!', and they a few steps behind. But just before reaching the corner where the lit up minarets would come into view, I stopped to wait for them and then we all walked together towards the open space in front of the entrance to the mosque. Dad looked on and smiled, but the childish expression he had earlier had now disappeared. He was moved by the sight of the minarets and of the columns of the Roman temple all lit up, almost as brightly as in the daylight. The darkness of the night enhanced the whiteness of the stone and the marble even more. And after a moment of silence filled with emotion, he pulled out a handkerchief that looked far too big for his face, dried the corners of his eyes and said: 'Don't look at me like that. They've been watering like this for years.' But they weren't watery before, they were completely dry in fact. Then, after a while, he said these words, like an old man who by this stage has broken off all his ties with the world and looks at it from a distance – not the distance of death but something quite close to it.

'What a wonderful thing progress is! I've always felt that there was a special light emanating from this place, and for years at the Friday prayer I tried to explain that the light of the mosque is like a light that shines on the path of each of us. And now the mosque is really made of light, and anyone can understand the meaning of my words!'

And so Masha and I also felt moved, not by Dad's words but by his ability to appreciate even the things he didn't understand and had never seen before. Everything was good, everything was beautiful: everything came for the Lord and was an expression of Him. Where any other old man would have complained that the lights and the beams spoiled everything, he saw yet another wonder of the Lord and praised Him with the enthusiasm of a teenager.

How many years had he led the Friday prayer at the Umayyad Mosque for? Thirty-five? Thirty-six? That's far more than I, who let my son take over from me last year. My dad for thirty-five years, myself for almost twenty-five, and my son for seven or eight…

I don't know, the idea of going home… Will Masha know? Won't she know? Or maybe she already knew everything before I left the house, maybe our son told her. I wish I still had many kilometres to walk, not just a few dozen metres. And I'm also getting more and more hunched.

Ah, here are the Amin brothers, the new owners of the hammam. They owned another bathhouse not too far from here… It was in a terrible state before they took it over! It used to be managed by that odd-looking man, a fellow who concealed himself, not very successfully, behind a courteous but all too obviously false expression. People used to say that under his management the hammam had become a sort of house of ill repute, where the city's homosexuals got together. It's the usual gossip you hear from people who don't really know how things actually are, but once a place begins to have that kind of reputation it's doomed. They said it was filthy and wasn't even run as a bathhouse. The people who went there were also a bit dubious, they seemed to be bad sorts. The brothers bought it for a trifle. They cleaned it up and fitted out a shop next door as a gym. Within a year it was completely transformed, and the young people of Damascus started going there regularly, as if it was their own meeting place. And now the brothers have taken on a new challenge, they've taken over this establishment, the oldest hammam in Damascus.

'Peace be unto you!'

'… And also unto you, Your Grace.'

'The weather has turned so cold; all my bones feel broken. I'm probably going down with something…'

'Come inside, Your Grace…' Oh, praise the Lord, now they'll want to know all about it as well. '… Do you remember that on our opening day you said you'd come and see us? That was two months ago, and you still haven't paid us the honour of a visit.'

'Two months ago? Has it been two months already?'

'It was the first of September, do you remember? Actually, it was over two months ago. Come, at least come and see how we've done up the main lobby.'

So I look in and who do I see? Selim, the Turk with the metal smile.

'What a surprise! You are here as well Selim!' And the fellow smiles, with that unfortunate smile, the work of an army dentist, and says to me:

'Your Grace, Hassan is here too! Hassan, come over here! Here's the sheikh of the mosque!'

And so, it's impossible for me not to go in, they are so kind. I sit down – just for a second – it's so warm, what a delightful temperature! And the other men turn to me and greet me. 'No, please, don't trouble yourself. Don't mind me.' And a fellow I've never seen before picks up an oud, which he had set down on the floor when he saw me coming in and starts playing it again. And everything seems to emanate the warmth and calm of bygone days, when I used to come here as a boy tagging along with my dad.

'You've done things very well. I think it all looks wonderful.'

'It's something we had promised our dad. We said that if we could, we would restore the old hammam and bring it back to its former glory. We're only at the beginning, but we are trying…'

'I think you are doing a splendid job! It's very clean in here, and you've also brought back all the people who used to work here in the old days! How did you manage that?'

Selim doesn't answer. He seems to want to show me something that is worth more than words.

'Oh, I say, what an old fashioned gesture!'

He smiles with satisfaction. He rolls up a damp cotton cloth into a ball. He tosses it up in the air so that it unrolls of its own accord, as if in slow motion, and when it comes down it opens out and falls onto a metal line hanging almost five metres from the floor.

'Oh, we're back to the old days!' I say. Selim smiles and with a long cane he stretches out the cloth high up on the line so that it doesn't crease and irons itself out naturally as it dries. Hassan appears through the door leading to the bathing area, almost naked and with arms that look as if they could lift a bull off the ground. He smiles at me and greets me with a nod before going back to the steamy baths and to the customers who are waiting for his massage.

And so I agree to stay and allow myself to be lazy. The two Amin brothers are kind; they offer me some tea and don't ask me any questions. They want me to take a look at the special cloths in linen and silk that used to be called "Queen of England". I sit there and look at these fabrics that are no longer manufactured these days being laid out before me. The man I don't know carries on playing the oud and I begin to be afraid of the cold. The brothers tell me about the money they spent, the trouble they had with the municipality over a particular licence, how disgusting the old bathhouse was and how it was in such ruins that the owners didn't even bother to clean the floors anymore.

'It was very brave of you to restore the hammam to what it was like in former days.' And they realize that I'm wondering whether they'll make it, and whether today, when everything has become so much faster, people still manage to find the time to spend a couple of hours at the hammam.

'The secret is cleanliness, a calm atmosphere and warmth: these three things never go out of fashion,' one of the twins tells me. As the other twin takes the payment from a customer, I see a young man coming in and the whole establishment automatically moving into action. One attendant takes the customer's wallet and documents, puts them in a locker and gives him the key. Another attendant is waiting in a corner holding a towel in front of him and looking the other way. The young man then gets undressed, wraps a towel around him and disappears behind the door of steam and misty warmth.

I've never been a "hammam sort of person", but now that I am here and there is this faint background music, and everyone is sitting around and relaxing, thinking about their own concerns, I wonder why I've deprived myself of this pleasure. Something reminds me of what I was like as a young man, and of my intransigence, not so much towards the hammam in itself but towards spending time unproductively. 'Our life,' I used to think, 'is the time granted to us by God for serving and honouring Him. It shouldn't be wasted like this, in this nothingness that doesn't lead to anything – in this feeling of wellbeing, so worldly as to be almost pagan in its shamelessness.' Once I said this at the dinner table, and maybe I said it with that excess of mental rigidity typical of young people when they want to show self-confidence. And Dad smiled at me but didn't respond. His only comment was: 'When will you grow up, Rabah? When will you become a grownup?'

I can still see him now: small, with his pale eyes and pointed nose, and his big, long, thin, hands. He had his usual ironic expression on his face. And my mum stood there – tall, with her huge bosom – almost scolding him with her look, which seemed to say: 'Don't mock your son, answer him instead!' And, of course, in the evening, in their bedroom, she would give him a long lecture before letting him go to sleep.

Dad was all irony and jokes; Mum had no idea of what these things even were. He always played with words, whereas to her they were carved in stone. His jokes she sometimes thought disrespectful, other times silly, but never amusing.

'You've been leading the Friday prayer at the Great Mosque of Damascus for years. You should remember that when you're at home, at least sometimes. I mean, you're an authority...' she kept repeating.

And Dad wouldn't reply. But after a while, with that twinkle in his eye, which I've never had, he would start talking about the cobblers, the porters, the pistachio merchants and the cotton traders who listened to him on Fridays, until he would laugh and say to us: '... So, always remember you are the children of the sheikh of the cobblers and porters! You have to live up to it! You have to be worthy of this important role!' ... And Mum would go to the kitchen in a temper, and you could bet that in the evening she would let out a torrent of words in their bedroom...

And so, of course my mind goes back to my son, and to Masha who is waiting for me at home and maybe doesn't know yet. But if she does, then I ought to phone her and tell her I'll be late. Otherwise she'll worry and think I've taken it really badly. I must hurry back.

It was a sad blow, but did I not expect it? Did I really not know that it would happen? Perhaps I didn't think I'd feel guilty, as if I were responsible for it. Maybe things would have been different if I had been there, if Ibrahim's family hadn't asked me to go and see them. But that very morning his son turned up at my house and said: 'Your Grace, my mum has asked to meet with you, she would like to speak to you.' So I got dressed in a rush, said goodbye to my son who was in his bedroom rehearsing his speech, and off I went. I had to go and listen to one of those stories which are so ordinary that they seem to have been devised by God in order to remind us to be humble: the husband, who is always driving his lorry, back and forth between Damascus and Kuwait, and the wife, who is fed up of waiting for him and wants a husband and a family. 'If she wants to leave, she can go ahead,' he says to me, 'but the children will stay with me.' 'Your Grace,' she says to me, 'do you hear him? How can I leave my children on their own for months, without a father or a mother? He's never here, who knows how many women he has around the world! The children need to have someone with them...' And I look at three children who are listening silently, only the youngest is crying. The others seem hardened and look as if they have shut themselves off.

But then I look at him and realize that there is more to it than that. I can tell he doesn't have other women and that he still loves his wife and is using the children to try and save something of the marriage. And maybe the children understand this and keep quiet, while their mother talks and talks and talks. She talks too much, as if she didn't want to see.

So I leave their house with an added burden of anxiety and promise I'll try to find Ibrahim a job with a transport company that does deliveries from Aleppo to Damascus, so he can be home almost every day. But the last thing I see as I leave the house are the children huddling up to their dad and their mother standing by the door. Although I can't be sure of it, I feel she is looking at me coldly. Maybe she's hoping I won't be able to find him a job. Or maybe she's saying to me: 'I'll leave anyway, whatever job you find for him. I don't love this man anymore. I don't want to live with him anymore.'

By the time I'm out in the street, it's already lunchtime. It looks like a beautiful October day, like many others. Yet there is something… I feel that something has happened. But I tell myself that the sadness of a family that's breaking up has got to me, and that the feeing will slowly pass, as the day goes on.

And then today, I get a call. They are waiting for me. I go over to the Awqaf, on this cold November day…

'The fact is… Did you hear your son's speech on Friday?' I look at the Awqaf official and I already know where this is leading to. 'It's not the first time, some people have already complained. Leading the Friday prayer at the Umayyad Mosque is a delicate task, Rabah. I'm sure you are well aware of that in your family.'

How many times had my father repeated it at home? How many times had I said the same thing to my son?

'We know very well that it isn't your fault, maybe it's nobody's fault, but speaking in public, and speaking in the Great Mosque of Damascus, requires discipline, or a certain amount of prudence at least.'

As if I didn't know that. Fifty-six years, between my father and I, of sermonizing on Fridays. Fifty-six years of listening to my dad repeating the same things over and over: that when we stand on the *minbar*, we have to be mindful of the world around us, we should invent nothing except when strictly necessary, and speak to everyone not just to a few select people.

'Leading the Friday prayer, Rabah, is an honour, but most of all it's an act of great responsibility. It's not you who is speaking; it's the community of believers. Sometimes you need to have the courage not to see, and to calm things down; remember that emotions are deceptive, and that even your heart can deceive you. Be humble: don't be ingenious or creative. Be useful: avoid the great issues and give advice. But, first and foremost, remember that you are leading a following. You'll need to be aware of everything, but your step must be prudent and wise.'

'Your son, Rabah, do you know what he did? And it's not the first time. He's a good young man, he is learned and will become a great preacher, but there are some things that it is not helpful to talk about, whether or not they are right. They make people uncomfortable; they create conflicts.'

'I don't think he said anything that can be so serious.'

'No, not serious. And your son's faith and his ability to speak to people are still a great resource for our community. But if there is no sense of balance, then maybe it's time to take a pause for reflection, and let time rebuild the necessary sense of proportion that has been somewhat lacking in his recent prayers.'

Then he had slipped off his glasses and rubbed his eyes.

'I know as well as you do, Rabah, that your family has been leading the Friday prayer in the Great Mosque for a great many years. Believe me, it's a matter of deep regret to us too.'

And that's when I understood. And I was so distressed that I didn't even manage to defend my son or at least extract an assurance that someday the decision might be reconsidered. The world collapsed on my head, my world, everything that we have been, that we are, and that we could have been.

'Will he be sent to another mosque to speak?'

'No, that would be too harsh a punishment. It would be humiliating for him, don't you think so?'

'I think that not leading the Friday prayer, even in a mosque in the countryside, would be unbearable to him.'

He had nodded slowly.

'I know, and your family still deserves a lot of credit for everything it has done for the city and the mosque. For almost sixty years you've served in a way that everyone has found very balanced...' And my son was being dismissed. 'The good you've done doesn't go away, Rabah, it comes back. It isn't lost. Even if everything should disappear, there will still be something left. And your family has really done the mosque and the city a great deal of good. I am sorry, believe me.'

So I get up, not knowing what to say. I stand there for a while, hoping he'll say 'Someday', 'In the future', 'With time…' But he says nothing. He is also standing, waiting for me to take my leave.

'Your Grace, why such a dark look on your face?' From the other side of the lobby Selim smiles at me and says: 'Come, get undressed, come to the bathing room, it will do you good…'

'Ah Selim, things are not what they used to be! I am so old I'll get lost in the steam!'

And he laughs and brings me another glass of tea. He sits down next to me.

Don't worry yourself like that, Your Grace. Whatever happened, it will pass. Come next door, come. I want to show you the old steam room, with the original domes. You'll feel better, you'll see, and your bones won't ache so much anymore.'

'Dear Selim, if only my problems were just my bones! And what about your mum, how is she? I haven't seen her in a long time.'

'She's well, thank the Lord… Come, follow me. Leave your worries outside this bathhouse for a couple of hours, whatever they are. If they are really that serious, they'll wait for you outside…'

And so, here I am, without having called Masha, in a cloud of steam so warm and thick that I feel as if I'm being reborn. An unreal blue light is streaming in from the glass tiles of the dome. It's dark outside, the daylight has gone, where is this glow coming from?

The perspiration is dripping from the tip of my nose, as if all the fat in my body were melting. Every now and then Selim comes by with a bucket of water and pours it on the searing rocks in the corner.

'Is everything alright, Your Grace?'

I watch him disappear in the steamy mist. I feel as if I'm shrinking by the minute, only my anxiety is unchanged. 'It's a punishment I have created for myself, I am the one to blame,' I say to myself. But I can't understand how and when it all happened.

We brought up all our children in the same way, as my father did, and as many other people do. Religion is something they lived with at home, they didn't study it. It's something they developed gradually and made their own. They got it partly from me, partly from their mum, from their grandad, and also from their uncles and aunts. We were all so proud that it was a path we all walked together, without forcing things, and without anyone forging ahead. Some people criticized us because we allowed our children to pursue whatever career they wished, without forcing anything on them at all. Our two boys became technicians and our daughter a lawyer. It all seemed so simple, so natural.

Then my son decided he would become a man of prayer and to continue the family tradition in the Great Umayyad Mosque. And for years he came to listen to me every Friday. Like one Sunday in November, many years ago, he came up to me as I was leaving the mosque and said to me: 'You know, Dad, I'm proud of you. You are not one person in the mosque and another person at home. You're always the same, you love God in the same way, and you celebrate Him in a simple way even in daily life. Many people are not like that.'

That's where the first mistake was. I mumbled something, embraced him in my happiness, and we went to the Fountain Café, as if to celebrate a happy event. I can still see myself there, peaceful and happy, gratified in my pride. And I pretended not to notice that there were at least two things that I didn't like: the fact that he judged me as if I were an ordinary person and not his father, and that he had gone to other mosques to listen to others speak and had judged them.

I should have acted then. I should have told him that at twenty-five years of age you shouldn't presume to judge others, you don't give them a pass or fail score. But I didn't, I could see the arrogance behind a harmless sentence, yet I chose to enjoy the moment, the café and the hustle and bustle around us.

When did this lack of respect begin? ... Or maybe it isn't a question of respect but of overconfidence. Yet that isn't something that has to do with character but with habit... I've always seen the

Great Mosque as a place connected to my existence but not as my home. It was a familiar place, but I would never have presumed to criticize anything about it. That's how it's always been for me, ever since my father's time. He went to the mosque and we would join him there, without mum or anyone else. It was only a few hundred metres from home, just past the souk, and everyone knew us along the way. But maybe this was already a mistake in itself, living the mosque like an extension of our house, and going there once, twice, maybe three times a day to call Dad, or just to meet other children. So, it was my mistake, passing on so much familiarity to my son that he had lost all sense of respect, all sense of distance. When I let him play with the other children in the big courtyard I didn't see anything wrong in all that. I thought it was right that he should feel it as his own home.

They could have found other ways. Or maybe it's just that everything has changed. So many things have happened in recent times, and nothing is what it used to be anymore. And yet the change wasn't so wrong. There was something good in it.

Like once, when my son came home and started talking about a souk merchant who is always in the front row at the Friday prayer, but is a bit too shrewd when it comes to doing business. And he went on to say that if a faith is limited to Fridays and prayers but doesn't become a way of life then it's too convenient. He said that if our faith in God is sincere, then it cannot but also becomes love towards our fellow men and towards life itself. It cannot but be honesty, sincerity and transparency.

Of course there was something excessive in his words, but the concept itself was not wrong, it didn't seem so bad to me, on the contrary, I was proud of it. I thought it was a good thing that young people felt God's presence in such a direct and personal way, that they weren't satisfied with the Friday prayer alone but tried to go beyond form. Not that my dad's religion and mine were mere form. But there was also a bit of that. It was a given, and it wasn't up for discussion. It was also a familiar habit, possibly quite convenient, sometimes superficial and generally lived less intensely and less directly.

Poor dad, listen to the way I'm talking… It must be all this steam that's getting to my brain and making me confused. My father was formal, I was formal… No, now I'm overstating it, I must be feeling weak from the heat. Yet it's true that we also saw what my son was seeing, we also noticed that some people's faith was somewhat too superficial, and maybe we didn't do as much as we could and should have done to set them right.

But neither he nor I would ever have presumed to criticize the mosaics in the mosque. One day, he and his sister started saying that they found all those mosaics too busy and that they disturbed concentration. That explosion of green, blue and lapis lazuli colours, they said, distracted one from the sense of God's presence. And I remember saying to them that the mosaics belonged to a distant and bygone era of our culture and that we had to be more tolerant. Whatever they thought of them, those decorations had been put there by deeply religious men. And God, I said, was not particularly interested in how a prayer is performed but in the prayer itself. And even though we can't say that every prayer is right, or that it can be performed any way we like, nevertheless, if the prayer is sincere, if it gives praise to God, then it is good and deserves respect.

But at the time, I remember, we talked about beauty, and how it comes to us from God. Yet – I wonder how I didn't see it then – there was something excessive in that criticism too. Today, I wouldn't say the things I said back then. I would ask him: 'How can you expect me to appreciate such lack of humility? What makes you think you can judge not only men but also the eras that came before us?' But why didn't I say that? Instead, I was almost tender with him. I tried to avoid any disagreements and said I actually found the mosaics somewhat disturbing too, but since they had always been there, we might as well enjoy them instead of decrying them.

Nevertheless, there was some good in him, in this different sensibility. But my mistake was not to realize that his familiarity had

turned into overconfidence and had become intolerance, and not to
see that he no longer had any regard for concepts such as "humility"
and "obedience".

'Your Grace…'
This time it's Hassan, appearing through the steam. He looks at
me and says: 'Your Grace, you've been in here for too long. It's not
good for you; you'll feel too weak… come next door.'
'How did they get you back here?' I ask as I get up. I am really
having trouble standing up. It's as if my whole body had gone to
sleep.
'That's right, I really am back. Have you seen what a good job
they've done? I like working with them. They are young, they know
what they are about, I'm sure they'll make a success of it. Come,
come and lie down here.'
And so he takes me to the bathing room with the stone tubs and,
a bit numbed from the intense heat, I lie on the floor next to one of
them… yellow and navy tiles, like the ones they had in the old days,
the sound of the water pouring into the tub from high up, Hassan
and his coarse, soapy black glove on my back.
'Have you already heard, Hassan?' He doesn't say anything. But
when I am about to turn my head he stops me and scrubs the back
of my neck and shoulders.
'I've heard something, just something,' I hear him say.
'You know, I would rather it had happened to me. I feel guilty
towards him, towards the Awqaf, towards everyone.'
'Guilty of what, Your Grace?'
'It would take too long to explain…'
Right there, under my right shoulder blade. Since I was a boy,
I've always liked this coarse glove massaging so easily the spots I
can't reach.
'You can't even relax in here…'

My wet cheek is resting on the hot floor. I feel like Ali's old dog, the one that when you walked into the shop just looked up at you with his eyes without uttering a sound.

'… You don't have to explain anything. I was there on Friday, I also heard you son's speech. He spoke very well, with all his enthusiasm. What is he supposed to be guilty of? He spoke the truth; he only spoke the truth.'

That's just what my son says. 'But the truth has to be adapted, Hassan. It can't be blurted out just like that.'

'I know, Your Grace, I know.'

'And then, what is the truth? Is a cloud passing in the sky the truth? When the shadow it casts vanishes in just ten minutes?'

'We have to be patient with young people, though sometimes they put themselves in situations where it's impossible to be patient with them…' Hassan sighs, as if he were me.

A spurt of hot water on my head. When I reopen my eyes I see the suds running off over the tiles. Another spurt, on my back. Hassan hits the plastic bowl twice against the bigger stone tub.

I've rolled over and now he's on top of me, lathering my chest and my belly, in his cloth with purple and green stripes, and with his usual relaxed expression on his face.

'Do you remember old Bashir? He used to come here, and whenever he rolled over he would always say: "Dear Hassan, what are we guilty of that we have to leave this place and go out into the world?"'

'He was always melodramatic in everything he did or said. He always spoke as if he was performing in a theatre.'

'Well, he did make life very difficult for himself…'

'… What a crazy idea marrying a girl twenty-five years younger than him! Leaving his wife and daughter to run after a young girl he met at university who worshipped him… As if a student could be a wife! Two days in heaven and a life of hell, ruined by her misery!'

'But it was she who wanted it!'

'… I know, I know. They say she was like that ever since she was a teenager, she used to fall in love with all the men who were much older than her. Do you remember how desperate her father was?'

'He used to come here too. But he preferred to lie on the massage table. He didn't spend much time here in the water.'

I know, I've been in here for too long. But this water that Hassan is pouring on my belly, which gets in everywhere then runs off after a while, seems to me to wash all the anxiety away. It's running off… How I wish it would wash everything away from me now.

'Wouldn't you like a massage?'

'No, Hassan, it's much too late. Maybe another time, when I'm less worried.'

Masha is waiting. I still haven't told her anything. I'm here, having my wounds treated, in this blue and yellow light, and now that I've stood up I realize that I'm in a hurry again.

A loincloth around my waist, a towel around my shoulders and another one protecting my head and neck. I look at Hassan, who is about to go back to the steam and the water.

'But tell me, when did you start going back to the mosque again? There were years when I never saw you there.'

'I liked your son; I liked his enthusiasm. Even though there were a lot of things I didn't find convincing, it was good the way he tried to shake us up, urging us to practice our faith in a less selfish and less routine way.'

'Do you mean to say I was old?'

'No, Your Grace,' he says, as he wraps a towel around my shoulders. 'When you are young, you're not particularly interested in the enthusiasm of other youths. But when you are old, as I am, you appreciate it. It makes you feel renewed.'

He is standing in a spot where the steam is thinning out, on the threshold of the intermediate room, before going back to the big entrance lobby. He smiles at me, ignoring with dignified composure the two customers who are waiting for him by the stone baths.

'Thank you, Hassan, my regards to everyone in your lovely family…' He smiles, without moving away. '… Why did you say: "I *liked* him," do you know everything already?'

'You know very well how it is with these things… But some people realized it after the Friday speech. They say he had already been warned… So, I suppose it wasn't hard to guess…'

He disappears in the mist. I go back to the entrance lobby, covered by a heap of towels. It feels cool in here. What a wonderful sensation to be in this large hall after the small, steamy spaces in the bathing area. One of the twins comes up to me, removes a damp towel and replaces it with a dry one. As I sit down I see my damp towel flying up in the air in the shape of a ball, then opening up and softly landing on the metal line. My eyes are half-closed and for a second, before seeing my wife's face in tears, I can hear the sound of the oud and then the tinkling of a glass of tea.

'Your Grace, would you like sugar in it?' With me eyes closed, I nod – a tiny movement and I notice that my forehead is beaded with perspiration.

'Rabah, I heard you son yesterday!' He had seen me walking past his fabrics shop. How many years ago was that? Was he emotional, or I am just imagining that now? Aziz had rushed out of the shop, elbowing his way through the usual crowd of women who were unrolling the cotton fabric, touching it, inspecting it and commenting on it. 'Rabah, I heard him yesterday!' he repeated.

I stopped. There was a great hustle and bustle. But he took no notice of all the jostling and the porters pushing him aside to get through. Like the curtains he sold, he just fell back into position, ignoring everyone around him.

'He spoke very well, very well indeed! I said to myself that I had to tell you. He made an excellent impression all round. He talked about the Surah, about the pilgrimage, and a few people next to me were almost moved to tears… He sounded like you when you were young, Rabah! You were so impetuous in your early days!'

He had studied for a whole week, rehearsing dozens of times the verses from the Quran he wanted to recite. I phoned him every so often, asking him how it was going. 'Son,' I said, 'you only have twenty minutes, you can't take up the time for the announcements to the worshippers. You won't be able to say all this in twenty minutes. Choose one of them and focus on that. Twenty minutes fly by!'

And he kept asking me how he could possibly not speak about this or about that. How could he not recite this verse or that? And while he spoke, I had an odd sensation that my time was already past, that I had completed a cycle of my existence. And whereas I had waited for my father to retire, my son was now pushing me out of the mosque, out of the pulpit from which I had spoken for so many years. But he had so much enthusiasm in him that I found it impossible to feel sad about it.

'Did he recite the verse "That they may witness things that are of benefit to them…"?'[33] At home he had rehearsed it countless times.

'No, I don't remember. But, actually, I don't think he did. He talked about the pilgrimage and the uplifting feeling of knowing that we are all equal in the eyes of God, regardless of our race, language, gender or culture. It was a beautiful speech, but he didn't recite any verses from the Quran. And eventually he got so carried away by his enthusiasm that he didn't notice that time had run on and he still hadn't read the announcements for the worshippers.'

So he had improvised – just what I had told him so many times not to do. Now that I think about it, I feel I almost agree with the suspension. The house of God is not my son's house: it is "also" his house. When will he understand the difference?

Not far from me, someone is speaking to one of the twins. He's asking about Mondays, when the bathhouse is closed to men and is only open to women.

'Is anything different then?'

'No, it's just that we have an all-women staff. And we have some hair removal specialists coming in. But apart from that, the bathhouse carries on just as usual.'

Someone says: '… And maybe they come here to look for a wife for their son.'

'… I suppose some women might,' somebody else adds, 'but nowadays children marry whoever they like.'

I open my eyes and at the opposite end of the room a fat, dark man – where have I seen him before? – laughs and says:

'I know what's different! When you have men here, one of them talks and everyone listens. When there are women, they all talk, and nobody listens!' And he laughs, greatly amused, along with some of the other men who are getting dressed.

And now I'm outside. It's turned so dark that where the street lighting is dim I have to slow down and watch my step. I get to my front door and walk in.

'It's me!' I call out.

But she has already seen me. She is sitting on a chair, holding a handkerchief. Her eyes are red from crying. I hug her:

'I've been told it's not going to be for very long, Masha, only for a few days…'

As I hold her tightly in my arms she starts sobbing like a young girl.

'Where did we go wrong, Rabah? What did we do wrong?'

Afterword

Prior to the publication of *The Minaret of Jesus*, there were long discussions among those who read the manuscript as to whether it was necessary to add a comment to the published interviews. The decision to write a brief essay prevailed when I realized that most of the readers believed them to be fictional narratives – not without an underpinning of truth but fiction, nonetheless. Since that is not the case, and the stories are – sometimes even literally – transcriptions of interviews, I felt it was important to provide some details on how the material was collected and used, and to supplement it with a number of concluding remarks, among the many possible ones.

Oral sources are important for the historian, even though they are difficult to handle, laborious to collect and complex to interpret. They provide an important vantage point from which to glean what eludes official history, which is mostly based on written documents. Moreover, in the last fifty years, the need to record the history of peoples and social classes that have not used writing has significantly widened the scope of oral history.

These issues were very topical during the Seventies, the years of my academic training. In Italy, those were the years of Danilo Montaldi,[34] Gianni Bosio and the *Edizioni del Sole* group,[35] and of the experiences of the *Nuovo Canzoniere Italiano*, a group whose show *Bella Ciao* at the Spoleto Festival in 1964 revolutionized the world of entertainment and the study of history at a stroke by suggesting that another kind of history existed in the world: "the other" history.[36]

Drawing on readings that I found both fascinating and remarkable,[37] I also followed this movement, whose development was marked by a seminal conference in which I participated as a student, organized by, among others, Carlo Poni.[38] The contributions of Paul Thompson,[39] Jan Vansina[40] and Jack Goody[41] had a deep influence on my academic development and led to my definitive involvement in oral history – a field that many of my professors still looked upon with scepticism despite the widespread formal recognition it had gained, including from "high" history, through the publication of a great classic on the subject.[42]

But nothing was so important for me than my meeting with Roberto Leydi. His wise and caring guidance through the bewildering, but to him very familiar, world of informants and the traps they can lead into, through what they say and what they conceal, helped to turn me into a "researcher". Our collaboration led to some important research projects. The most fruitful among them was an investigation I conducted in the Apennines of Italy's Emilia region, which brought to light a musical and fiddle-playing tradition of huge interest for the field of musicology.[43]

Another, also very successful, study dealt with the Italian peasant revolt against milling taxes in the mid-19th century. Its history was reconstructed through a dual research path involving, on the one hand, written sources (reports on the interrogations of those arrested in the revolt, procedural documents and pleadings), and, on the other, oral sources (what is still being passed down about this revolt in the countryside of the Emilia region today, one hundred and fifty years on).[44] Through the course of these investigations I developed the growing conviction – shared by other experts – that what is passed down orally in the world of ordinary people not only encapsulates the historical subjectivity of the narrators, but, if properly analysed and carefully considered, can also provide some very useful information on the event itself, that is, on "what actually happened".

When I first visited Syria, in the 1980s, I was surprised to recognize a series of signals – and I hope the reader will forgive me for not describing them in detail – that were very familiar to me. Although it was a profoundly different world from that of the Po Plains and northern Italy, everything in Syria denoted a society still firmly structured around oral culture. Interviewing people would therefore make it possible not only to reconstruct their historical subjectivity (their lives) but also to trace an initial outline of their society as a whole.

Many things happened after that visit, and the project had to be put aside for fourteen years due to work commitments and many other events. Then, in the spring of 2003, I felt ready for this experience.

The work, which would have been impossible without the active cooperation of many Syrian friends, got very rapidly off the ground. The interviews, which were recorded on tape and immediately transcribed before the next meetings, revealed lives of wonderful complexity and richness. Some of these were fragments (minor, brief and anecdotal, episodes), while others were veritable epic cycles that started with the life of the interviewee's grandfather, father, and parents more generally, eventually ending with their own.

There is no point my going into each of the testimonies, detailing which of them were fragmentary and which were of an "epic" nature. What is more important is for me to explain that the sense of book that was taking shape was determined by the "epic" testimonies, which I felt required to be left intact, with their errors, omissions and silences. So, when using the "fragments", the choice was already made. I had to invent nothing, limit the narrative to bare essentials and confine myself to providing functional but basically unimportant details (such as stating the time, for example). I could intervene – or, at least, I felt I could intervene – but under the following conditions:

1) in no way could I alter the history of a family; while some of the stories may seem almost fictional (e.g. the Kurd who gives away all his properties so as not to be guilty of the pain they cause), they are in fact only transcriptions of the accounts;

2) I could not set right incorrect information, conceal prejudices or attribute to the interviewees knowledge that they didn't have;

3) I could not introduce elements into the narrative that would change the interviewee's personality, namely his cultural and historical world.

Accordingly, my intervention has been confined to coordinating the stories, developing some sort of continuity between them, and building a framework around them – which is what my work specifically involved – that would transform what were difficult and laborious interviews into readable narratives.

None of the important contents of the book are invented. Everything is true and everything is what I have been told. The reader who really wishes to know where reality ends and where fiction begins should turn to the most insignificant, almost colourful, moments, which constitute the heart of every narrative but rarely become the subject of the story told by those who provide testimonies of their lives. This, however, doesn't necessarily mean that everyone will find my reconstruction convincing, but that is a different matter.

I owe special thanks, first and foremost, to the families of Bashir al-Ash and to Hussein Hinnawi, for their invaluable collaboration and delightful hospitality. Without their friendship many of these interviews would never have been held. I will always cherish the memory of their caring and attentive support as well as the hours we spent together.

My friend Maurizio Harari offered me precious advice that helped me to avoid awkward and sometimes dangerous blunders. Thanks to him I have adopted the scholarly terminology of the ancient world (Near East and not Middle East). Roberto Leydi, who recently passed away, taught me a great deal and it grieves me deeply that I cannot show him this work.

Finally, I would like to thank the many individuals in Damascus, Aleppo and Palmyra who received me as a friend and agreed to tell me about themselves and their lives, without asking for anything in return and in the certainty that their names would never be published. To those whose story is not featured in this book, I would like to give my assurance that they have nevertheless been crucial, and that their contribution to my development and understanding has been equally decisive.

The geographical space

This is the most homogenous perspective of the interviewees. Their world stretches from the Arabian Peninsula to the Taurus Mountains, and from the shores of Lebanon to Iran and Iraq, sometimes reaching into present-day Turkmenistan and Uzbekistan. One is impressed by the precise references they give, evincing an extensive knowledge of Lebanon and the whole of western Iraq, from the area west of the Euphrates River through to the port of Al Basrah (Basra).

What emerges is a rich and composite picture that highlights, albeit without politically challenging it, the basic inconsistency between the region's political borders drawn after the two World Wars and its cultural borders. The interviewees did not raise the question of borders as a crucial problem, but it is nevertheless clear that the structure given to the region after the fall of the Ottoman Empire has cut across ancient routes and severed traditional links, while the new political units established as a result have hardly achieved any real cultural autonomy.

Only the northern border with Turkey is viewed as real. The interviewees expressed no opinion about this border, either negative or positive. They seem to have no particular interest in the fact that the Anatolian Plateau belongs to another state and another community.

Feelings run high, especially in Aleppo, when it comes to the region of Antioch (Turkey), which, as one is constantly reminded, had been the city's natural outlet to the sea through the ages. Without going into details which are beyond the scope of this investigation, and whether or not it is true that the region of Antioch once belonged to Syria, the fact that the cession of Antioch to Turkey has cut off western Aleppo's access to the sea is perceived as seriously damaging to the economy of the city and of the whole country, and is still a very active source of tension with its powerful northern neighbour.

Lebanon is talked about with daily regularity, as if it were just another province of Syria where people go all the time, as they always have done, for trade, business or religious purposes, and to visit relatives. Lebanon is very familiar to the Shiites and the Druze, who are often of Lebanese origin. It is a land of trade and business for merchants from Aleppo and Damascus alike. There is detailed knowledge not only of Lebanon's large cities but also of its lesser valleys and small towns, as well as of its most important families, including the community they belong to and their religion. There is just as much familiarity with Lebanon's specialty foods, its most beautiful landscapes and its classical ruins. Knowledge of Lebanon is both widespread and comprehensive, and Lebanon's economy and social life appear to be strongly integrated with Syria's.

The testimonies show that there is considerable, almost astonishingly detailed, knowledge of Iraq, and particularly of Mosul, Karbala, Najaf, Baghdad and Al Basrah. The main factors contributing to this are religious (the holy cities of Karbala and Najaf), economic (Mosul and Al Basrah), and related to trade, with Iraqi cities providing intermediate stops on the way to the Iranian Plateau (Tabriz) and Teheran itself. The interviewees have very precise knowledge of each of these locations. They know – in the kind of perfect detail that is typical of an ancient tradition – the halfway points, the changing landscape, the most difficult and the most dangerous places, and the traditional as well as the most isolated routes. As a result, the space of a citizen of Aleppo and of Damascus stretches far and wide, reaching borders so distant as to remind one of the well-known universality of Arabic culture.

The interviews show that there is generally less knowledge of Jordan, tinged with a vague sense of superiority. People don't go to Amman, it is a city without history and without a past, it has only developed out of Jordan's separation from Syria. Jordanians, as such, don't exist: they are either Palestinians or Bedouins.

The citizens of Damascus and of Aleppo are not beguiled by the riches of the Emirates, Oman and Arabia. In these regions, even the humblest lorry driver acts the part of the intellectual or city dweller. Here, people spend fortunes on things that the citizens of Damascus wouldn't dream of having in their homes; the women are simple and welcoming; and there is widespread sense of admiration for Damascus across the whole population. We glean from some of the interviews that being from Damascus in itself confers an honorary status that allows unimaginable upward leaps on the social and cultural ladder. The police are corrupt, customs officers are corrupt, and the man in the street is corrupt. But, as the interviews suggest, the cause of this corruption is not the fact that the people are bad or are out to speculate. Corruption seems, rather, to be regarded as a necessary evil that is bound to thrive in a country which knows nothing about urban culture or about the art of government and administration. 'Oh, you're from Damascus!' the lady shouts from the car window. All it takes is a Syrian number plate, or the suspicion that someone comes from the great Syrian metropolis, for the most ill-tempered Saudi Arabian to adopt a respectful and sometimes even deferential attitude. In the Damascus souk, people comment that the wealth of Dubai, Abu Dhabi and Mecca is vast compared to Syria's. But the souks are unsophisticated, and the decorations provincial. They try to amaze with rudimentary and "rural" techniques. 'They are not bad people,' some say, 'but until forty years ago they were almost savages.'

The interviewees' geographic horizon moves confidently across a vast area encompassing all of the Near East, part of Iran and Central Asia, and the Arabia Peninsula up to Ashkhabad, in a world which they feel themselves to be full "citizens" of. Despite all the borders and barriers that have gone up, there is an enduring knowledge, both widespread and non-bookish, of the different dialects, customs and traditions and, more generally, of the different attitudes. The

Syrian border is certainly important from an administrative, political and military point of view, but for the interviewees it simply doesn't exist.

The city, the countryside and the desert

Damascus and Aleppo, both with an ancient history and among the oldest continuously inhabited cities in the world, constitute the pride and the cultural dimension of the interviewees, who are conscious of being the expression of an urban culture that has little in common with the countryside. The clear-cut boundary between the city and the countryside evidenced by their testimonies seems insurmountable. The interviewees have no relationship, except of an occasional and in any case superficial nature, with a countryside that they do not describe, are unfamiliar with and essentially ignore. While the cultural world of a citizen of Aleppo or Damascus seems to stretch with ease from Beirut to Central Asia, it becomes immediately awkward with regards to the outskirts of their own city and comes close to ignorance when it comes to the rural world. The testimonies paint a picture of a thankless and abandoned countryside, an inhospitable place where it is challenging and unpleasant to live. The boundary between the city and the eastern desert areas is just as clear-cut. Although the desert and its peoples are clearly striving to break out of their isolation (viz. the ubiquitous television dishes on the tents and the efforts of the schoolmaster in Palmyra), it is equally apparent that all this seems to be happening amid the basic indifference of the citizens of Aleppo and Damascus.

The latter live in the present while displaying attitudes that are the product of centuries-old but bygone experiences. The desert – at least between 2003 and 2006, when these life stories were recorded – is no longer dangerous, or a place of anguish and human dramas. No one is attacked by Bedouins or robbed on the way to Mosul or Baghdad. Yet this means nothing to the citizens of Aleppo and Damascus – the desert is simply a place you don't go to. Those who go there either have Bedouin relatives or are Western tourists.

The cities and the citizens

The citizens of Aleppo and Damascus, in different ways due to the different history of the two cities, offer a remarkable array of ethnicities, cultures and religions. In both cities, there are Arabs, Armenians, Kurds, Bedouins and Jews, as well as a host of minority groups, including Caucasians, Iranians and, naturally, Europeans. The Druze, contrary to what most of the historiography suggests, regard themselves as a separate people with its own religion. Whether or not the Druze community constitutes a separate ethnic group, their sense of belonging means that we have to talk about the Druze people and their religion as an autonomous unit. In terms of languages, Arabic, Turkish, Armenian, Kurdish, as well as countless Bedouin dialects are spoken fluently. A high percentage of the population can speak English or (people over 60) French. The most widely practiced religions are Sunni and Shia Islam, countless varieties of Sufism, Judaism, Armenian and Chaldean Christianity, Iranian-type monotheistic cults (Kurds) and Catholicism. Each of these groups includes a multiplicity of sub-units, the most numerous of which is certainly the community of Christian-Chaldean Arabs.

In other words, the two cities have been required by their history to provide an answer to the question – which is causing so much anxiety in the West today – of how different groups can co-exist without losing their identity and without coming into conflict with one another. The testimonies provide a very specific frame of reference that all the interviewees seem largely to adhere to, regardless of their ethnic, religious or language group.

Within the two cities there is a traditional and well-established division of the spaces and districts that has developed over thousands of years, each with its own ethnic, religious and socioeconomic features. It cannot be said that there are reserved areas, inaccessible to anyone who is not from a given religious or ethnic group. If such boundaries do exist, they seem to be vaguely hinted at, rather, and to be more the result of economic circumstances than of choices related to ethnic background. Thus, in 1980-2000, the Kurds occupied the districts that the Armenians had settled in during the 1910-1925 period and then gradually abandoned as their economic situation improved and they became integrated into the life of the city.

Tour guides take great pains to show visitors that in both cities there is an Armenian, a Jewish and a Christian quarter. While this may have been true in the past, it is no longer the case today, when the only difference is between those who can afford to live in certain districts and those who cannot. Also, the choice to observe certain customs and behaviours (women covering their hair even if they are Christian or Armenian) is not so much to do with whether or not one is going through a Muslim neighbourhood, but with a sort of widespread and mature 'unspoken' rule which is one of the cornerstones of the urban culture of Aleppo and Damascus.

It is a sort of constantly changing map, a detailed knowledge of which constitutes the dividing line between those who "are" citizens of Aleppo or Damascus (i.e., those who have succeeded in becoming citizens) and those who, as yet, are not. There are streets you don't go through after a certain time of day, and restaurants where it is a good idea to go with your family but not with your boss from the office. There are some invitations to restaurants or clubs that can be accepted, others that should be declined, and others again that herald a success and a small step up the social ladder. In this urban setting, the student from Latakia feels rejected by Aleppo, while the citizen from Aleppo feels rejected by the citizen of Damascus and vice versa. It is a subtle and ruthless game of relations and knowledge that slowly and gradually leads the generations in both cities to achieve a higher status and grow in prestige, even without being financially successful, until they reach the centre of the city – its ancient heart, sometimes in ruins, but nonetheless prestigious.

The city is open to all, with no restriction of any kind. The different "peoples" (talking about social groups would not be accurate) tend to settle in different neighbourhoods. Sometimes this boundary is easily discernible but is not presented to the interviewer as an insurmountable or particularly relevant barrier. There is an important unwritten rule, broadly observed by all the communities, whereby a young Armenian woman who goes shopping in an Islamic street will tend to dress appropriately, often covering her hair, albeit with a certain freedom of style. It is a sort of statement of respect ('Since you cover your hair, I'll do likewise') and freedom ('I'll cover myself up but I'll do it my own way, maybe with a brightly coloured scarf that doesn't quite cover all my hair'). Similarly, a young Muslim woman going out to see a film or to eat with her female friends in a non-Muslim neighbourhood will tend to take greater liberties, which she will give up as soon as she returns to the area perceived as being that of her own community. There is another unwritten rule, carefully observed everywhere by all the different groups, whereby any behaviour and any display that may challenge or offend the sensibility of a fellow citizen of a different religion or culture must be avoided. Religious feasts, for instance, once had an echo through the city, spilling over into the streets, but that is now avoided. One of the interviewees blames it on the traffic, yet the impression, although certainly subjective, is that the traffic is not the only reason. Religious processions, whatever their nature, tend to be avoided and to be confined within the community's temple or place of worship. Thus, Shia Muslims don't set a great deal of importance on the external celebration of the holy days in their calendar (specifically the birth and death of Ali), Sunni Muslims limit their "visible" presence in the urban fabric to the muezzin's call to prayer, and Christians (Armenians and Chaldeans) perform their rites inside their churches, which, significantly, often feature a fairly large enclosed area that might be interpreted as a metaphor or representation of the outside world. The priest often stops on the church steps to speak to the faithful as they leave the church, much as the Muslim sheikh does after the Friday prayer. It all takes place very discreetly, however, with a preference for spending time with the religious community inside the building itself or in the area immediately outside it.

All this is worth noting in order to highlight not only the political prudence of this kind of conduct but also the extent to which it is something new. In the 19th century, Syria's cities were described as fanatical. According to an eminent 19th-century traveller, a European could not stroll down the street in European clothes without putting himself in danger and had to wear Oriental attire.[45] Alphonse de Lamartine defines Damascus as a holy, fanatical and free city, which nothing must upset.[46]

This diversity of ethnic backgrounds does not appear to influence the kind of work people do, although it is still the case that the traditional occupations of these groups through the centuries have become a component of their identity. So, it is quite possible to find Muslim jewellers and Armenian carpet sellers, yet, by and large, Jews and Armenians tend to be bankers, jewellers and goldsmiths, Christians and Armenians are generally in the liberal professions, and Arabs (regardless of their religious faith) are usually traders, businessmen and sometimes farmers.

The greater mobility of the modern era means that these job categories have generally become less rigid. The one in which there seems to be the strongest continuity is the propensity of the Druze to pursue a military career, a profession ignored by the non-Islamic communities.

In places of leisure (cafés, Turkish baths, parks and high streets) and entertainment there are no barriers of any kind. In all of these, the communities rub shoulders, each in their own groups, taking no notice whatsoever of the presence or the behaviour of others.

The place where this considerable degree of tolerance is lacking, and where there are still barriers that seem insurmountable, is the family and the family's space, defined as the place inhabited by the family unit or by communities that share the same economic activity (the "communal" house of the merchants). Here, the tolerance shown outside turns into intransigence. The things that people are proud of as citizens (the openness of Aleppo and Damascus) or which they enjoy in their daily lives (meeting places, the workplace and entertainment venues) become a taboo that no one is allowed to break. It is significant, however, that only the Druze talk openly about this.

In the Druze family, if the children care about their relationship with their parents and the family, they have no alternative to marrying a Druze. Due to a peculiar and inevitable demographic trend, however, the proportion of women is constantly increasing and, as a result, there are girls in many Druze families who have no hope of marrying. When Druze girls were asked about this during the interviews, alongside their parents, they confirmed that a different choice would have disastrous consequences for a society in which the family is pivotal to its organization – even though many of them said that at some point in their lives they had actually fallen in love with a man from a different community. If a Druze girl decided to marry anyone outside her faith, the whole of Druze society would expect her father to banish her from the house and break off all relations with her, including their bonds of affection and economic ties. It is not, at least at the time of writing, an individual choice, or, at any rate, there is no room for subjectivity. Anyone who fails to observe this rule, and their family with them, is excluded from the community, and even moving to a different city does not provide a solution.

This particular Druze position is criticized by all the other communities in Aleppo and Damascus. Druze behaviour on this point is stigmatized for being too rigid. Yet, behind the criticisms and sometimes the ironic remarks, one senses that something very similar is practiced by the other groups as well. Although all groups (except the Druze) espouse freedom at the theoretical level, in practice, relationships appear to be hindered. 'Not because it's forbidden, but by personal choice,' is the refrain voiced by the interviewees. Palestinians marry Palestinians, Shia Muslims marry Shia Muslims, Armenians marry Armenians, and Chaldeans marry Chaldeans. 'It's a functional choice,' they claim, 'it's for the children's education, for the happiness of the marriage,' and so on. But when couples — following feelings that will not always be constrained by such rigid barriers — break the mould and decide to go on with a difficult coexistence regardless, the whole of society hardens. Society does not forget and, one is inclined to say, does not forgive. There is a vast array of retaliatory measures deployed by the communities of Aleppo and Damascus against lovers who break the barriers. Sometimes, they say, these measures are deliberately designed to put the love that exists between them under strain, in order to test how strong it really is and whether it can cope with life's challenges. These considerations appeared reticent, instrumental, and sometimes totally in bad faith.

Those who marry a member of another community are disinherited. The woman — if she doesn't adopt the husband's religion — ceases to be a member of her own community and is not accepted into that of her husband. Even if the couple have the strength to go on with the relationship and fight against the difficulties that society puts in their way (if they are prepared to give up the family inheritance, for instance), this neither changes the nature of the problem nor does it resolve the conflict. On the contrary, the difficulties are then extended to their children. Which community does the child of an "irregular" couple belong to? When in doubt, Aleppo and Damascus seem to take a retrograde step: children from mixed marriages don't have the same opportunities as their peers to start a family except with people who share their family history.

This is a burning issue, made all the more complex to explore by the almost total absence of female interviewees, since both the interviewer and the interpreter are male. It is not a subject that the interviewees are happy to discuss; it causes the immediate hardening of the interviewee's position and pushes the interview onto contentious ground where things could explode at any moment. The impression is that the citizens of Aleppo and Damascus are thoroughly convinced that this parallel track – closure at home and openness in society – is the only way to enable such a diversity of peoples to coexist. Yet, since their culture is almost European (in terms of their education, readings, and tastes in music and films), they are well aware that all this is difficult for Europeans to understand.

The relationship with the Turkish universe

Turkey holds a particular place in most of the testimonies collected. It is a constant presence in the interviews, in which we can say that no other people or nation features so prominently. The relationship is not a positive one, nor is it simply the product of the kinds of conflicts that naturally develop between bordering states all over the world, particularly when they share a boundary stretching hundreds of kilometres.

Although Turkey features widely, when it comes to the traditional economy and its related trade routes, it is most notable by its absence and scarce significance in the interviewees' perception. Turkey is not a place people go to for religious reasons, nor is it the destination for the migrations of semi-nomadic peoples. The Bedouins who settle in the various regions of the Near East travel as far as to the Taurus Mountains but never cross this major physical boundary.

Turkey is also not a traditional trade destination for travelling caravans, once made up of camels and nowadays of trucks. All the trade routes and spiritual routes lead west (Lebanon) or east, particularly towards western Iraq and Iran (Tabriz and Tehran). Turkey, with its densely populated and in some ways flourishing cities, does not appear to represent a traditional economic hub but seems, rather, to occupy a sort of area of "geographic darkness" that is not worth talking about or is a distressing subject to discuss.

However that may be, Turkey is problematic and hostile to all the communities in Syria.

The Turkish world is portrayed through cursory and negative caricatured images. It only appears through its worst aspects, depicted as distinctly prejudicial and cruel. The Turkish economy, however important for the region, seems to live in a sort of gloomy and menacing darkness. No place in Turkey is exempt from this "cancellation" of space that occurred during the interviewees.

As we have seen, however, the oblivion to which the Turkish geographic space is consigned does not apply to its history. On the contrary, Turkey is the only significant exception in a romantic and somewhat dreamy emphasis on the past. The interviewees, who are all prone to paint an almost idyllic picture of anything that doesn't belong to current history, make an exception for Turkey, which in their narratives becomes, if not the cause of all their misfortunes, certainly the leading player in them.

There is an enduring and deep-seated memory of too much bad Ottoman administration that has become engrained in the culture of the cities and is surprisingly alive even many decades on. During Ottoman rule, the Turks took no interest in the desert and its problems. The only Ottoman concern was to protect the droves of people that left Damascus for the annual pilgrimage to Mecca, but even this was badly managed, and the pilgrims' caravans were sometimes attacked.

The Turks did not protect trade, and the merchants of Aleppo and Damascus thus had to disguise themselves as pilgrims. The Turks organized pogroms in the city of Aleppo, thereby forcing the persecuted ethnic minorities (Jews and Armenians) to dig underground shelters. The Turks massacred the Armenians, driving them almost completely out of their homeland, something they are repeating today with the Kurds, who in some ways were their allies against the Armenians in the past.

Beyond the historical aspect, in a sphere that is both broader and without chronological references yet no less homogenous on that account, the Turks are described as having taken possession of a religion, along with a literary, urban and architectural culture and a craftsmanship tradition, that is not theirs and to which they have only made a negligible contribution. The Turks say one thing, and systematically and blatantly do another. The Turks are the enemies against whom the nation organized its great epic feat: the Arab revolt during World War One. They also allied with the West to expropriate Aleppo's coastal region including its port city of Antioch.

Resentment towards the Turks is homogenous and shared by all the interviewees with the sole exception of those with an Armenian background. This has to do not only with their higher cultural level but also with a sort of deep self-awareness. It is as if they didn't need to add anything else: the very history of the Armenians, they seem to suggest, is an eloquent anti-Turkish and anti-Kemalist manifesto.

In today's anti-Turkish sentiment we pick up echoes reminiscent of the sense of liberation felt by the citizens of Damascus and Syria when their country was liberated, and the Turks were driven out. This feeling of joy at the liberation of Damascus was vividly described by one of the key players in those events, Thomas Edward Lawrence (Lawrence of Arabia), who wrote:

'Damascus went mad with joy. The men tossed up their tarbushes to cheer, the women tore off their veils. Householders threw flowers, hangings, carpets, into the road before us: their wives leaned, screaming with laughter, through the lattices and splashed us with bath-dippers of scent.'[47]

Nostalgia for the past

Many of the testimonies revolve around the past, which seems to be portrayed as a happy and in some ways better time compared to the present. After a while, however, it becomes clear that this "nostalgia" is only the formal setting for a story dealing with the past. Beyond this edifying and sweet-sounding narrative backdrop – 'everything was much better, we had stronger friendships, everything was greener' –, what transpires is a world of such harrowing pain as to explain, of itself, the desire to relieve the strain by setting the memory of it into a more peaceful and almost nostalgic context.

The world evoked by the testimonies reminds the listener of epochal massacres (Armenians and Kurds), tragedies that caused unspeakable suffering (leaving Palestine) and military and ideological defeats from which Syrian society still doesn't seem to have recovered (the Arab revolt against the Turks "stolen" by France and Britain, and the anti-French uprising in Damascus). On the whole, the individuals who appeared before the microphones may have told their stories in a charming and engaging way, but they spared no details about past traumas that still have the poignancy of unforgotten sufferings and, to some, are still real nightmares to this day. Nothing has been forgotten – the contrast between the lofty social and political values of the French Revolution and French colonial policy, the protection offered to the Armenians, the challenge to the Druze, Antioch, Lebanon, and so on.

On the one hand, the interviewees' "oral tradition" shows a remarkable degree of precision in recollecting events that ended many decades ago and which they could not, therefore, have participated in personally. On the other hand, their enduring memory of these events, in itself, shows something that is not necessarily obvious: peoples do not forget.

The damage caused by centuries of occupation (Turkey) or by decades of colonial policies (Britain and France) does not disappear with the end of occupation. From listening to the testimonies, the Western delusion that all has been forgotten and relations can restart on the basis of trust and equanimity would seem to be illusory. The West may have forgotten its central role in the mistakes and horrors of the past; it may even sincerely regret its actions and believe that the colonial era is over for good. But "the others" have not forgotten and do not forget. Their memory may no longer be open bitterness and resentment, but it is still diffidence, fear and distrust.

What is far more surprising than the so-called nostalgia, or the watered-down version of traumatic events, is the paralyzing vision of the present and the absence of the future. The interviewees had ample freedom, and after being interviewed for a few hours, the rules of the interview were eventually ignored. If things went as hoped, and even the slightest degree of familiarity was established, the interviewee would end up talking about everything, whether or not it was of any interest. Within this "everything", the present struggled to emerge, as if it were unimportant. Only in rare cases (the Sunni sheikh, the Bedouin schoolmaster and the Palestinian refugee, who has managed to integrate quite successfully) was the present preferred to the past and dwelled upon, proving that satisfaction and success (and the Bedouin schoolmaster is certainly a case in point) naturally encourage people to talk about the present and to envisage or fantasize about the future.

The published stories all seem as if they had ended a few years before the interviewer actually went to Damascus or Aleppo. It is as if nothing worthy of note was happening at the time of the interview, and as if the future either did not exist or caused so much anxiety that it didn't deserve to be mentioned. It is difficult to hide the fact that this impression is conveyed not only by individuals but also by the cities themselves. There are many reasons behind all this which have to do with complex political issues and also have a major economic impact. It is not the task of this essay to identify the reasons for the obvious economic decline, but when there is no future to look forward to, it is only natural to turn the past into legend.

Anecdotes, meeting places and music

The remarkable wealth of anecdotes, traditional stories, legends and narratives featured in many of the published interviews deserves special attention. The oldest among them is the legend of Christ's descent on one of the minarets of the Umayyad Mosque. According to the records, the legend has existed since very ancient times, yet is still so alive among the whole population that it was also immediately noticed by Western travellers. According to the *Nouvelle Géographie Universelle* published by Hachette in 1884,[48] one of the three minarets of the mosque is called "the tower of Jesus", and the people of Damascus believe it is where the Son of Man will appear on the Day of Judgment and gather before him the living and the dead.

The legend provides perhaps the strongest evidence of the continuing presence in Damascus and, possibly to a lesser extent, in Aleppo, of a sort of archaic and thriving oral tradition of place. Almost everyone takes part in it, within the family, in the streets and the souk. These stories are mainly passed on in cafés, hammams and barber's shops. *Hakawatis* and musicians are the real masters of this great tradition, which had already made an impression on Western travellers in ages past. The memory of the city's recent and 19th-century history also lives on in the barber's shops where, symptomatically, musical instruments are sometimes displayed.

The beauty of Damascus

All the testimonies are marked by a fond memory of the long-gone splendour of Damascus. It is true that a feeling of "nostalgia" for what cities were like in the early 20th century applies to all cities, not just in Syria. Nonetheless there is something more to this *leitmotiv* that has been a constant feature through Arabic and local literature since the 7th century AD. Damascus shines for its wonderful souk, its cafés and magnificent hammams. Yet, the economic decline of the 19th century is all too obvious. Period photographs of Damascus at the end of Ottoman Empire offer no splendour to yearn for. What the images show of the city is the quintessential expression of what can only be described as "urban decay".

As a matter of fact, what the interviewees talk about is not the city itself but the vast and luxuriantly green area (the Ghouta) created by the waters of the Barada River running across the plain of Damascus. These waters, flowing down from the Anti-Lebanon Mountains towards the desert, once tempered the heat of the desert, made the evenings cool, enriched the city's inner gardens and made the oasis resplendent and recognizable from afar.

It is curious to note how this sensibility (not so much towards the city as towards its greenery) echoes that of someone who was well acquainted with both the art and the history of Damascus, and whose wealth of knowledge was far superior to that of other Western visitors to the city. This is how T. E. Lawrence describes his entry into Damascus after its liberation:

'When dawn came, we drove to the head of the ridge, which stood over the oasis of the city, afraid to look north for the ruins we expected: but instead of ruins, the silent gardens stood blurred green with river mist, in whose setting shimmered the city, beautiful as ever, like a pearl in the morning sun [...]. We drove down the straight banked road through the watered fields, in which the peasants were just beginning their day's work. A galloping horseman checked at our headcloths in the car with a merry salutation, holding out a bunch of grapes. 'Good news -- Damascus salutes you.' [...] Quite quietly we drove up the long street to the Government buildings on the bank of the Barada. The way was packed with people, lined solid on the side-walks, in the road, at the windows and on the balconies or house-tops. Many were crying, a few cheered faintly, some bolder ones cried our names.'[49]

Interestingly, Lawrence himself, despite his awareness of the importance of the artistic and architectural heritage of Damascus, did not actually devote a great deal of attention to it. What he describes with literary mastery is not a city but an oasis. The focus is not on the buildings but on the waterways running through Damascus which turned it into one huge garden. There is no reason to believe that Lawrence's perception was any different from that of the Arabs he led into the capital. That is because, as we have already gathered, the fascination held by the city is not that of an urban centre as it might be interpreted in the West, but springs from the reification of what has been an absolute *topos* of Arabic literature through the ages. Damascus is the garden of delights; it is heaven on earth – the defeat of the desert and of its barrenness.

The object of so many nostalgic moments is not the city of Damascus itself but its oasis – it is the Ghouta as a metaphor of the heaven offered to those who can earn their way into it. It is the same recurring theme found in the courtyards and gardens of Granada and Esfahan, in *The Thousand and One Nights*, in Cairo, in the Umayyad castles of the Syrian Desert, in the gardens and decorated pavilions of Yazd, Kashan and Shiraz, in the poems of Omar Khayyam, in Firdausi's *Shahnameh* and in the works of Ibn Battuta.

In their own way, the testimonies collected are once again exceptionally useful to the historian. They may not represent the memory of a city as we might generally understand it, but they are evidence of an enduring literary tradition which, blurring the boundary between metaphor and reality, celebrates neither a place nor a physical space but man's encounter with something superior and immanent: the God who defeats the deserts and whose waters quench all thirst forever.

'As for Damascus, may Allah protect it, she is the Paradise of the Orient, and dawning-place of her resplendent light [...] She is adorned with the flowers of sweet scented plants, displaying silk-brocaded garments in the form of gardens [...] its rivulets twist snake-like in all directions; its orchards generate gentle zephyr injecting life into souls [...] its gardens encircle it like a halo around the moon; they contain it as a calyx contains a flower [...] They told the truth who said: 'If Paradise be on earth, Damascus must be it.' [Ibn Jubayr, 12th century].

---

[1] The *souk*, or *bazaar*, is the marketplace found in almost every Arab city.

[2] *Hakawati* is the Syrian term for storyteller.

[3] The First World War.

[4] 'As for Damascus, may Allah protect it, she is the Paradise of the Orient, and dawning-place of her resplendent light [...] She is adorned with the flowers of sweet scented plants, displaying silk-brocaded garments in the form of gardens [...] its rivulets twist snake-like in all directions; its orchards generate gentle zephyr injecting life into souls [...] its gardens encircle it like a halo around the moon; they contain it as a calyx contains a flower [...] They told the truth who said: "If Paradise be on earth, Damascus must be it."' Ibn Jubayr, 12th century.

[5] 'On the slopes of Mount Qassioun is the Cave of Blood, where they say that Hābīl was killed by Qābīl', al-Harawī, 11.

[6] The Kurdish word for "brocade" is *brocar*. The Kurds interviewed in Damascus believe that the word comes from the combination of *Bro* ("Abraham" in Kurdish) and *car* ("work" in Kurdish).

[7] Hadith in Islam is generally seen as a narrative or communication and, according to tradition, specifically refers to the deeds and words of the Prophet and his companions. The Hadiths form the Sunnah, namely the custom, tradition and rules of conduct inherent in the actions, statements and tacit approval attributed to Muhammad, which, through these, is presented as a model that Muslims are required to follow.

[8] Quran, Surah 16:121-122

[9] The person appointed by the community to recite the *adhan*, the call to prayer

[10] Plural form of *Waqf*. It stands for properties and assets donated by private individuals to religious associations and institutions for charitable purposes. By extension, those in charge of the *Awqaf* are also responsible for the mosques and the activities carried out within them.

[11] The so-called Turkish baths.

[12] Occupied by Israel in 1967.

¹³ Bedouin protection lasts the time it takes for the body to eliminate the food and liquids consumed under their hospitality. After three days, when everything the guest ate and drank is thought to have been expelled, the protection granted as part of Bedouin hospitality ceases.

¹⁴ Tripoli, a city in northern Lebanon.

¹⁵ Basra or Basrah, a city located in Southern Iraq, on the Persian Gulf.

¹⁶ *Lawrence of Arabia* (1962), directed by David Lean, starring Peter O'Toole, Alec Guinness, Anthony Quinn and Omar Sharif.

¹⁷ Holy pilgrimage to Mecca.

¹⁸ A string instrument similar to a lute which is still the most commonly featured instrument in every Middle Eastern music genre. Musicians consider the lute as important as the piano is in Western culture. It is only through the lute that the player and the singer can learn to engage with the other "voices" that make up the orchestra.

¹⁹ String instrument of Persian origin found throughout northern Syria and in the Turkish-Iranian plateau up to the plains of Central Asia.

²⁰ Small red hat made of felt and shaped like a flat-topped cone, better known as *fez*.

²¹ Also known as 'Embellished song', generally based on love themes.

²² Epic songs frequently based on transcriptions of poems drawn from Arabic literature.

²³ Leading Egyptian singer who became such a legend and was so worshipped by her fans that her popularity in the Near East was comparable to that of Maria Callas in the West.

²⁴ A prominent singer from Cairo and a leading performer of Arabic music from the 1940s through to the 1960s.

²⁵ A current that cuts across all sects of the Islamic faith, usually seen as having a more emotional and less rational relationship with God, often built on singing, playing music, reciting poems or dancing. This form of mysticism, also very popular in Central Asia and India, has frequently been the target of persecution by the various Islamic currents which – wrongly rather than rightly – have identified pagan elements in the religious ecstasy that draws the *Sufi* faithful towards God.

²⁶ Nusrat Fateh Ali Khan (Faisalabad, Pakistan, 1948 - London, 1997). He came from a family with a 600-year old Qawwali (Sufi devotional musicians) tradition and achieved great international renown.

[27] Liqueur made from aniseed fermentation.

[28] Guernica, near Bilbao. The bombing was carried out by aircraft sent by Hitler to support Franco's forces.

[29] A play on words. The full stop written out as the word "point" turns the meaning of the French motto into "Liberty none Fraternity none Equality none".

[30] Farmers

[31] Almost one hundred and twenty-five hectares

[32] *21 Hours at Munich* (1976), directed by William A. Graham, starring Franco Nero and William Holden.

[33] Quran, Surah 22:28.

[34] Danilo Montaldi, *Militanti politici di base*, Turin, Einaudi, 1971, and *Autobiografie della leggera*, Turin, Einaudi, 1978.

[35] Gianni Bosio, *L'intellettuale rovesciato: interventi e ricerche sulla emergenza d'interesse verso le forme di espressione e di organizzazione spontanee nel mondo popolare e proletario*, Milan, Edizioni del Gallo, 1967.

[36] Roberto Leydi, Filippo Crivelli and Il Nuovo Canzoniere Italiano (eds.), *Le canzoni di Bella Ciao*, Milan, I Dischi del Sole, 1965.

[37] Albert B. Lord, *The Singer of Tales*, Cambridge (Mass.), Harvard University Press, 1964.

[38] Bernardo Bernardi, Carlo Poni and Alessandro Triulzi (eds.), *Fonti orali: antropologia e storia*, Milan, Angeli, 1978.

[39] Paul Thompson, *Oral History and Working Class History*, in *ibidem*, pp. 35-58.

[40] Jan Vansina, *Oral Tradition, Oral History: Achievements and Perspectives*, in *ibidem*, pp. 59-74.

[41] Jack Goody, *Oral Tradition and the Reconstruction of the Past in Northern Ghana*, in *ibidem*, pp. 285-296.

[42] Paul Thompson, *The Voice of the Past: Oral History*, Oxford, Oxford University Press, 1978.

[43] Stefano Cammelli, *Musiche da ballo, balli da festa. Musiche da ballo dell'appennino bolognese*, Bologna, Alfa editrice, 1982.

[44] Stefano Cammelli, *Al suono delle campane. Indagine su una rivolta contadina: i moti del macinato*, Milan, Angeli, 1983.

[45] Domingo Badia y Leblich, *Travels of Ali Bey (Domingo Badia y Leblich) in Morocco, Tripoli, Cyprus, Egypt, Arabia, Syria and Turkey between the Years 1803 and 1807*, London, Longman, 1816, t. 2, p. 273.

[46] Alphonse de Lamartine, *Souvenirs, impressions, pensées et paysages pendant un voyage en Orient, 1832-1833 ou notes d'un voyageur*, Paris, Pagnerre, Hachette & Fume, 1856, t. 2, p. 50.

[47] Thomas Edward Lawrence, *Seven Pillars of Wisdom*, Chapter CXIX.

[48] *Nouvelle Géographie Universelle. L'Asie Antérieure*, Paris, Hachette, 1884, vol. IX, p. 790.

[49] Lawrence, *Seven Pillars of Wisdom*, op. cit.

www.ingramcontent.com/pod-product-compliance
Lightning Source LLC
Chambersburg PA
CBHW051949150726
47999CB00004B/1307